Educational Excellence for Your Child

Educational Excellence
for
Your Child

Kenneth Kimball, Jr., Ed.D.

Leesome Associates

Copyright 1996 © Kenneth Kimball, Jr.

All rights reserved. No part of this publication may be reproduced, stored in a retrieval system, or transmitted, in any form or by any means, electronic, mechanical, photocopying, recording, or otherwise, without prior written permission of the publisher except for brief quotations embodied in articles and reviews.

Produced in association with Tabby House
Author photo by K. Kimball, III
Manufactured in the United States of America
Library of Congress Catalog Card Number: 96-076518
ISBN: 0-9652071-0-2

This publication has been written to provide helpful information in regard to the subject matter covered. It is sold without warranty or guarantee, expressed or implied, respecting its contents, quality, merchantability, or fitness for any particular purpose. Neither the author, nor its publisher, dealers or distributors shall be liable to the purchaser or any other person or entity with respect to any liability, loss, or damage caused or alleged to be caused directly or indirectly by this book.

Additional copies of *Educational Excellence for Your Child* and individual worksheets, forms, and lists can be ordered from Leesome Associates. Please call or write for current prices.

Cataloging-in-Publication Data

370.19 KIM	Kimball, Kenneth R., Jr., 1929 Mar. 13– Educational excellence for your child / Kenneth R. Kimball, Jr. Wellfleet, Mass. : Leesome Associates, ©1996
	256 p. ; cm Produced in association with Tabby House. Includes bibliographical references and index.
	Summary: A guide to what parents can do to insure the best possible education for their children, from determining the child's educational needs and evaluating schools to interacting and communicating with teachers and school administrators.
	ISBN 0-9652071-0-2 1. Education - Parent participation I. Title
	370.19'3_dc20

Provided in cooperation with Unique Books, Inc.

Leesome Associates
P.O. Box 1494
Wellfleet, MA 02667-1494
(508) 349-0528

Contents at a Glance

How to Get the Most Out of this Book   xxiii

1. Introduction to Educational Excellence   25
2. Getting to Know Your Child Better   33
3. Determining Your Child's Needs   43
4. Looking at School Organization   55
5. Understanding Curriculum, Resources and School Calendar   63
6. Preparing for Your School Visit and Survey   73
7. Visiting the School, Conducting the Survey, Reviewing the Results   87
8. Background Information on Goals   97
9. Developing an Education Action Plan   101
10. Getting Your Child's Education Action Plan Implemented   111
11. Becoming Involved in Your Child's School   121
12. Opportunities for School Volunteers   133
13. Dealing Effectively with Change   139
14. Preparing Your Child for Optimal Learning   147
15. Establishing a Home Learning Center   155
16. Home Activities That Increase Learning   163
17. Community Activities and Resources That Increase Learning   193
18. Assessing Progress and Moving On   209

Appendixes
    A. The National Education Goals   215
    B. Blue Ribbon Schools Program   217
    C. Letters and Memorandums   219

Resources: 225
    Books
    Magazines
    Other resources

Index   239

About the Author   253

Aa Bb Cc Dd Ee Ff Gg Hh Ii

Words and Ways

Words are important,
but so are our ways.
They each describe something
the other conveys.
When used all alone,
words work just great.
But most know our actions
will seal our fate.
Use them together,
and you will agree.
You can do anything,
try it and see.

Dedication

This book is dedicated to all who seek excellence.

To my wife, Betty, and our children, Ken III and Kay. To you and your children. May your efforts coupled with those of dedicated parents and educators throughout America make excellence a daily occurrence for every child.

To my parents, Dorothy and Ken, who taught me the joy of learning, and my New Zealand students who taught me the joy of living.

To the Farnsworth Middle School staff, parents and students for their efforts in seeking educational excellence for all.

Contents

Contents at a Glance . . . . *vii*
Dedication . . . . *ix*
Worksheets, Forms and Lists . . . . *xvi*
Acknowledgments . . . . *xvii*
Preface . . . . *xix*
How to Get the Most Out of This Book . . . . *xxiii*

Chapter 1
    Introduction to Educational Excellence 25
        The education of our nation's children
        What is educational excellence?
        Excellence is not always what it appears to be
        Who can best identify excellence?
        Some excellence exists in every school
        Successful schools have common attributes
        Responsibility for your child's education
        Schools are in business to serve the public
        Examples of parent successes
        Average children also require extra parent effort
        Obtaining excellence need not be difficult
        Set high goals and go for them
        Remember, each child is different
        Most differences are normal
        Let's get started

Chapter 2
    Getting to Know Your Child Better 33
        Building a foundation for excellence
        Developing a file of educational records
        Filing system helpful hints
        Introduction to the Child's Interest Interview
        Conducting the Child's Interest Interview
        Take a more comprehensive look at your child
        Educational Records File Inventory Form
        Child's Interest Interview Form

Chapter 3
    Determining Your Child's Needs 43
        Step back and look at your child
        Section A - Interests and Activities
        Section B - Work Habits

Section C - Skills and Mental Abilities
Section D - Physical Characteristics
Using the information from the Know Your Child Worksheet
Introduction to the Parent Recommendations Summary
You are becoming a wise consumer
Know Your Child Worksheet
Parent Recommendations Summary

Chapter 4
Looking at School Organization 55
Excellence is a journey, not a destination
Learn all you can about schools
Your experiences will help you understand today's schools
Which grades should be included in a school?
Student population; how important is school size?
Compensating for large or small school disadvantages
House plans can be found at any level
Class size is something to consider
Self-contained classrooms for younger children
What is team teaching? Can it improve instruction?
Individualized instruction
How and when does independent learning occur?

Chapter 5
Understanding Curriculum, Resources and School Calendar 63
The curriculum: who decides what will be taught?
The scope of the curriculum
The school's role in educating children is not exclusive
Library/media centers support curricula
Computers have become a very useful resource
Adequate human resources are very important
Successful schools are part of the community
The school year is based on tradition
Lengthening the school year
Reducing the long summer vacation
The school day: how long should it be?
The school day: starting and ending times
Before and after school programs
Time in school vs. time learning
Modular schedules
Sources of information about schools

Chapter 6
Preparing for Your School Visit and Survey 73
The School Survey Form, a valuable tool
Understanding the educational bureaucracy
Principals provide leadership and operate schools
Principals want to meet parents
Things to do before calling the school
Using the School Survey Form
Determining which questions apply to your situation

Educational Excellence for Your Child

    Adding questions to the School Survey Form
    Planning your school visit
    Deciding what to see at the school
    Determining your visit sequence
    Keep your observations in perspective
    What to expect on your tour
    Determining which staff members to meet
    Determining how much time to request for your visit
    School Survey Form

Chapter 7
   Visiting the School, Conducting the Survey, Reviewing the Results 87
    Scheduling an appointment
    Your visit, your agenda
    Appointment questions and answers
    Telephoning the school for an appointment
    Ensuring a successful tour and school survey interview
    Visit suggestions
    Tour suggestions
    Survey suggestions
    Concluding your school visit
    When returning home
    Identifying advantages and disadvantages on the Survey Form
    Using the School Survey Balance Sheet to refine your data
    Do a reality check
    Still undecided, try this
    Summary of your efforts to date
    Sample School Survey Balance Sheet
    School Survey Balance Sheet

Chapter 8
   Background Information on Goals 97
    Excellence seldom occurs by chance
    Excellence in education, excellence in life
    Setting goals and communicating them to the school
    Heading in the right direction
    Some goals will change
    Before writing your first goal
    Discussing goals with your child and others

Chapter 9
   Developing an Education Action Plan 101
    An Education Action Plan is an itinerary for life
    Long-term goals are normally realized after four or five years
    Long-term goals should include vocational objectives
    Intermediate-term goals can be met in one to three years
    Short-term goals can be reached within a year
    The Education Action Plan Worksheet helps you write goals
    A few clearly defined goals are best
    Writing goals and strategies
    Completing additional Education Action Plan Worksheets

Educational Excellence for Your Child

Thinking ahead
Sample 1 - Education Action Plan Worksheet
Sample 2 - Education Action Plan Worksheet
Education Action Plan Worksheet

Chapter 10

Getting Your Child's Education Action Plan Implemented 111

Working with the school to realize your child's goals
It takes an entire village to raise a child
Let the school's organizational structure help you
Preparing for your follow-up conference
Copies and folders help establish credibility
Conference attendees: Your child? Advocate? Staff member?
Making an appointment
Conducting a productive conference
Meeting with other staff members
Realize the school has options
Strengthening your commitment by offering to help
Persuasion can work for you
Knowing when to "back off"
Change often takes time
Send a follow-up memorandum of understanding
What to do if you are not successful
Legal action, a last resort
The importance of monitoring
Where do you go from here?

Chapter 11

Becoming Involved in Your Child's School 121

You should become involved in your child's school
Employers realize the importance of monitoring
A wise consumer monitors
Set aside time to monitor
Becoming involved in your child's school educates you
Choose your level of involvement
First-level involvement—reading/phoning
Make sure you receive notices and memos
Use the phone to keep in touch
Separated and divorced parents and the information loop
Understanding the school's reporting system
Deciphering report cards
Second-level involvement—attending
Attending functions will help you learn about the school
Understanding open houses
A conference is a very effective way to communicate
Third-level involvement—participating
Parent/teacher groups help children and schools
Parent/teacher groups influence education
Serve on a study committee or board
Participate in educating your community

xiii

You can help the school meet its increasing responsibilities
Participate in the school budget process
Take an interest in your child's cocurricular activities
Learn more about the school through volunteering

Chapter 12
Opportunities for School Volunteers 133
What can volunteering do for my child?
What are the benefits of volunteering?
Develop new vocational skills as a volunteer
Volunteering can prepare you for greater responsibility
What can volunteering do for my child's school?
How do I get involved?
What volunteer opportunities exist in today's schools?
Volunteer in your child's future school
Serve as a volunteer while at home or in the community
Investigate school/business partnerships

Chapter 13
Dealing Effectively with Change 139
Challenges facing families
Challenges facing schools
Develop personal attributes in a supportive family setting
Adopt positive family moral values
Teach key skills to help your child adapt to change
Help your child avoid exploitation
Know who is supervising your child
Meet your child promptly after activities
Collaborate with the parents of your child's friends
Parent groups can be organized any time
A positive home atmosphere encourages learning

Chapter 14
Preparing Your Child for Optimal Learning 147
Parent interest and guidance are keys to success
Ten "Super Things" to do immediately
Ten steps to physical excellence
Eight personal traits that can accelerate success
Increase learning with a home learning center

Chapter 15
Establishing a Home Learning Center 155
Learning center environment
Learning center furniture
A folder, book bag, or backpack is essential
Learning center supplies and equipment
Learning center supplemental books and materials
Start a home library/media center
Computer information services
Ten effective ways to use a home learning center

Chapter 16
- Home Activities That Increase Learning 163
  - Activities can enhance your child's formal education
  - Educational activities can be fun and inexpensive
  - Every experience can be a learning experience
  - Selecting activities
  - Some activities have limited lives
  - Your interest and enthusiasm are important
  - Getting your child started on a home activity
  - High Interest Home Activities List

Chapter 17
- Community Activities and Resources That Increase Learning 193
  - Obtaining information about community activities
  - Determining if a program or activity is appropriate
  - Selecting activities
  - High Interest Community Activities and Resources List

Chapter 18
- Assessing Progress and Moving On 209
  - Continuous monitoring of a continuing journey
  - You have already begun to determine progress
  - Review your child's Education Action Plan
  - Where to get feedback
  - Tests as indicators of success
  - Indicators to look for in your child
  - Indicators to look for in the school
  - Moving toward increased excellence
  - Helping others achieve excellence
  - The future prospects for excellence

Appendix A:
- The National Education Goals 215

Appendix B:
- Blue Ribbon Schools Program 217

Appendix C:
- Letters and Memorandums 219

Resources 225
- Books 225
- Magazines 229
- Other resources 232

Index 239

About the Author 253

Worksheets, Forms and Lists

Educational Records File Inventory Form	37
Child's Interest Interview Form	40
Know Your Child Worksheet	47
Parent Recommendations Summary	52
School Survey Form	79
School Survey Balance Sheet	95
Education Action Plan Worksheet	109
High Interest Home Activities List	166
High Interest Community Activities and Resources List	195

Acknowledgments

Many people, past and present, have provided me with the knowledge and inspiration necessary to write this book. I have heard their voices and seen their faces as I have written each sentence. I hope they realize the importance of their contributions. They should take pride in what they have done to help children experience educational excellence.

I am especially indebted to my wife, Betty, to my children, Kay Kimball Gruder and Ken III, and to my daughter-in-law, Karen, for listening to my ideas, offering suggestions, and their assistance in planning and reviewing *Educational Excellence for Your Child*. I particularly appreciate Kay's help and valuable advice at all stages of writing, editing and publishing.

Preface

Educational Excellence for Your Child has been written with one purpose in mind, to help you increase the possibility your child will receive an excellent education. It is based on the author's experiences, observations, and strong belief that, while education has come under harsh criticism for its mediocrity, there are examples of excellence in every school. In fact, more and more teachers and schools are demonstrating that when one considers the quality of the programs they offer, and the results they are getting, they are worthy of recognition.

By acting as an informed "parent consumer," and working with the school, excellence can become a part of your child's life. Through your efforts, you can make an important contribution to his or her future, and to a substantial degree, the quality of education received by all children in your community. You should also experience personal satisfaction and enjoyment in the process.

Anyone can use this book

The suggestions and procedures described in this book can be used effectively by parents, family members, child advocates, or friends who have assumed all or part of the responsibility for the education of a child. Educators should also find it useful in helping parents become more involved in their children's education. It describes a "how-to-do-it" program, and includes hundreds of valuable ideas. These ideas have been used successfully by others, and can work for you. Many of the suggestions will be useful even if you know very little about your child's school and have only limited time to learn more about it.

In order to increase your understanding of the information presented, pertinent background information has been provided. Also, to simplify reading, educational jargon, abbreviations, dated facts, and fads have been avoided. *Educational Excellence for Your Child* can be easily understood and used by lay people, now and in the future. This information can be applied while working alone or with other parents and school staff members interested in achieving educational excellence.

Are you a wise consumer of education?

You may think of yourself as a wise consumer, but have you ever considered whether or not you are a wise consumer of education? Like many parents, you may spend hours, even weeks, deciding which stereo, automobile, or other consumer product to buy, but, for one reason or another, may not devote much time to ensuring your child receives a quality education. Could it be that you are satisfied with the job the school is doing? Possibly, but there are strong indications many children are not receiving the quality education their parents feel they deserve. If you suspect your son or daughter might be one of these students, the chances are very good that your involvement could make a difference.

Schools must serve parents as well as children

Schools, like most organizations, are bureaucracies. As such, they respond in somewhat predictable ways to the concerns of their constituents. For example, they often function in a traditional manner unless the government, parents, or students suggest, or insist on, change. Many parents do not realize that schools operate this way. Also, they often forget that schools have a responsibility to serve them as well as their children.

Unfortunately, many parents assume schools are doing the best they can to educate their children when this is not necessarily the case. All too often, parents hesitate to ask for help when problems occur. Unsatisfactory school experiences in the past, combined with a hesitancy to confront the power structure, lead many parents to avoid contacting their child's teacher or principal. If you are one of these people, the insights, ideas, and confidence you can gain from reading this book should help you overcome these obstacles.

Parent involvement can produce positive results

The suggestions that follow are based on sound educational principles, and take into account how change occurs in schools. They reflect the author's understanding of children and schools, as well as the successful real life experiences of hundreds of students, parents, and school staff members he has known. These observations and experiences have revealed something you might expect. Almost without exception, the parent who shows an interest in his or her child's education, and communicates this interest to the school, gets attention. More often than not, this attention leads to an improved education for that child. You can be one of these parents.

If after a thorough investigation you find you are satisfied with the education your child is receiving, sections of this book will continue to be useful. Of particular value is the information on preparing your child for optimal learning, Chapter 14, how to set up a home learning center, Chapter 15, and scores of suggestions describing how the resources of the home and community, Chapters 16–17, can be used to fill the gaps or to enrich your child's education.

Limitations of this book

Educational Excellence for Your Child recognizes the fact that profound changes are occurring in families and society. Some of these changes, particularly those affecting children and their schools, are discussed in Chapter 13. There is, though, no attempt to analyze all of the reasons behind these changes. There is a continuing flood of information available on this subject if the reader wants to learn more. What this book does do, is help you identify the strengths and weaknesses of your child, your family, and the school, so that with careful planning and effective persuasion you can increase the probability that your son or daughter will receive an excellent education.

You should not expect the information presented to solve all of your child's problems. This is especially true if your son or daughter is having great difficulty dealing with learning and life. Likewise, it cannot be the sole means of turning around a school that has fallen into a state of disarray. It does, though, present hundreds of practical hints that can be helpful to any child, parent, or educator.

As in using any how-to guide, you must recognize your limitations and the limitations of the approach you are planning to use. Seek professional assistance if the seriousness of the situation exceeds that which you are qualified to handle. The old adage, "if in doubt, don't" is a good one to follow, if only until you have determined the approach you have selected is within your capabilities, and that it has a good chance of success.

Things you should accomplish

You should accomplish the following while carrying out the program described in *Educational Excellence for Your Child*.

- ★ Start your child on the road to excellence.
- ★ Develop an Educational Records File for your child.
- ★ Determine your child's interests, needs, and learning style.
- ★ Develop a better understanding of the ways schools are organized for teaching and learning.
- ★ Using the School Survey Form, do the research necessary to gain important information about your child's present or future school.
- ★ Analyze the information you have collected so that you can make enlightened decisions.
- ★ Develop an effective Education Action Plan for your child.
- ★ Learn how to best present your plan to the school.
- ★ Gain the school's cooperation in providing excellence for your child.
- ★ Become an effective monitor of your child and the school.
- ★ Learn how you and other members of your family can make your lives more conducive to learning.
- ★ Set up a home learning center.
- ★ Utilize the resources of your home and community to enrich your child's education.
- ★ Determine if you have been successful.

Let's begin to obtain educational excellence

You are now ready to begin the process of obtaining educational excellence for your child. Take the time to review "How to Get the Most Out of This Book," which follows this section. This will save you time and energy. Before long, you will begin to realize that by spending a little time each week following the suggestions in *Educational Excellence for Your Child*, you will be able to gain substantial control over your child's education. By doing this, you can greatly increase the chances your son or daughter will receive a much better education than otherwise would have been the case. Also, you can expect your efforts to bring about changes in your child's school that will benefit all children.

How to Get the Most Out of This Book

Educational Excellence for Your Child consists of eighteen chapters. Each deals with one or more topics that will help you accomplish your objectives. The greatest benefits will accrue to your child if you carry out the suggestions described in the first ten chapters in the order presented. If this is done, you should find your activities occurring in a natural sequence. This is certainly the best approach if you are dissatisfied with the education your son or daughter is receiving, or if you would like your child to attend a different school, either locally, or in a new community.

You should realize, though, that each child, parent, family, school, and community is different. Your focus, and the specific approach you decide to take after reviewing this book and considering its suggestions, should be guided by your understanding of these differences.

I would encourage you to use any of the hundreds of suggestions found in later chapters whenever you like. It would be a shame, for example, to delay making a change that might increase your child's self-esteem or readiness to learn because you are still studying your child's needs or planning your school survey.

Begin by scanning the information included in this book. The easiest way to do this is to spend a few minutes reviewing the contents of each chapter. If you find something of interest turn to that page and read about it. Consider how you can use this information to improve your child's education. If a suggestion appeals to you, mark it, and plan to use it as you begin to develop your own approach.

Next, read the first few chapters. You will find specific information about things you can do to accomplish your objectives. Make notes in the margin or on a separate sheet as you study the suggestions. Review the worksheets and begin to customize them. Talk with others about what you have learned and begin to assemble your child's Educational Records File. At this point, you will be moving in the direction of educational excellence.

1

Introduction to Educational Excellence

The education of our nation's children
Children need it, parents are concerned about it, politicians promise it, and teachers and principals work on it. What is it? The answer, of course, is the education of our nation's children.

As people search for ways to improve education in the United States, there are three conclusions that seem to rise above all others:

★ there is a vital need for all schools to become excellent schools,

★ responsible parenting is essential in preparing children to take advantage of educational opportunities, and

★ parents, educators, and governmental and community leaders must work together if children are to reach their greatest potential.

Tens of thousands of people who have telephoned the U.S. Department of Education's Information Resource Center have heard the following recorded message emphasizing the importance of the family in obtaining a quality education. "Thirty years of research show that greater family involvement in children's learning is a critical link to achieving a high quality education and a safe, disciplined, learning environment for every student."

While most communities are making progress in improving their schools, some are not. Real change on a grand scale may take years. Unfortunately, your son or daughter cannot wait for these changes to occur. *Educational Excellence for Your Child* has been written to help you deal effectively with this situation. It will prepare you to identify your child's needs, increase your understanding of your role and the role of the school and community in the teaching/learning process, and provide you with practical suggestions so you can begin immediately to increase your child's chances of receiving an excellent education.

What is educational excellence?
Are there excellent things happening in your child's school? If this is the case, do you know what they are? How can you ensure your son or daughter has the opportunity to benefit from them? These are important questions that you should consider.

When describing excellence, most people tend to give several examples. Ask for a definition, and they use words like "quality" or "the best." They are, of course, right. Common dictionary definitions indicate the noun "excellence" means a high degree, or the highest degree, of good qualities. Other words associated with excellence include superior, virtue, and perfection. In education, as in life, excellence is admired and desired. As such, it is certainly important to every parent and child.

> Aa Bb Cc Dd Ee Ff Gg Hh Ii Jj
>
> Picture "excellence":
> If a picture is worth a thousand words, picture excellence.

The adjective "excellent" is used frequently in schools to describe a teacher's lesson, a child's behavior, or the quality of something a student has produced, as in the case of a written assignment or an art project. In some schools, the term is used on report cards to identify a category of performance far exceeding average. No doubt, you can think of other examples of things that either you or the school considered excellent.

Excellence is not always what it appears to be

People who visit a school for a brief period may feel it is excellent if they observe children moving quietly through the corridors. Parents have been known to judge a school by the amount of homework that is assigned. A school board member once said he could tell the quality of a school by how well the lawn was mowed during the summer. These things may be good, some even excellent, but they tell only part of the story.

School administrators can usually identify excellence, but occasionally they too have difficulty. A principal might assume a school is excellent because there are so few complaints about the building. A superintendent might equate excellence with a school's ability to stay within the budget. There is a possibility these people could be right. There is an even greater chance they could be wrong.

These conclusions may or may not be indicators of excellence. Even if they are, it would be a mistake to rate the quality of a school on so few factors. In reality, while the children are quiet, the homework is being assigned, the lawn is manicured, and the parents seem satisfied, the overall educational program, or important parts of it, could be far less than adequate. Thus, it is important to consider many factors when attempting to determine the quality of education provided by a school.

Who can best identify excellence?

One might think it would be the teachers, or perhaps the students, as they spend hundreds of hours each year in school. Yet, even these people may have difficulty. Often, children have not experienced schools other than their own. For some, their only comparisons are the television situation comedy classrooms or cartoon schools, with frustrated teachers and class clowns. Others form their opinions from conversations with parents or siblings, based on "when I was in school," or "when I was in that grade." Teachers, on the other hand, have had a variety of educational experiences. They have spent at least four years in formal training, during which time they learned to evaluate both students and programs. They talk daily with other teachers, administrators, children, and parents, and spend most of each working day in school. They are in an excellent position to see the positive and negative things happening in a school, and often do. Yet, even teachers can become so involved in the day-to-day operation of their classrooms, lesson preparation, lunch duty, and record keeping, that they may not fully recognize excellence when it exists. As a principal, I often had the opportunity to praise teachers who were totally unaware that something they had recently done was truly excellent.

Some excellence exists in every school

In spite of the current criticism of education, examples of excellence occur millions of times each day in schools across America. They can be found in the quality of the curricula, the attitude of individual students, and the efforts of teachers. You, like many parents, may already be aware of signs of excellence in your child's school. Indicators might include the introduction of a new enrichment course, discovering that a teacher had provided your child with an unusual amount of help, or learning the school had substantially improved its standardized test scores. You may also have recognized some of the more subtle indicators like your child telling you that he or she had a great day at school, getting out of bed early on school days, wanting to get back to classes after a vacation, or not bothering to watch a favorite television program because he or she is so engrossed in homework or a class project.

Identifying educational excellence is not always easy, yet it need not be difficult. By reading *Educational Excellence For Your Child*, you will learn to evaluate what is happening at school. You can then develop an informed opinion about what is excellent and what is not, particularly as it pertains to your child.

Successful schools have common attributes

The U.S. Department of Education has found that successful schools have common attributes (*Blue Ribbon Schools, Schools Recognized 1982–83 Through 1994–95*, U.S. Government Printing Office, Washington, D.C., 1995). These qualities have received extensive publicity, and have been adopted by many schools as they attempt to achieve excellence.

* ★ strong visionary leadership
* ★ a sense of shared purpose among faculty, students, parents, and the community
* ★ a school climate that is conducive to effective teaching and teacher growth and recognition
* ★ an environment that conveys the message that all students can learn
* ★ programs that challenge gifted, average, and at-risk students
* ★ evidence of impressive academic achievement and responsible student behavior
* ★ actively involved parents and broad community support
* ★ a commitment to an ongoing program of student assessment and school improvement
* ★ a "can do" attitude toward problem-solving, preferring to view "problems" as "opportunities"

These attributes should be kept in mind as you work with the school in achieving excellence for your child.

> Aa Bb Cc Dd Ee Ff Gg Hh Ii Jj Kk
>
> Educational Expertise: Each of us feels we are an expert on education by virtue of the fact that we have attended school.

Responsibility for your child's education

It is your responsibility, working closely with your child, professional educators, family members, and others in the community, to ensure your son or daughter receives an excellent education. This will not happen by chance. While some teachers may be able to provide the quality program and individual attention each child requires, this is a difficult task. All too often it is the exception rather than the rule.

You may have experienced crowded classrooms or poor teaching when you were a student. You may also have realized you were not getting the attention you needed. Similar situations occur today. Yet, the difficulties a school is experiencing does not lessen its responsibility to your son or daughter. Knowing this, you should feel comfortable in using the suggestions in this book to make sure your child receives the education that he or she needs and deserves.

Schools are in business to serve the public

Unfortunately, some parents have had negative experiences, either as children or as adults, when dealing with the school. Also, a small minority of educators behave in a manner that leaves parents feeling discouraged or inferior. As a result, parents are often reluctant to contact the school when attempting to bring about changes that will benefit their children. Additionally, many parents assume principals, guidance counselors, and teachers have authority over them. This could not be farther from the truth. Schools and school personnel are in business for only one purpose, to serve the public.

Educators have an obligation to listen to, and work with, parents. This is not to say that school officials do not have major control over what goes on in today's schools. They do, and as a consequence often must make decisions benefiting the greatest number of students rather than any one individual. You though, with few exceptions, are the ultimate authority when it comes to decisions relating to your child.

It is important to realize that as an adult and parent you have an entirely different relationship with the school than you had when you were a student. You should put aside any lingering reservations, or feelings of inferiority, and expect school officials to serve you as they would any other adult. Most educators, when properly approached, will work diligently to help you carry out your objectives. They, like you, realize that children are most likely to learn and to be successful when parents and schools work in unison.

Examples of parent successes

Every educator and most parents can recall situations when the efforts of a parent made the difference between a child's success or failure. You may know of examples from personal experience or from talking with friends. A child's success may have resulted from informing the school of an interest in art, writing, or sports, so that he or she could be encouraged in one of these areas. Success could also have occurred after a teacher was made aware of a physical problem or an incident at home that might have temporarily limited a child's ability to perform well or to be attentive in school.

It could have been more dramatic, as in the case of a concerned businessman whose son had Tourette's Syndrome, a rare disorder of movement that often includes repetitive grimaces, noises, or gestures. Knowing his child would attract attention in a new school, this parent offered to talk with the staff and his son's future class. This gave him the opportunity not only to describe the infliction, but also to point out his child's strengths. As a result, the students and staff of the new school were prepared to ensure a successful transition. This child became one of the most popular and respected children in his class and went on to become a very successful student and adult.

It also could have been the parents who reminded the principal that while their first two children had difficulty in school and had discipline problems, their third child was different and much more should be expected of her. They were right. As a result of one brief conference the child's teachers established higher expectations than those that might have been developed if the parents had not contacted the school. They were not disappointed with the result of their efforts.

Average children also require extra parent effort

By definition most children are considered average. As such, they seldom attract as much attention from the school staff as children who are having difficulty or those who are performing exceptionally well. They may not receive the individual attention required to capitalize on their ability. To overcome this problem it may be necessary for parents of average children to play a more significant role than might be realized in getting the school to provide an excellent education.

You understand your son or daughter in ways that are known only to you. If you want the school to be effective in educating your child, you must make a conscious effort to share some of this information with the school. It is interesting to note, but also a tragedy, that pet owners often provide kennel operators with more information, suggestions, and recommendations, when boarding their animals for a few days than parents give classroom teachers who will be teaching their children for a full year.

Effective communication usually requires more than one telephone call or a meeting at the beginning of the school year. Rest assured, though, that hundreds of millions of success stories have begun with a chance conversation with a teacher in the supermarket, or a brief memo or phone call to the school. Why leave communications to chance when it is relatively simple to keep in touch with your child's teachers, counselor, and principal?

As a concerned parent you must also realize that opportunities to improve the education of any child exist outside of school. You will find many suggestions of how to locate and use these resources in the latter chapters of this book. By doing more at home, and utilizing challenging programs available in your community, you can customize your child's education so that he or she will benefit greatly from these experiences. To do this, you will need to know what is available. You will also need to be sure the people offering these opportunities are familiar with your child's ability and needs. Talk with others about your child, and begin to utilize the world as a learning environment. This is one of the ways parents are ensuring that children who might otherwise go through life somewhat unnoticed, receive the benefits of excellence.

Obtaining excellence need not be difficult

Up to this point, you have gained some understanding of excellence and should be thinking about what it can mean to your child. You are aware of your responsibilities, and more than likely have thought about some of the things you would like to do in order to achieve excellence for your son or daughter. You might wonder if your child's school, or any part of it, offers an excellent education. You might also like to know what you can do if this is, or is not, the case. You may be asking the question, "How can I be more effective in communicating my concerns and desires to the school?" "How can I promote excellence?"

Some schools publish parent handbooks describing ways parents can provide input to maximize their children's education. Most hold orientation programs to familiarize parents with effective ways of communicating with the school. An increasing number have "home pages" that can be accessed by computer. The vast majority have parent/teacher organizations that can be of help. Some schools have counselors or other staff members who are assigned the responsibility of communicating with parents and the public. As a parent and taxpayer, you should use all of these resources.

Parents often hesitate to ask for help in shaping their children's education. This is not unusual, as most people have a sense of pride that tells them to take care of their problems themselves. While you can work alone, there is comfort, and quite often efficiency and strength, in working with others. Friends, relatives, and professionals within the community, can help you obtain a quality education for your child. You should not hesitate to request their assistance.

Time is at a premium in most households. *Educational Excellence for Your Child* has been written in a way that should help you conserve time by capitalizing on your previous experiences as a student and later as a parent. Using the knowledge you possess, and the information, guidelines, and suggestions included in this book, you should be able to proceed with confidence. This should result in the school serving you and your child in an efficient and effective manner.

You should keep the following guidelines in mind as you begin to plan and "make" the school work for your child.

- ★ Begin now! Don't wait until a problem occurs to try to improve your child's opportunities for excellence.

- ★ Don't apologize for taking a school staff member's time. It's part of the job. While this person's primary responsibility is to the students, parents come next.

- ★ Do ask for information. You have a right to know about things going on in school, to review your child's records, and to learn the reasons for decisions affecting your son or daughter.

- ★ Make it a point to know with whom you are talking. Be sure this person knows who you are, i.e. Becky Kelley's mom. Take notes for future reference.

- ★ As words can have several meanings, you should not assume your child's teacher or principal is using a word as you would define it. While you may be reluctant to ask what something means, educators are usually glad to answer your questions.

- ★ Make sure others realize your child has great potential. If you must err in describing your child, err in the direction of his or her "talents." When parents and teachers think children are smart, children learn more. This is also the result when a child feels confident about his or her ability.

- ★ After studying a situation, don't hesitate to make what you, or the school, might consider special requests. I can assure you that you will not be the first or last parent requesting something special to provide a better education for a child.

- ★ Smile! Be pleasant, understanding, and appreciative. These qualities can go a long way in helping you accomplish your objectives.

Set high goals and go for them

Many parents do not establish high goals for their children. How often have you thought or heard, "If it was good enough for us when we were in school, it's good enough for them today?" Let's look at this statement. Are you sure the education you received was good? How do you know? Are you willing to settle for "good" when "excellent" might be available? Are you willing to accept a "good" education for your child while some children attending your child's school are receiving an excellent education? Of course not.

To be effective in seeking excellence you must also be realistic in recognizing your child's strengths and weaknesses. Be candid in discussions with school personnel. To minimize serious weaknesses may complicate the process of obtaining an excellent education, and even deprive your son or daughter of needed remediation or supplementary services.

In today's highly competitive world, the child who receives a quality education stands the best chance for future success. Other things being equal, he or she will enjoy a better choice of post high school, college, and vocational opportunities. For most people, economic benefits will increase, as will the person's health and overall quality of life. For many, leisure will become more pleasurable and meaningful. Thus, it is fitting for you and your child to make a sincere effort to raise your sights from "good" to "excellent."

Remember, each child is different

Before beginning the process of obtaining educational excellence for your child, you will want to keep in mind that each child is different. It would be helpful to have a general idea of what causes differences, as they play a role in the education of each child and each child's response to education. Most parents and teachers are well aware of the fact that each child is different from all others. They do, though, sometimes have difficulty deciding whether or not to consider some of these differences when making decisions.

Differences come from either heredity or environment. Our initial mental and physical characteristics stem from our biological parents. They are acquired by heredity. Some of these characteristics remain with us during our entire lives. Others are modified by the experiences we have as individuals, as part of a family, and as members of society. These relationships and experiences are an important part of a person's environment. Not only is each child different from all other children at birth, but these differences are continually changing as a child grows and develops.

Parents often wonder why brothers and sisters who live in what they consider "the same family" can be so different. They tend to overlook the fact that their family is constantly evolving. Each of their children has lived during a different time. Children also experience different social situations. Beginning at birth, interactions with family members vary. For example, there is a big difference between being the oldest or only child in a family, as compared to being the youngest, or being sandwiched between two or more children. Family schedules, economic resources, and varying experiences add to a mix that makes each person unique.

Most differences are normal

What would be worse than "all children being different?" The answer, of course, is "all children being the same." People generally accept children as they are, as most differences are normal. It is only when a child has difficulty functioning within the accepted norms of the family, school, or society that anyone expresses much concern.

Each child should be viewed as a unique individual who has certain strengths and weaknesses. Parents and teachers must recognize individual differences in order to provide children with the kinds of nurturing they require. It is, though, particularly important not to dwell on these differences. The exception would be when a difference makes it difficult for a child to function effectively. It is then the job of parents and teachers to address the problem by providing the education and experiences necessary to help the child achieve his or her greatest potential. A good way to do this is to gain a better understanding of your child, and to use this information in planning for the future.

Educational Excellence for Your Child

Let's get started

You are now ready to obtain an excellent education for your child. First you will ensure that all of the reports and other data you have accumulated about your child are at your fingertips. Then, using the worksheets provided, you will learn more about your child. This information will be used when working with your child and the school. Many of the things you will do to obtain educational excellence for your child can be done at home. Thus, they can be completed in private and according to your time schedule. This is especially true for the activities described in Chapters 2 and 3. Completing this process should increase your enthusiasm and strengthen your confidence to earnestly pursue educational excellence for your child.

2

Getting to Know Your Child Better

Building a foundation for excellence

The information presented in this chapter will help you establish a foundation on which you can begin the process of obtaining an excellent education for your son or daughter. It will help you review your child's past, evaluate the present, and aid in planning the future. This will result in an up-to-date working record that will make you more aware of your child's likes, dislikes, strengths, weaknesses and needs. This information can help you understand what motivates your son or daughter to learn. It will be most beneficial if you gather this information before proceeding further in working with the school to achieve educational excellence. You will take the following steps to accomplish this task.

- ✓ Set up an Educational Records File for your child.
- ✓ Gather your child's records from around your home.
- ✓ Obtain copies of missing records.
- ✓ Inventory and file all records that should be saved.
- ✓ Conduct your Child's Interest Interview.

If you are like most parents, you know the kinds of information and documents you already have about your child. You also have a pretty good idea of the additional information you may want to obtain. This is good, as it will save you time and energy. It is important, though, to organize this information in a way that makes it easy to use. The suggestions included in this chapter will help you do this.

The steps described to obtain and organize data can be completed at your convenience. They should not require more than a couple of hours, unless you become fascinated with what you are doing and decide to become lost in your child's past, present, or future.

Developing a file of educational records

One of the first things you will want to do is to become familiar with the Educational Records File Inventory Form and directions for using it. A copy of the form has been included at the end of this chapter. It will remind you of the numerous documents that should be saved. Begin by reviewing the form. Next, set up the suggested folders or envelopes. Finally, gather all of your child's papers and documents and file them in the appropriate folder or envelope where they can be easily located when needed.

Unfortunately, more than one child has ended up waiting in line to get an unnecessary inoculation, simply because the parent could not find a record of the initial immunization. Your child's Educational Records File is so important you should take the time to set it up now, even if you don't follow another recommendation in this book.

Parents often maintain better records for their motor vehicles than they do for their children. Perhaps newborn infants should be sent home from hospital with manila expanding folders attached to their wrists, in which essential documents could be kept. If this were done, it might be as easy to find a child's birth certificate or the previous year's standardized test scores, as it is the automobile registration or proof of vehicle insurance.

Your initial efforts in gathering information and organizing your child's Educational Records File will not require special supplies or an inordinate amount of time. A few large, new or used, envelopes will work just fine. If, on the other hand, you have a personal computer, you may want to use it to create a filing system for storing information. After all, there is little value in saving dozens of old report cards or forms with test results when they can be summarized, or scanned and stored electronically for future reference.

If your child is quite young, it will only be necessary to set up two or three categories for information. For children who are already in school, five or six categories will usually be adequate. It is suggested that you file documents in the following folders:

- ✓ general information documents folder, which will contain items that might be needed at any age (medical reports, duplicate Social Security card, birth certificate and the like)
- ✓ preschool documents folder
- ✓ elementary school documents folder
- ✓ middle or junior high school documents folder
- ✓ high school documents folder, which can include items related to future education and/or employment. You could also set up a separate post-high school folder if you would like.
- ✓ additional items folder

As your child grows older, you may feel additional categories would be desirable. If this is the case, you are encouraged to create them. The important thing is that you are comfortable with your system, and that you are able to quickly file and locate the items you need.

Filing system helpful hints

Keep your filing system simple. Your primary objective is to assemble documents and other information related to your child in one location. This way they will be readily available for your use. Manila folders, large envelopes, or even one or two shallow cardboard boxes are probably better than what you are now using. Expanding folders are available in office supply and discount department stores. These are already divided into individual sections for various categories of documents. Be sure to set up a separate file for each of your children.

Your folders or envelopes should be large enough to allow the documents to be kept flat. It is a good idea to place these folders or envelopes in a box, drawer, or protective container. This will prevent papers from falling out of a folder, or the loss of an envelope. For additional security, records should be stored in a safe, file cabinet, or metal box specifically designed to protect documents from insects, fire, mildew, and water damage.

Label the outside of each envelope or folder. A simple way to do this is to letter your child's name, and the title of the information contained, at the top of the folder where it can be easily seen. Then list the contents, in pencil, directly below the title. Another possibility is to use a copy of the Educational Records File Inventory Form. Place check marks next to the items on the form, and attach it to the folder. Pencil is much better than pen as it will allow you to make changes more easily. If the Inventory Form is used, a copy should be included with your records while another copy can be kept in a separate location.

It is important to keep an up-to-date account of the documents in your child's file. Note the removal date and new location of any item removed for even a short period of time.

Use photocopies of valuable documents. Your child's birth certificate, passport, citizenship papers, Social Security card, and other official documents should be stored in a secure place such as a fireproof safe, cabinet, or bank safe deposit box. Copies of these documents will serve most educational purposes and can be placed in your child's Educational Records File. You should include a notation in your child's file stating where each original document is located.

Date all information. One of the most perplexing problems a parent can face is that of trying to establish the identity or date of a document, sample of a child's work, or photograph. This is especially true if substantial time has elapsed since it was filed. The task often becomes impossible if there are several children in the family. A simple notation on the front or back of the item is all that is needed. Do it now!

It is a good idea to do as some other parents have done and preserve samples of art work, writing assignments, and the like. These can be placed in a "portfolio." Portfolios of various size are available at art supply stores. These samples will help your child see the progression that occurs as he or she matures, learns more things, and becomes more skilled. Sample work should be reviewed periodically. Some of the better examples can be used when applying for enrichment programs, college, or work.

Keep your child's Educational Records File up to date. This cannot be overemphasized. Once you have set up a file, entering new items becomes simple. If you are in doubt as to whether an item should be saved, I would recommend that it be included. It is much easier to remove an item at a later date than it is to search for it when you finally realize it is needed. When you have set up your Educational Records File, you will be ready to conduct your Child's Interest Interview.

Introduction to the Child's Interest Interview

Quite likely, you have found that one of the best ways to obtain information is to talk with an expert. Who is a better expert on your child than your child? This is the reason for interviewing your son or daughter at this time. The Child's Interest Interview Form will help you do this in a manner that will provide information that will be useful in working with your child and the school to achieve excellence.

There are, of course, some situations where parents know their children better than the children know themselves. Examples would be, very young children and children with certain handicapping conditions. Also, some children do not have the language skills required to verbalize their likes and dislikes. You, on the other hand, are very much aware of the significance of each smile, sign, gesture, or cry.

Educational Excellence for Your Child

The Child's Interest Interview should be conducted only if your child is able to express opinions in a meaningful fashion. If this is not the case, you will have an opportunity to record your observations and impressions of your child when you complete the Know Your Child Worksheet. A sample form and directions are included in Chapter 3.

One of the best ways to determine if an interview with your child will be productive is to try it. You will quickly learn whether or not the process is working. If there is not a free flow of information, it is usually best to discontinue the interview. If this is necessary, it is still a good idea to become familiar with the Child's Interest Interview Form. You will quite likely have the opportunity to ask these questions at a later date, and in a less structured setting.

Conducting the Child's Interest Interview

The key to a successful interview is to keep it short, simple, and relaxed. The Child's Interest Interview Form has been designed to meet the first two requirements, while the task of creating a relaxed atmosphere is up to you. It is recommended that you do the following things to ensure a successful interview.

- Become familiar with the interview questions. By doing this, you may not need to have them in front of you during the interview.
- Consider using a discussion format rather than asking formal questions if you would be comfortable with this method.
- Set aside about forty-five minutes when you and your child will not feel distracted.
- Choose a comfortable location, where you will not be interrupted. If this is difficult to do at home, go out for a sundae, take a walk, or find a quiet place in a park.
- Tell your child why you are doing the interview; in other words, to learn some things that will make it possible to get a better education.
- Be careful not to let your personal feelings dominate the discussion.
- Refrain from being judgmental.
- Stop or reschedule the interview if you sense it is not going well.
- Write down your child's responses. This can be done during the interview or shortly thereafter if you feel you can remember what he or she has said.
- Flag any unexpected or questionable information requiring follow-up.

You are now ready to review the Child's Interest Interview Form included at the end of the chapter. While doing this, think about how you might ask each question. You should feel free to change the wording of any item if it will help you get a more accurate or detailed response. Space has been provided at the end of the form to record your child's answers to any additional questions you might ask. This is also a good place to add other information that might emerge from your discussions.

Take a more comprehensive look at your child

When you have completed the steps described in this chapter, you will be ready to proceed to Chapter 3 where you will take a more comprehensive look at your child. After reading the information it contains, you will record your personal impressions of your child on the Know Your Child Worksheet. This information, along with the data you already have, will be used in developing your Parent Recommendations Summary which will serve as an important tool as you take further steps to achieve educational excellence for your child.

EDUCATIONAL RECORDS FILE
INVENTORY FORM

Child's Name: _____ Date: _____

The following documents should be included in your child's Educational Records File. If an item is not in your possession you may wish to obtain the original or a copy. If this is not possible, record its location, along with a name and telephone number, for future reference.

If your child is young, you will want to include all information to date. For an older child it is recommended that you first file the "General Information" documents, along with key items from prior years in order to establish a baseline record. Current information can then be added as it becomes available.

General Information Documents Folder	Comments	Date
Birth certificate (copy)		
Finger and/or footprints		
Social Security card (duplicate)		
Medical and dental reports, including immunization records, blood type, and eyeglass prescription		
Test results (mental and/or physical)		

File these items here or in grade level folders:
   Educational Records File Inventory Forms
   Child's Interest Interview Forms
   Know Your Child Worksheets
   Parent Recommendations Summaries
   School Survey Forms
   School Survey Balance Sheets
   Education Action Plan Worksheets		

Preschool Documents Folder	Comments	Date
Registration forms		
Day-care records and reports		
Preschool records and reports		
Notes from teachers		
Summaries of meetings and telephone conversations		

Elementary School Documents Folder	Comments	Date
School registration forms		
Report cards		
Standardized test results		

	Comments	Date
Individualized Education Plans (if applicable)		
Notes from teachers		
Summaries of meetings and telephone conversations		
Awards		
Middle or Junior High School Documents Folder	**Comments**	**Date**
School registration forms		
Report cards		
Standardized test results		
Individualized Education Plans (if applicable)		
Comprehensive exam results		
Notes from teachers		
Summaries of meetings and telephone conversations		
Labor Department working papers (if applicable)		
Resumes		
Letters of recommendation		
Employment applications		
Job evaluations		
Awards		
High School Documents Folder	**Comments**	**Date**
School registration forms		
Report cards		
Standardized test results		
Individualized Education Plans (if applicable)		
Comprehensive exam results		
Notes from teachers		
Summaries of meetings and telephone conversations		
Labor Department working papers (if applicable)		
Resumes		
Letters of recommendation		
Employment applications		
Job evaluations		
Diploma and awards		
College entrance test results		

College applications and acceptance information		
Scholarship applications		
Student financial aid applications		
Student loan application		
Selective Service Acknowledgment and military information		
Driver's license information		

There are additional items that might be useful. You may wish to place them in a separate folder or portfolio reserved for less official information.

Additional Items Folder	**Comments**	**Date**
Samples of original writing, drawings, etc.		
Newspaper articles related to your child or the school		
Photographs		
School newsletters noting relevant programs		
Articles indicating the overall quality of school programs		
Information about summer school or camp programs		
Information about your child's volunteer experiences		
Special programs and travel experiences		
Videos showing physical or mental accomplishments		

Other: _____

_____

_____

_____

_____

_____

_____

_____

_____

_____

_____

_____

_____

(Copyright © 1996 Kenneth R. Kimball, Jr.)

CHILD'S INTEREST INTERVIEW FORM

Name: _____ Age: _____ Date: _____

1. What activities do you most enjoy?   Why do you like these activities?
   a. _____   _____
   b. _____   _____
   c. _____   _____

2. What activities do you least enjoy?   Why don't you like these activities?
   a. _____   _____
   b. _____   _____
   c. _____   _____

3. Do you prefer to work or play alone? Y (Yes) N (No)   With others? Y / N
   Why? _____
   _____

4. Do you prefer to do things with a particular age group?
   Your age? Y / N   Why? _____
   Younger?   Y / N   Why? _____
   Older?   Y / N   Why? _____
   Adults?   Y / N   Why? _____

5. Think about some of the best teachers you have had, past or present. Did you learn a lot from them? Y / N Were they strict? Y / N Lenient? Y / N Describe some of the things these teachers did to make you feel they were the best. _____
   _____
   _____

6. Let's talk about some of the things you have learned in and out of school. Examples might include reading, writing, math, science, history, art, music, world languages, cooking, sewing, carpentry, physical fitness, sports, and hobbies.
   Which have been the easiest to learn?

   _____   _____   _____
   _____   _____   _____

   Why have these been easy to learn?_____
   _____
   _____

Which have been the most difficult to learn?

_____   _____   _____

_____   _____   _____

Why have they been difficult to learn? _____

_____

Do you want to learn more about some new things? Y / N What? _____

_____

What kinds of help do you need to do this? _____

_____

7. Would you like to spend more time on any work, school, or recreational activities?
   What are these activities?   Why do they interest you?

   _____   _____

   _____   _____

   _____   _____

   When would you like to do these things? Now? ____ Next summer? ____
   Next year? ____ After you finish high school? ____ Other? _____

8. People learn in different ways. Do you learn things best by:

	Often	Sometimes	Never	Why?
Hearing or being told?	___	___	___	_____
Seeing or observing?	___	___	___	_____
Figuring things out?	___	___	___	_____
Discussing them?	___	___	___	_____
Memorizing?	___	___	___	_____
Writing things down?	___	___	___	_____
Drawing?	___	___	___	_____
Actually doing things?	___	___	___	_____
Other?	___	___	___	_____

9. Additional questions and comments: _____

   _____

   _____

   _____

   _____

   _____

(Copyright © 1996 Kenneth R. Kimball, Jr.)

3

Determining Your Child's Needs

Step back and look at your child
Completing the forms in this chapter will enable you to establish long-, intermediate-, and short-term goals for your son or daughter. These goals will give direction to your child's life. Your efforts will also produce information that will be helpful in planning and conducting your school visits. The Know Your Child Worksheet encourages you to step back from your daily routine, and to take a more comprehensive look at your son or daughter. You will record your personal observations, impressions, and other data about your child. When completed, it will be used along with information compiled in Chapter 2, to help you determine the school program that would best benefit your child. The information you have gathered can be summarized by completing the Parent's Recommendations Summary included in this chapter.

Do you feel you know your child well? Quite likely, your answer is "yes." Why, then would you want to take the time to fill out the Know Your Child Worksheet? The primary reason is that it will give you an opportunity to look at your child in a more objective, and consequently more useful manner than is usually the case. You will consider your child's interests and activities, work habits, skills and mental abilities, and physical characteristics.

The information that follows will introduce you to each section of the worksheet. You will want to read it carefully prior to answering the questions. You will find some questions are purposely similar to those you asked when interviewing your child. The difference is that you will be answering them this time.

Section A - Interests and Activities
One of the best ways to determine people's interests is to observe how they spend their time when they are free to choose what they want to do. As an adult who is responsible for a child, you are in a good position to do this.

It is also helpful to be aware of any interests your child has that cannot be pursued due to time constraints, geographic location, cost, or other factors. Examples might include participating in certain sports, visiting distant relatives, or engaging in costly hobbies. An awareness of desired activities can be as important in understanding your child as the things he or she finds more readily available.

When using this form, you will record your child's activities, and briefly describe how he or she developed the knowledge and skills to participate in them. This information will help you determine the way your son or daughter learns best. This can be of great value when describing the kind of teacher, classroom, curriculum, and school that would meet his or her needs.

You should not be concerned if your child's interests or activities seem to be ever changing. This is not unusual. It is one of the reasons why there is a continuous supply of used athletic equipment and hobby items on the market. Look for patterns of interest your child might display, as they usually reveal much more about a person's likes and dislikes than a single activity.

Section B - Work Habits

The way people approach and perform various tasks determines, to a substantial degree, their success or failure in life. Often referred to as "work habits," these actions and attitudes become especially important when one attempts to obtain a quality education. Teachers and parents agonize over, and teach work habits. Business, industry, and government spend millions of dollars a year trying to improve the work habits of their employees. Unless parents and schools are more effective in instilling good work habits in children at an early age, some individuals and society will continue to suffer.

If after completing this section, you confirm that your son or daughter has good work habits, you are fortunate. If this is not the case, you will want the school to consider your assessment when making teacher, classroom, or grade assignments.

Section C - Skills and Mental Abilities

The mind is, by far, the most complex and certainly one of the most studied parts of the human body. While scientists are learning more about it each day, they still find there is much they don't understand. One thing that is known is that a person seldom uses more than a small percentage of his or her mental capacity.

Testing is one way to learn more about a person's ability. It is important to realize, though, that in spite of decades of research and testing, the assessment of mental ability is less than an exact science. Language barriers, cultural experiences, reading problems, motivation, physical well-being, emotional state, attentiveness, and a variety of other factors can and do affect the results of any mental test. Thus, the information gained from intelligence tests, especially the rather short group tests conducted by schools, should be used guardedly.

The results of a test may provide new information about your child or substantiate previous tests. The results could also be inconsistent with earlier testing, or quite different from the way your child performs. If the latter is true, you should insist on further testing before drawing conclusions. When making decisions regarding your child's education, the results of mental tests should be considered, but only along with other relevant information that either you or the school might have.

Most teachers, and indeed many parents, find it is much better to look at how a child functions on a daily basis rather than relying on test results to determine ability or potential. Does your son or daughter remember important things

> Aa Bb Cc Dd Ee Ff Gg Hh Ii Jj Kk
>
> The value of knowledge: While knowledge is essential, knowing how to find and use it is equally important in everyday life.

and retain newly acquired skills? How well does he or she use reading and writing skills, handle money, or play a musical instrument? As a parent, you are aware of how quickly your child "catches on," and whether or not he or she has difficulty figuring things out. This information can be very helpful in guiding your child's education.

Your child's teacher observes your child in a variety of social and intellectual situations, and usually has a good idea of his or her ability to learn. You should consider performance at school as well as at home, when establishing goals that will benefit your son or daughter. These goals should be challenging, while not being so high that they lead to discouragement. This is essential if your child is to receive the kind of education and level of instruction necessary to reach excellence.

When completing Section C of the Know Your Child Worksheet, you should consider the following:

- ✓ your personal assessment of your child's skills and mental ability
- ✓ assessment of your child's skills and mental ability by present and former teachers
- ✓ intelligence test and standardized achievement test results
- ✓ reports you have received from professionals or agencies
- ✓ impressions or observations of people who know your child

Section D - Physical Characteristics

Your child's physical well-being is a key factor in learning. Think of your own participation in everyday activities. How well do you concentrate and learn when you have a headache or a backache? Has fatigue ever prevented you from performing physical or mental tasks as well as you would have liked? Does your physical comfort, or how you sense you appear to others, ever affect your disposition? Your answer to each of these questions is probably "yes." A similar response could be expected from most people. When completing this section, it is important to accurately characterize your child's physical condition, as this information will be helpful in maximizing learning.

Using the information from the Know Your Child Worksheet

When you have completed the Know Your Child Worksheet, you will have a written record describing your current impressions of your child. You will also have completed a process that may be as important as the final product. You elected to think about a number of aspects of your child's life and education in a way not considered by most parents. Undoubtedly, you will know your son or daughter better now than before you completed the worksheet. This should help you guide your child's education in directions that will be acceptable to you both. I would recommend that you update this worksheet on an annual basis, or more often if necessary.

The Know Your Child Worksheet and other data you have collected will be used on several occasions as you begin to bring about the changes necessary to achieve excellence. It will serve an immediate purpose as you fill out your Parent Recommendations Summary. This is the third and final form you will complete before planning your school visit.

Introduction to the Parent Recommendations Summary

The Parent Recommendations Summary will help you organize the information you have obtained as a result of setting up your child's Educational Records File and conducting the Child's Interest Interview in Chapter 2, and completing the Know Your Child Worksheet in this chapter. On this summary you will describe the educational program and setting that you feel will most benefit your son or daughter. This information will be used in preparing for and conducting your school visit, as described in Chapters 6-7, and in developing an Education Action Plan for your child, Chapter 9.

First, review the Parent Recommendations Summary Form. You will find it has been designed to be as open-ended as possible, while providing enough structure to channel your thinking about important aspects of your child's education. At this point you have probably begun to realize that your child can benefit from certain kinds of schools, classrooms, teaching styles, and the like. If you have not reached this stage in your thinking, do not be concerned. Review your previous work, and by all means, read Chapters 4 and 5. These chapters include information on school organization and programs that will help you complete the first three items on the Summary. While parents who have had other children in school may be familiar with this information, others may not. These chapters must be considered essential reading for those who do not feel ready to complete the Parent Recommendations Summary.

It is important to have your child's Educational Records File and other pertinent background information available while completing your Summary. Refer to it as necessary. Do not spend too much time on any one question. You can always think about what you have written for a day or two before writing your final version. You should be more than satisfied with the results.

You are becoming a wise consumer

Your Parent Recommendations Summary will probably take about thirty minutes to complete. Once this is done you will have an outline of the educational setting and program you want for your child. This will be helpful when you conduct your school survey, and later when you attempt to obtain the most desirable arrangement for your child. It will also be useful in establishing goals and strategies for change, and in setting up experiences to maximize learning in the home and community.

By now you have made a conscious decision to ensure that your child receives maximum benefit from school and various other educational experiences. You have decided to be a wise consumer of education. Interestingly, even though you have already completed a number of the steps suggested in this book, you have probably spent less time on this task than doing the back-to-school shopping or watching television for a few hours. It should be reassuring to know that if you do nothing further to seek excellence, you will have done more to understand and help your child than all but a small percentage of today's parents. Now you have an opportunity to really make a difference.

If you have not already read Chapter 4 in connection with your Parent Recommendations Summary, you should do so now. You will learn about different ways that schools are organized. What grades should be included in a school? Does it make any difference? Should your son or daughter attend a small school or large school? What are the advantages and disadvantages of a self-contained classroom? Could your child benefit from team teaching? These are just a few of the concepts and practices currently used by schools. Becoming familiar with them will greatly increase your ability to talk with school officials and will help you guide your child's education.

KNOW YOUR CHILD WORKSHEET

Name: _____ Age: _____ Date: _____

This worksheet will help you organize and record the insights and information you presently have about your child. It will provide a record of things you have thought about but may not have written down. It is an important part of your data collection process and will be of value, along with information from other sources, in determining what is best for your child. It is for your personal use and need not be shared with others, unless you choose to do so. You will want to be as candid as possible in considering your responses.

This worksheet consists of four sections. You will respond to several questions about your child in each section. Answer each question as accurately as possible, based on the information you have. As your first thought is often your best thought, it is unnecessary to dwell too long on your responses. You can usually make changes later on. Completion time is less than one hour.

A. Interests and Activities:

1. When working or playing "alone," my child spends a lot of time pursuing the following activities:

   Activity   How did your child learn about, and get started in, each activity?
   _____   _____
   _____   _____
   _____   _____
   _____   _____

2. When "playing with others" my child spends a lot of time pursuing the following activities:

   Activity   How did your child learn about, and get started in, each activity?
   _____   _____
   _____   _____
   _____   _____
   _____   _____

3. My child has indicated an interest in pursuing the following additional activities if the opportunity arises.

   _____   _____
   _____   _____
   _____   _____

4. My child is a good_____ leader_____ follower_____ both_____ neither.

Educational Excellence for Your Child

5. My child watches approximately _____ hours of television each week.
6. My child averages the following amount of sleep each night:
   Sun.–Thurs. nights _____ hours   Fri. and Sat. nights _____ hours

B. Work Habits:

	Circle one			
	Always	Usually	Seldom	Never

My child:
a. Is able to plan and carry out activities	4	3	2	1
b. Begins work without being told to do so	4	3	2	1
c. Follows directions	4	3	2	1
d. Performs chores and work with little supervision	4	3	2	1
e. Follows through on work and play activities	4	3	2	1
f. Gets things done on time, without a reminder	4	3	2	1
g. Is able to evaluate how well he or she is doing	4	3	2	1
h. Works well with others	4	3	2	1
i. Works well alone	4	3	2	1
j. Works best in a structured situation or classroom	4	3	2	1

Comments:_____
_____
_____

C. Skills and Mental Abilities:

Rate your child's skills and abilities in each of the following areas. If he or she is quite young, or has not taken a particular subject, you can still respond by thinking about what each subject area includes. For example, in the case of art; consider drawing, painting, modeling with clay, and craft-type activities. Add any additional skills or abilities that you feel are helpful in understanding your child.

	Circle one			
	Always	Usually	Seldom	Never

1. My child displays strong ability in:

a. Reading	4	3	2	1
b. Writing	4	3	2	1
c. Speaking	4	3	2	1
d. World languages	4	3	2	1
e. Mathematics	4	3	2	1
f. Social Studies	4	3	2	1
g. Science	4	3	2	1
h. Computers	4	3	2	1

i.	Sports	4	3	2	1
j.	Art	4	3	2	1
k.	Music	4	3	2	1
l.	Drama	4	3	2	1
m.	Dance	4	3	2	1
n.	Life skills	4	3	2	1
o.	Industrial technology	4	3	2	1
p.	Problem solving	4	3	2	1
q.	Creative thinking	4	3	2	1
r.	Mechanical tasks	4	3	2	1

Other/comments:_____
_____
_____

2. Have you received oral or written information from the school or another source that has helped you understand your child's mental characteristics? Y / N
   Summarize:_____
   _____
   _____

3. Has remediation (extra help) been recommended? Y / N
   Summarize:_____
   _____
   _____

4. Has your child received remediation? Y / N
   Summarize:_____
   _____
   _____

5. Has enrichment been recommended? Y / N
   Summarize:_____
   _____
   _____

6. Has your child participated in enrichment activities? Y / N
   Summarize:_____
   _____
   _____

Educational Excellence for Your Child

When answering the following questions, consider how your your child behaves as compared to others in his or her age group. You should try to recall feedback you have received from your child's teachers, peers, family members, and friends, as well as your personal knowledge.

7. Does your child maintain self-control in stressful situations?
   ____ Often ____ Sometimes ____ Seldom ____ Never
   Comment:_____
   _____
   _____

8. Is your child the recipient of other children's pranks or thoughtlessness?
   ____ Often ____ Sometimes ____ Seldom ____ Never
   Comment:_____
   _____
   _____

9. Does your child have serious misbehavior problems?
   At home: ____ Often ____ Sometimes ____ Seldom ____ Never
   Comment:_____
   _____
   _____

   At school: ____ Often ____ Sometimes ____ Seldom ____ Never
   Comment:_____
   _____
   _____

D. Physical Characteristics:

Circle one

	Always	Usually	Seldom	Never
1. My child:				
a. Feels well physically	4	3	2	1
b. Is well coordinated	4	3	2	1
c. Likes physical activity	4	3	2	1
d. Enjoys competition	4	3	2	1
e. Is satisfied with his or her physical appearance	4	3	2	1
f. Participates in sports	4	3	2	1
g. Avoids accidents	4	3	2	1
h. Takes responsibility for personal hygiene	4	3	2	1

i. Is rested and alert	4	3	2	1
j. Functions well as a team member	4	3	2	1
k. Has demonstrated leadership in sports	4	3	2	1

Other/comments:_____
_____
_____

2. My child is: ___ short ___ average ___ tall compared to his or her peers.
   Comments:_____
   _____
   _____

3. My child is: ___ underweight ___ average ___ overweight compared to his or her peers.
   Comments:_____
   _____
   _____

4. Briefly summarize any information you have received from physicians, nurses, therapists, dentists, eye specialists, or other dependable sources, which has helped you better understand your child's physical well-being: _____
   _____
   _____
   _____

5. My child has the following physical problems that limit his or her activities or may require special arrangements or remediation: _____
   _____
   _____
   _____

   Additional comments regarding my child: _____
   _____
   _____
   _____
   _____

(Copyright © 1996 Kenneth R. Kimball, Jr.)

Educational Excellence for Your Child

PARENT RECOMMENDATIONS SUMMARY

Child's Name: _____ Age: _____ Date: _____

Using information from your child's Educational Records File, Child's Interest Interview, Know Your Child Worksheet, and other data and descriptions you might have, briefly describe the kind of school, classroom, teacher, and curriculum you feel would be best for your child. Also suggest any remediation or enrichment you would recommend. You may wish to use additional paper for your responses.

1. Describe the characteristics of a school (size, location, grades, program focus, schedule, etc.) that would be most desirable for your child.

2. Describe the kind of classroom (self-contained, team teaching, size, curriculum focus, etc.) that would most benefit your child.

3. Describe the qualities and teaching style of the teacher that you feel would be best for your child.

4. List academic areas in which your child might do well.

5. List nonacademic areas in which your child might do well.

   _____
   _____
   _____
   _____
   _____
   _____
   _____
   _____

6. Describe any remediation you feel your child might need.

   _____
   _____
   _____
   _____
   _____
   _____
   _____
   _____

7. List any enrichment or cocurricular activities that would benefit your child.

   _____
   _____
   _____
   _____
   _____
   _____
   _____
   _____

8. Other comments:

   _____
   _____
   _____
   _____
   _____
   _____
   _____
   _____
   _____

(Copyright © 1996 Kenneth R. Kimball, Jr.)

4

Looking at School Organization

Excellence is a journey, not a destination
A good way to think of excellence is to consider it the journey one takes through life, rather than the destination at the end of the trip. Just as a traveler discovers excellence traveling through cities, small towns, and rural areas across America, the learner finds excellence in the daily experience of learning. To the traveler, it is a quiet campsite, a magnificent view, or a superb meal at a highly acclaimed restaurant. To the learner, it is being taught by a "Teacher of the Year," perfecting a new skill, or receiving several "A's" on a report card. Yes, excellence is the journey not the destination.

In this context, educational excellence is not limited to graduation day, college acceptance, or getting a job. It is not even limited to what goes on in classes during the more than thirteen years a student attends school. It is, rather, an unlimited array of positive experiences that take place in the school, home, and community throughout a person's entire life. As one who realizes the importance of education, you can appreciate this concept. Like the rest of us, you are still making this journey.

Unfortunately, not all journeys are smooth. You have probably heard about children who have learned very little, or who have seemed to regress during a school year. While this may or may not be the school's fault, it is still tragic. You may also be aware of school programs where the diplomas are of little value when applying for college, or when trying to get a good paying job. What a shame! These situations need not exist. There are ways to correct or avoid them. Some solutions lie within the school while others lie at home. It has been demonstrated over and over again that children are more likely to become better educated if their parents do the following important things:

★ show greater interest in their children's lives

★ offer direction and encouragement

★ become more involved in the schools their children attend

★ provide greater opportunities for learning at home

If you do these things, you can help your child avoid many of the shortcomings of today's schools and society, while reaping the advantages of excellence along the way.

Learn all you can about schools

On the average, one family in six moves each year. Many of these families have school age children. If you are planning to move to a new community, you may be presented with the opportunity to select from several residential areas and school situations. If so, you will want to learn all you can about the educational possibilities by planning school visits and meeting with key educators.

There are a number of ways to obtain information about any school, the most important of which is to visit the school, look around, and talk with people. By doing this, you can acquire the information you need to make informed decisions. A well thought out plan will help you avoid missing anything important. It should be realized though, that educators, like anyone else, have personal preferences and biases. This is normal. It is mentioned only to remind you that you should obtain information from as many sources as possible.

As a principal, I was "interviewed" a number of times by parents who were shopping for a school or school district just as they might shop for a house. Most felt it was important to first select the school. This made a lot of sense. It demonstrated their concern for their children. It was evidence that they were wise consumers. What could be more important, when making a move, than including the quality of the school a child would attend in the equation with employment and selecting a house or apartment?

Your experiences will help you understand today's schools

Historically, educational change has occurred slowly, requiring as much as fifty years from the time an idea or practice began to take root in one school, until nearly all schools had adopted it. More recently, improved communications and an emphasis on in-service education for teachers have accelerated change. Yet, some of the current arrangements for teaching and learning were probably in use when you, or even your parents, were in school. They may not have changed much since that time. If this is the case, your experiences will help you understand today's schools. Of course, new concepts and practices that may be unfamiliar to you, are being introduced all the time. The following topics are presented so you will become better informed before meeting with school officials.

grades included in schools	self-contained classrooms
school size	team teaching
house plans	individualized instruction
class size	independent learning

The words used to identify school organizational patterns and teaching practices often do a less than satisfactory job of describing what is actually going on in schools. This is especially true of expressions like "team teaching," "individualized instruction," and "independent learning." If you feel you already have a good understanding of school patterns and practices, you may need only to scan this information at this time. If, on the other hand, some of these terms are unfamiliar I would recommend that you read about them before going on your school visit or conducting your interview. This will prepare you to ask questions that will help you understand what people are actually saying when they describe things being done in a school.

Learning about the ways schools are organized will help you better understand the school your child now attends, or one he or she might attend in the future. It is important to be aware of the more common ways students, staff, facilities, resources, and time are organized for teaching and learning. It is beneficial to know the advantages and disadvantages of different arrangements and to understand some of the misconceptions surrounding them. Using this information, you should be able to discuss educational issues with your child, other parents, and school officials. You will also be able to make more enlightened decisions.

Which grades should be included in a school?

Parents often express concern about which grades should be included in a school. This discussion probably began long ago when elementary schools with only one or two rooms became overcrowded. One of the solutions to this situation was to build an addition on the existing building. Another plan may have involved sending older students to other school districts. A third alternative was to build new facilities up the road for the "big kids," which in some cases students from surrounding school districts were also allowed to attend. No doubt, the question arose as to whether twelve year old children should be in the same building as seventeen and eighteen year old young men and women. What about the differences in levels of maturity?

More recently, intense discussions have taken place when parents have struggled with whether fifth or sixth grade students should remain in an elementary building with the younger children or move to a middle school with seventh and eighth graders. Fortunately, these discussions can end amicably if parents, teachers, and others concerned about children understand (and accept) a conclusion that I and a number of other educators reached some time ago. After looking at students and programs in a number of schools, it became obvious that it makes very little difference which grades are included in a school. It is what is done to meet the children's social, emotional, and educational needs after they get there that is important.

With this in mind, many schools are organized so that children of various ages are mixed when desired, and separated when necessary, all within one building. If student and staff schedules and building use are effectively organized, the curriculum is in place, and the staff is doing its job, students will more than likely benefit from the arrangement. Of course, it also helps if children and parents are properly prepared for, and have a positive attitude about the school. If a school you are exploring is doing these things, you need not be concerned about age differences within the building.

Student population; how important is school size?

The size of the student population in schools is a continuing concern of both parents and educators. Most people favor smaller schools at the preschool and elementary levels but are willing to accept larger schools as children grow older. There are good reasons for this position. Among others, it creates a natural progression for children as they move from their family situations, with a limited number of personal contacts, to a much larger and more complex world.

Parents who continue to favor small schools, at the middle and high school levels, usually feel these schools will help their children avoid some of the problems prevalent in society. Often, they are right. Parents who favor larger schools are usually willing to give up some of the security small schools offer in order to gain program enhancements. Advanced academic classes, certain special education programs, world languages, specialized math and science courses, library/media centers with greater resources, and some music and athletic programs can be found more often in larger schools. It is usually more feasible to provide teachers, facilities, and equipment, if programs serve a greater number of students. Additionally, it is easier to attract competent full-time teachers if they will be teaching all or most of their classes in their areas of specialty.

It is important to point out, though, that the quality of a school can be affected by many factors other than size. A small school that does not take advantage of its smallness may not provide the security and individual attention you might expect. Similarly, a large school that does not offer a broad curriculum and wide array of services may not be any better for your child than a small school that does not offer these programs. In other words, either a large or small school, if effectively organized and properly administered, can serve the educational, social, and emotional needs of most children. The important words here are "effectively organized." While it might seem natural to have your child attend a small school, you should seriously consider a larger school if it provides opportunities for a better education. The most important thing you can do at this time is to remain open minded about school size until you have completed your school visits.

Compensating for large or small school disadvantages

There are a number of things small schools are doing to provide children with the program advantages of larger schools. You will want to look for them as you visit schools. Electronic libraries, fax machines, interactive television, programmed learning materials, computer assisted instruction, on-line information services, and other innovations and devices make it possible for even the smallest or most remote school to offer specialized instruction and activities.

At the other end of the spectrum, educators have found ways for larger schools to provide many of the advantages of smaller schools. One of the most common arrangements is to divide the building into several distinct subdivisions. Students and staff are assigned to these subdivisions, often called "houses" or "halls," for much of the day. While a child might be in the same building or on the same campus with perhaps twelve or fourteen hundred other students, he or she could be part of a much smaller "house" that might have only three or four hundred students.

House plans can be found at any level

House plans are most common at the middle and high school levels but can be found in some large elementary schools. One of the most desirable house plan arrangements is when each house includes several consecutive grades, for example, grades five, six, seven and eight, in a middle school. Ideally, students are assigned to a house and remain there for their entire middle school experience. Academic teachers, guidance counselors, administrators, and other support staff are assigned for extended periods of time. Each house can conduct its own classes, assembly programs, intramural sports events, parent's nights, and the like. This arrangement can provide closeness and stability as numbers are limited and relationships between students, staff, and parents continue over several years.

Special area facilities, large group instruction rooms, gymnasiums, auditoriums, and cafeterias are shared by students from all parts of the school. The character and curriculum emphasis of each house can be the same or different. Some middle and high schools have set up houses that emphasize certain programs such as language arts and humanities or science and technology. This is a feature that appeals to many students, parents, and teachers.

Class size is something to consider

A subject that receives more discussion than any other is probably class size. Boards of Education, parent groups, school administrators, and teachers have shown continued interest in controlling the number of students a teacher has in class. In the case of special area subjects, there has also been concern about how many different students a teacher should teach on a daily or weekly basis. This is understandable, as it is generally accepted that teaching and learning become more difficult as numbers increase.

Children come to school with many factors affecting their readiness to learn. Some have had good experiences the previous evening, others have not. Some may be exhausted, others may be wide awake. Some feel well, others may be under the weather. Each of these factors affects learning. Educators refer to a phenomenon they call "the teachable moment." This is a period of time, however brief, when conditions are just right for a child to learn. Unfortunately, a teachable moment can be just that, only a moment. As you can imagine, it rarely occurs simultaneously for all students in a class. The possibility becomes even less as class size increases.

Even if children are physically and mentally ready to learn, they do not all learn in the same manner or at the same rate. Some children are attentive and stay on task, others become easily distracted. Some ask questions, others do not. It is a rare child who does not daydream, if even for a few moments. The teacher must be alert to the needs of each child, and respond accordingly for optimal learning to take place. Mini-lessons within the larger lesson must be taught if the objectives are to be accomplished for all students. Having too many students in a class makes this job very difficult, if not impossible.

It is hard for a person who has not faced a classroom full of children to understand and appreciate the variety and complexity of problems a teacher must deal with each day. The ideal teaching/learning situation may still be, as the old adage describes, the teacher on one end of a plank and the learner on the other end. This is not to say that children should be educated in isolation. Many of the lessons taught in modern schools require children to discuss issues and topics and to work together, much as they will in the adult world. But, even in a group, learning is an individual experience as the information one acquires is being processed in the brain. Consequently, many children still require individual attention in order to maximize group experiences.

While there is no universal guideline regarding class size, some states, and many school districts have adopted policies limiting the number of students in a class. Also, many teachers' union contracts include provisions on this subject. One might expect to find preschool classes of ten children or less, and nursery school classes under fifteen. Elementary school classes might run from fifteen to twenty-five, with all except kindergarten exceeding twenty. Middle and high school classes of twenty-five are quite common with all too many reaching or exceeding thirty. Teacher aides are added to some classes in order to accommodate more students.

> Aa Bb Cc Dd Ee Ff Gg Hh Ii Jj Kk
>
> **Overcrowded Classrooms:** Some communities try to solve school overcrowding by placing temporary children in temporary classrooms with temporary teachers for a temporary number of years. In some cases the temporary years have added up to more than three decades.

While there are indications that class size, within reasonable limits, may not be as important as some other factors, the fact is, that small class size is considered desirable by most who understand the teaching/learning process. This view persists despite attempts to compensate for larger classes by using technology or a variety of alternative teaching techniques and classroom arrangements.

There are several additional class size factors to consider if you expect to achieve excellence for your child. First, the ability and behavior of the students in a class have a lot to do with how effective the teacher can be. If, for example, one or more children require an extraordinary amount of attention, the teacher's efforts will be diverted from the remaining students. Second, you may feel more comfortable with your child in a large class if the school has added an aide or teaching assistant. This person can free the teacher to prepare and teach effective lessons while helping to provide the individual attention children require.

Finally, there is a key factor that could be your greatest concern. While class size is important, you would certainly prefer to have your child in a class of thirty students with the best teacher in the school, rather than in a class of ten with the poorest teacher. Keep this in mind as you discuss your child's education with representatives of the school.

Self-contained classrooms for younger children

A self-contained classroom is one in which children are assigned to one teacher, in one room, for most of the day. The teacher is usually responsible for all of the academic subjects but may also teach one or more special area subjects to the group. It is a common teaching arrangement for preschool, kindergarten, and early elementary grades. This is in contrast to an upper elementary school or middle school organization where two or more teachers often share the same group of students, or high school where students usually move from teacher to teacher and room to room throughout the day.

If you are a parent of an elementary school child, and feel as most parents do, you are happy having your child assigned to a self-contained classroom. In most cases this arrangement works well. An exception would be if your child has a teacher who lacks either the skill or ability to teach at the high level you expect. A personality conflict between teacher and child, although rare, could also be a problem. While these situations can occur with any class arrangement, it is much more serious when a child spends most of every day with the same teacher for the entire school year. This is a situation you can hope to avoid by learning more about the school and its teachers.

What is team teaching? Can it improve instruction?

Team teaching, as its name implies, consists of assigning groups of students to two or more teachers, thus forming a team. This arrangement is usually preferred by older children over the traditional single teacher, self-contained classroom. Most students appreciate having several teachers, each of whom is an "expert" on a particular aspect of the curriculum. They also like being taught in classrooms that have been designed and equipped for particular subject areas. Science is perhaps one of the most common examples.

Team teaching also appeals to many teachers. They have found that students can benefit from having a small group of teachers who know them well. They see value in meeting regularly to discuss the needs of individual children and to plan lessons. They also enjoy teaching subjects that most interest them, and for which they have been trained. For example, in upper elementary or early middle school, one teacher might prefer to teach math and science while another might like language arts and social studies. These two teachers could form a team and be responsible for teaching these academic subjects to their students. When this is done, each teacher can specialize in his or her favorite subjects while integrating the curricula when appropriate. This arrangement can lead to more productive planning time and, in many cases, better instruction as the teacher improves the lesson as it is presented to each section of the team.

Upper middle, and early high school teams often consist of four teachers. Each teaches a separate academic subject; language arts, social studies, mathematics, or science. They meet on a regular basis, often daily, to discuss their students and to plan and integrate their programs. For example, during team planning, they might decide a particular mathematics concept would be more meaningful if taught as a part of a science lesson, or that a descriptive writing method could be reinforced by all teachers on the team. This can lead to more effective teaching and more relevant learning.

At the high school level, teams are often organized by subject area. For example, several history/social studies teachers, each specializing in a particular aspect of the curriculum, would form a team. Students from all parts of the school could be assembled for large group lessons by these teachers. Following this instruction, they might meet in smaller groups, or move to the library/media center where the students would work independently. Not only do older students appreciate the benefits of specialization, but they also like the added excitement and perspective team teachers can give to their lessons.

If team teaching is to be successful, there is one essential requirement. Sufficient team planning time must be scheduled. Be sure to look for evidence of this when visiting schools or conducting the survey included in Chapter 6.

Individualized instruction

Individualized instruction is instruction tailored to the interests, needs, and learning style of the student. Fine, you say, but how can this be done when a teacher has twenty-five or thirty students in a class? Fortunately, good teachers know how to set the stage for learning. They can even create teachable moments. They are also aware of children who are having difficulty, and often understand the reasons why. Knowing this, they adjust their lesson planning, preparation, and teaching techniques to meet the needs of individual children or small groups.

When you think about your childhood, you can probably remember teachers who seemed to be aware of what you needed to know, and whether you and others in the class were ready to learn. They were able to help you in an efficient and effective manner. These were good teachers. They were the kinds of teachers you now want your child to have.

By definition, average students make up most of each class. Individualized instruction is very important if teachers are to be effective in teaching those who are either above or below average in ability. It is even more critical for those students at the extreme ends who should be receiving remediation or enrichment. Exceptional children must, by law, have "Individualized Education Plans (IEP)." Each plan must include clear objectives, techniques to accomplish them, specific time frames for completion, and ways to determine if the objectives have been met.

> Aa Bb Cc Dd Ee Ff Gg Hh Ii Jj
>
> Teaching:
> Teachers who focus on teaching children rather than on teaching curricula are more likely to reach their lesson objectives.

Educational Excellence for Your Child

It can be argued with merit that it would be good to have written individualized plans for all students. This possibility is becoming more feasible as teachers make greater use of computers and other forms of technology to plan lessons, instruct students, assign work, and to evaluate and record progress. While your child's school may not have reached this point, responsible teachers recognize the need for individualization, and plan and teach their lessons accordingly.

The faded portrait of the teacher standing in front of a group of thirty or forty students, lecturing to the average student has, in most cases, become a thing of the past. If you think of the teacher's role as that of teaching children, rather than teaching the curriculum, the importance of individualization becomes evident. As a wise parent-consumer, you should determine if your child's teachers are individualizing, and if so, how they are measuring progress. The School Survey Form will help you do this.

How and when does independent learning occur?

When a person learns by himself or herself, we have independent learning. There is nothing unusual about this phenomenon. It goes on every day and would continue even if the institution we know as "school" did not exist. It is important for educators and non-educators to keep in mind that while independent learning places significant responsibility on the learner, it does not in any way relieve the teacher, or parent, of the responsibility to teach.

For a person to participate fully in our rapidly changing world, he or she must become a lifelong learner. Much of our new knowledge and skills will be acquired away from the formal classroom setting. It is important for your child to develop the ability to learn, think, and act independently. When you visit your child's school or potential school and conduct your school survey you should look for signs of independent learning. Most educators are more than willing to show you examples or to describe what they are doing.

In the next chapter, you will read about curricula, school calendars, schedules, and some of the programs and resources that make independent learning possible. This will be helpful information to have before visiting schools.

5

Understanding Curriculum, Resources and School Calendar

The curriculum of a school describes the school program. Each subject or course taught in a school has its own curriculum. These curricula define what teachers teach and thus much of what students learn. Once a course curriculum has been developed, it is the human and material resources, and the assignment of time that control its implementation. Who determines what will be included in a course and how it will be taught? Your understanding of this important aspect of education will help you become a more effective advocate for your child.

The curriculum: who decides what will be taught?

The primary responsibility for education in the United States by law and tradition rests with individual states. While the federal government has some responsibility, for the most part it concentrates on health and safety issues and ensuring equal educational opportunity for all children. This includes the education of disadvantaged and handicapped students, women, and minorities. It is also responsible for the education of children in schools operated by the Bureau of Indian Affairs and Department of Defense. Most of what is taught in elementary, middle, and high schools is determined at the state or local level.

In those states assuming the greatest responsibility and leadership for education, curriculum guides, or syllabi, are developed at the state level by specialists working with teachers and experts from the field. Some curriculum guides, for example, mathematics, science, and world languages, are quite specific as to the concepts and skills that must be taught. In other cases, they outline broad topics that should be included in each course. The specifics of these courses are left to the school districts to develop at the district, department, or teacher level. An example would be the teaching of social studies. The state syllabus may require that United States history be taught in a particular grade and even define the specific periods of history and concepts that must be included in the course. Decisions regarding a significant portion of the content, though, may be left to the local schools. This gives teachers the opportunity to customize their courses, thus making them more relevant to students in their local communities.

The curriculum of a school is also influenced to a degree by textbook publishers. Their desire to produce books and resource materials that will be adopted by the greatest number of schools means they must follow state curriculum guides when determining the scope and content of their textbooks. Once a textbook is adopted and distributed to a class, it is more than likely that the teacher will include most of the material in the course. Even if portions of the book are not required reading, the fact that students have the additional information in their possession and may read it, can influence what they learn.

The scope of the curriculum

If you were asked what should be taught in schools, you might list reading, writing, arithmetic, and a number of other subjects. On the other hand you might answer thinking skills, critical analysis, decision making, and study skills. Another response might include getting along with others or how to obtain and keep a job. Considering the broad responsibilities assigned to schools, all of these answers would probably be correct.

The basic school curriculum is somewhat the same in most schools throughout the United States. Schools teach a core program of required subjects. They also offer elective courses, primarily at the middle and high school levels. As might be expected, the number and description of the electives vary, based on school size, district wealth, community expectation, and location. Except for an occasional new course, the list of core subjects has remained much the same over the years. While there will be differences between schools, they are usually less than might be expected. Most differences relate to the contents of the courses or when a particular topic or skill is introduced rather than whether or not it is taught. This is one reason why most children can change schools, even moving from one part of the United States to another without experiencing great difficulty.

Aa Bb Cc Dd Ee Ff Gg Hh Ii Jj Kk Ll Mm

> The importance of curricula: Health education, physical education and driver education can save lives. Art, music and drama make life worth living. Of course, there are a number of other courses like reading, math, science and history that are pretty important too.

A school district should provide a comprehensive program that will move a child from his or her home environment to a point where he or she is a fully functioning member of society. This is accomplished through thousands of lessons and experiences that are incorporated into the curriculum of the school. When conducting your school survey, Chapter 7, you will have the opportunity to determine the scope of the curriculum in any school you choose to visit.

The school's role in educating children is not exclusive

The school is not the only organization that educates children. The family and a nearly endless number of community organizations can play major roles in the education of any child. As an education advocate, you should seize the opportunity to arrange, coordinate, and monitor the learning experiences your child has in these vastly different worlds.

Unfortunately, not all education is positive. Most children, like adults, are exposed on a daily basis to some negative factors and experiences. Their peers, or others with whom they come in contact may try to influence them adversely. Radio, television, computer on-line services and print media offer their own agendas for learning. Studies show the average child spends more time watching television, including advertisements than attending classes in school. These factors along with many others make it necessary for you to take an active role in determining what is included in your child's formal and informal educations.

In addition to providing courses, most schools offer a number of material resources. These resources are designed to support the various curricula. Perhaps the most common resource and one that is easily recognized by today's parents is the library/media center.

Library/media centers support curricula

The term "library/media center," "learning center," or "resource center" usually designates one or more areas within a school that house books, magazines, and other print material as well as electronic and nonelectronic resources. The library/media center is essential to a school just as the traditional library has been for decades. In a well planned, adequately stocked and staffed center, the student will find materials that follow the regular curricula as well as resources that support remediation, enrichment, special interests, and leisure. In a modern library/media center the learner can choose from a variety of materials and select those matching his or her personal learning style. For more and more students, computers have joined books and periodicals as a resource of choice.

Computers have become a very useful resource

Computers are having a significant impact on the way teachers teach and children learn. Prior to the early 1980s, it was unusual to find a computer in any school, other than a large high school. With the increased availability of personal computers and acceptance by business, industry and the general public, their importance became apparent. Within a short time, schools set up computer centers, or began to acquire personal computers for the classrooms. Computer literacy became essential for all students and teachers.

Realizing there was much more to computer education than bringing the equipment, called hardware, into the schools, educators began to look for ways to use computers in teaching. This created a need for programs, called software, related to the curricula. With the development of these resources, and the linking of computers to other electronic media, computers have proved to be an effective and efficient tool in most subject areas. One of the greatest benefits is that they have made it easier for teachers to individualize instruction.

Computers have been used successfully to teach basic skills and to provide reinforcement, enrichment, and remediation. It is unlikely, though, that computers will either replace or lessen the need for teachers in the foreseeable future. Increasingly, teachers are reaching their time and energy limits while attempting to meet the rapidly growing needs of children. They will continue to be necessary until the time when children no longer have these needs. Most parents and educators do not see this happening.

Computers are performing an increasing number of important tasks that affect our everyday lives. Most businesses and industries depend on computers. More and more families have purchased computers and are using them in their homes. In an information world, those who develop, disseminate, and understand information using computers have a decided advantage over those who do not. It is essential that schools teach computer literacy, and use relevant software to support the curriculum. When evaluating a school, you should ask for a description of the kindergarten through grade twelve computer program, as well as a list of educational software used in the school.

Adequate human resources are very important

Students, teachers, parents, and administrators agree on the importance of having adequate human resources in their schools. Except for the students, staff is considered by most to be the single most important component of a school. Principals are very much aware that even small gaps in staffing can reduce learning and create teaching, supervising, safety, and morale problems.

> Aa Bb Cc Dd Ee Ff Gg Hh Ii Jj Kk
>
> School support staff: The main reason for staffing a school with administrators and support staff is to make it possible for teachers to teach and children to learn.

Children want to be helped promptly when they have questions. Teachers like to feel they can spend sufficient time with each child to maximize learning. Parents want the school staff to be effective in educating their children and they also want to be served promptly when they contact the school with concerns.

In your conversations with the principal, teachers, and other parents, you should ask if your child's school or a school that might interest you is adequately staffed. You will find that most schools do not have all of the personnel deemed necessary. Knowing this, it is a good idea to ask if the positions that most affect your child exist and if they are filled with competent people. This is particularly important if your son or daughter has difficulty learning and requires extra help. The information you gain from these discussions can help you make critical decisions regarding your child's education.

It is also important to ask if teachers feel positive about their jobs and the results they are getting. The School Survey Form, Chapter 6, Section D, Staff, has been designed to help you obtain this information. When doing your survey, you also should be able to determine if the staff members at your child's school or another school you might be considering are using all of the resources that are available to them. The community can be one of a school's most valuable resources.

Successful schools are part of the community

Schools that are most successful in generating and maintaining student interest and enthusiasm function as an integral part of the community. They take children into the community and bring the community into the schools. The kindergarten teacher who arranges a field trip to a fire station or dairy farm is making learning real for the children. Likewise, the high school history teacher who involves students in an archeological dig or asks them to interview older residents of the community helps students understand the past.

It is quite likely that some of the information you gained as a student from field trips or hearing guest speakers made a lasting impression. Your parents also may have provided you with enrichment experiences in the community. It is possible that one or more of these experiences may have sparked your interest in pursuing your present career.

The office manager, engineer, or artist who comes to the school as a guest speaker, or serves on a committee to revise a course curriculum or to plan a new building brings expertise from the job and community into the school. There is no substitute for the services provided by these people. At the least, you will want to ask whether your child's school or one you are considering is using the community as a resource. You may also want to learn how you can become personally involved in uniting the school and community. This information is covered in Chapter 12, "Opportunities for School Volunteers."

By building bridges connecting schools and communities, education can be greatly enhanced, and residents will receive more education for their tax dollars. In Chapter 17, you will learn about community resources that can be tapped, by either you or the school, to enrich your child's education.

Time is another important factor that must be considered in educating children. The resources that we have discussed can only benefit your child if adequate time is available for their use, and if this time is used effectively. The following information is presented to increase your understanding of the relationship of time to schools.

The school year is based on tradition

What might be considered the "regular school year" has not varied much from the time of its origin in colonial America. In many respects, it was determined by the weather and agricultural cycles. School classes began near the end of the summer harvest and ended in time for spring planting. This provided three to four months when children could work in the fields or perform other farm work. Schools also closed during harsh weather. Similar schedules, with the addition of a few days, have been maintained for over two centuries, even though more than three-quarters of today's children live in metropolitan areas.

The closing of schools for holidays can also be traced to the colonies, and even back to Europe. Most days off and longer vacation periods were based on traditional Christian holy days. As there has been very little change in the time set aside for these occasions, the school year, while somewhat longer than in colonial times, remains at a few more than one hundred and eighty days in most districts in the United States.

Lengthening the school year

It has been suggested that children in this country would benefit from a longer school year. One hundred and eighty days is far short of the two hundred or more days students attend school in some industrialized nations or the approximately two hundred and forty days many workers spend on the job. It should be pointed out that while these examples are used to support a longer school year, they may or may not be relevant. Cultures differ greatly, and there are few educational reasons to support the notion that children of any age should attend school the same number of days that adults work.

Proponents who would like to increase the number of days schools are in session often point to the success countries with longer school years are having in educating their children. On the other hand, those who feel the present calendar is adequate remind us that there are countries where children attend school approximately the same number of days as they do in the United States that are very successful. They also cite the widely varied results schools in this country are getting even though most follow quite similar schedules. The latter supports the position that there are factors other than increased time in school to consider when deciding if you want your child to attend school a greater number of days.

Critics of the longer school year point out with some confidence, that more of the same curricula and teaching is not necessarily better for children. If your child's school or a school that interests you has or is considering a longer school year, there are a number of questions you might ask.

- ✓ Would new courses be added?
- ✓ Would the content of existing courses be increased?
- ✓ Which subjects might receive greater emphasis?
- ✓ Does your child now have a problem with too much free time?
- ✓ Would your child benefit from a longer school year? How?
- ✓ How would your family's daily activities and vacations be affected?
- ✓ Would the possible results justify the added expense to the taxpayers?

Parents, community members, and educators at all levels should be involved in studying calendar, personnel, and program changes that might result from a longer school year.

There is an additional factor that must be considered. Education can be very intensive. One must be careful not to "burn out" teachers and students. The school year should not be lengthened if the primary purpose is to provide child care or to keep youth off the streets. This is an inefficient and expensive way to provide these services. The result may even be detrimental to children, their teachers, their parents, and their community. If Americans are sincerely interested in providing their children with a better education, there are often better solutions than increasing the length of the school year.

Reducing the long summer vacation

Parents and educators are increasingly questioning the desirability of the long summer vacation as compared to several shorter recess periods throughout the year. They know a long vacation can lead to boredom or behavior problems for some children. Teachers realize children forget important skills if they are not used or reinforced on a regular basis. They know it often takes days, even weeks, of review before optimal learning takes place following a long vacation.

In an attempt to avoid this down time, many districts offer summer school programs. More recently, some have adopted "year-round school" schedules. These usually consist of three or four sessions, or semesters, interspersed with periods of two or three weeks when parents can opt for either vacation or additional time in school for their children. The latter is often called inter session. While year round school schedules reduce the long summer vacation they do not necessarily increase the total number of days children attend school.

Whether summer school programs or inter sessions focus on remediation or enrichment, or just keep a child's mind more active by providing an opportunity to take additional courses, they can benefit many children. A school offering one of these year round calendars may be able to provide a better education for your child. Be sure to consider alternatives like summer camps with educational offerings, community programs, work, and family plans before making your final decision.

The school day: how long should it be?

Minimum times for the length of the school day are generally established at the state level. Often they are tied to funding, which gives local school districts a good reason to meet the requirements. Some states offer incentives to districts exceeding minimum instructional time or scheduling additional class periods at the middle or high school levels. The latter practice is especially important as it is often difficult for students to take all of the courses they need or desire during a minimum length day.

The length of the school day will probably not vary greatly between schools with similar grades within your immediate geographic area. In most cases, the elementary day will be shorter than either the middle or high school day. This can be justified if one considers the short attention span and limited physical endurance of younger children. The longer day at the middle and high school levels provides additional time for special area subjects and electives. It also allows time for students to meet laboratory requirements and, in some cases, to participate in cocurricular activities.

The way the school schedules your child's time is extremely important. It is the responsibility of the administration to ensure the school not only meets or exceeds the minimum time requirements, but also that the use of all time is maximized. There is little benefit in keeping students in school for an extra half hour or forty-five minutes if it means having unnecessary study halls or extra long homeroom or lunch periods. When looking at schools, you should determine how your child's time would be used rather than just how long he or she might be in school. Request a copy of the schedule. In your discussions with school officials, ask if they feel there is adequate time for the required academic and special area subjects.

> Aa Bb Cc Dd Ee Ff Gg Hh Ii Jj Kk
>
> The value of time:
> Time is one of the most valuable, yet least expensive, resources available to educators, parents and children. It must not be wasted.

Students in high schools having less than seven periods per day report difficulty scheduling the courses required for acceptance at some colleges. This may entail making other plans to meet the requirements for admission to a preferred college or university. Determine when your child would take electives, go to the library/media center, or work on assignments. Finally, inquire about the scheduling of music lessons, performing-group rehearsals, athletic team practices, and cocurricular activities if your child would be participating in any of these programs.

The school day: starting and ending times

Starting and ending times of individual schools are often based on non-educational factors. These factors include visibility when students are going to and from school, efficient bus utilization, staff availability, and even the work schedules of major employers in the area. Some districts plan their schedules so that older children will be at home when younger siblings arrive from school. Others make it a point to end the high school day relatively early so that students can work, or participate in interscholastic sports or other cocurricular activities.

A factor worth considering when selecting a school is that most children are at their best in the morning, although not necessarily during the first hour or so after they arise. If they have had adequate sleep, they are more rested, have longer attention spans, and are often better able to tolerate adversity without becoming upset. Principals and teachers realize this, and usually do what they can to focus on academic subjects at this time. The problem is that in districts where many students are transported, cost alone may necessitate using the buses for multiple trips. This creates a need for staggered opening and closing times. As not all schools can open at what might be considered an ideal time for your child, you may want to consider these factors in selecting a school.

Before and after school programs

Changes in the family and society have made it necessary, in most cases, for both parents or the sole parent to work outside the home. An increasing number of children are unsupervised for significant periods at either the beginning or end of the day. Unwise use of this time can create complex problems, not only for the children, but also for their parents and community. This has prompted agencies to plan and operate before and after school programs primarily aimed at keeping children occupied and off the streets. Most programs provide a safe place for young people to hang out or to participate in recreational activities in a safe setting. If children can also receive help with their homework or learn new skills there can be added benefits. The school can and should be a partner in these programs by providing materials and facilities.

If you are a working parent, and your situation warrants, you may want to consider a school that provides early morning and late afternoon supervision and activities. These programs are sometimes arranged by parent/teacher groups. An alternative would be to select a school that would allow your child to ride the school bus to a community recreation program or child-care facility. This often works well when a program is not within walking distance of the school, or does not provide its own transportation.

Time in school vs. time learning

When you think about your childhood, you probably remember spending some of your time in school doing things that did not seem educational. This is not unusual, as a portion of every school day is spent waiting, eating lunch, taking care of personal needs, and participating in procedural activities. For example, in cold or wet climates it takes time for young children to remove and put on their outside clothing. This occurs at the beginning and end of the day, but also before and after recess. If kindergarten students attend a full-day program, it is very likely that they will have a quiet or rest time.

Schools attended by older students set aside time at the beginning, and often the end of the day, for attendance and announcements. Also, schedules allow time for eating, personal needs, socializing, and moving from one class to another. Most of these activities are necessary if schools are to keep students alert and in a proper frame of mind to participate fully in the educational process. It must be realized though, that most of these activities decrease the time devoted to serious learning.

Your child will benefit most if the school is aware of the importance of time and is managing it efficiently. When conducting your school survey, Chapter 7, you should review a student schedule similar to the one your child might follow. By doing this, you can get a pretty good idea if adequate time is allocated to classes and other serious learning situations. If you have questions you should ask for an explanation.

Modular schedules

In order to maximize learning time, many middle and high schools have adopted modular schedules. Modules are blocks of time, generally fifteen to thirty minutes in length. They can be used individually, or in combination, to vary the length of classes, study times, labs, and other school activities. This is in contrast to a traditional schedule consisting of six to eight longer periods. The latter are usually of equal length and can be varied only with difficulty.

Under a modular plan, individual teachers, and/or teaching teams are assigned groups of students, blocks of modules, and classrooms or other instructional areas. Using these modules each team can establish its own schedule. Schedules can be varied as necessary in order to carry out the team's objectives. It is a very efficient way to use time.

As you talk with your child, or conduct the survey provided in this book, you should look for indications that the school is maximizing the time available for learning. While some of your hunches and opinions will be based on subjective information, if you feel time is being wasted, you should discuss your concerns with your child's teacher or the principal. This is one of the ways your efforts can benefit all children in the school.

Sources of information about schools

It is essential to ask the right people the proper questions when trying to learn about schools. Your objective should be to acquire a broad array of information and ideas for comparison purposes. To assist you in doing this the School Survey Form and instructions for its use have been included in the next chapter.

Before conducting your survey, it is important to do some preliminary research on your own. One of the best ways to do this is to contact others who have knowledge of your child's present or future school. For example, let's look at what can be done to obtain information if you are moving to a new community.

Your first step would be to get the names and addresses of schools where your child might legally attend. These should be located within a reasonable distance from your new residence or work location. This information can be obtained in a number of ways. You might start by asking a real estate agent or by checking at the closest school district administrative office. The Chamber of Commerce or local government office can also help answer your questions. A more comprehensive list of information sources is included in this section.

As school district boundaries do not necessarily coincide with other jurisdictions, you will need to make specific inquires if you are looking at houses located near the edge of a district. Check with your real estate agent, the seller, a neighbor with children, or better still, ask to see a recent tax bill. This should include the name of the school district in which the house is located. It will not, though, indicate a particular school building. For more complete information, it will be necessary to provide the school district office with the present owner's name and address, and the lot number of the property under consideration. The district office will also need to know the ages or grade levels of your children.

The district office or individual schools can provide other valuable information. Ask for copies of student and parent handbooks, school newsletters, and annual reports. The latter should include the results of annual testing programs and information on staff, curriculum, and budget. Many schools have standard information packets for parents. These are usually quite useful, but don't hesitate to request additional information.

A call to a newspaper in your new community might produce a copy of the annual back-to-school supplement. This can be very helpful, especially if you are moving to an area where bus transportation is a factor. This publication often includes school bus routes and schedules. You may also want to talk with the newspaper's editor or a reporter who covers school news in the community.

In addition to these sources, you can contact a number of other people for information. Take the opportunity to ask education-related questions even if you are calling someone about an unrelated matter. It is important, though, to remember the responses you get from individuals are their personal opinions, nothing more, nothing less. Before arriving at your conclusions, it is your responsibility to evaluate these opinions along with the more objective information you obtain.

The people listed below will usually be more than pleased to discuss schools and education with you.

- ✓ friends or relatives
- ✓ future employer
- ✓ employees who work where you will be working

Educational Excellence for Your Child

- ✓ real estate representatives
- ✓ employees you meet at the court house, post office, or other governmental agencies
- ✓ members of the clergy, librarians, physicians, bookstore owners and the like
- ✓ Chamber of Commerce, Better Business Bureau, civic and service organization representatives
- ✓ school principals, teachers, or others in your child's present school who might have knowledge of the area to which you will be moving
- ✓ Parent/teacher group representatives in your present school, or in the schools under consideration
- ✓ State Education Department officials, who can often provide information on a school's ranking based on such things as standardized test results, dropout rate, percentage of students winning scholarships or going on to higher education. These people can also refer you to schools with particular programs that might benefit your child
- ✓ representatives of colleges and universities who are familiar with the competencies and academic standings of students graduating from area high schools. It is a good idea to talk with faculty members who are doing research in area schools, or who are working with schools on curriculum development, in-service education, or student teaching

When asking questions, it is best to be sincere and as natural as possible. You may want to begin with a simple, "I expect to move to this area; what can you tell me about the schools?" In some cases, you may wish to be more specific and refer only to a particular school, grade level, or program. If you need further direction regarding appropriate questions, review your completed Parent Recommendations Summary, Chapter 3, or the School Survey Form, Chapter 6. Introductory and follow-up questions should be fairly evident.

6

Preparing for Your School Visit and Survey

The School Survey Form, a valuable tool

The School Survey Form has been designed to guide your questions and discussions in order to obtain specific information when you interview the principal and, if necessary, other school personnel. Yes, that's correct, "The principal!" It is important to have your questions answered by the person in charge. It is equally as important to have this person meet you and at a later time, your child. This can lead to a relationship that can be beneficial well beyond the time your son or daughter attends a particular school.

Understanding the educational bureaucracy

School districts are assigned the task of educating children. In most cases, they are operated by elected or appointed boards or committees of representatives that set policy. Leadership is usually provided by a superintendent or supervising principal who is responsible to carry out the program.

Historically, school districts and individual schools have been known for their specialization of function, adherence to rules, inflexibility, and hierarchy of authority. These are the characteristics of a bureaucracy, a term that does not produce favorable visions in the minds of most people. Fortunately, this situation has improved in recent years as more and more superintendents and principals have begun sharing responsibility for decision making with teachers and parents.

Many schools have established advisory committees composed of community representatives, parents, and teachers. Others have involved teachers in the management of the school. This has led to significant improvement in some, but certainly not all, districts and schools. If you hope to bring about changes benefiting your child and other children, it is important to understand the power structure of the school you are considering.

Principals provide leadership and operate schools

In most districts each school of reasonable size has a principal. This person provides leadership and is responsible for the day-to-day operation of the school. The principal also coordinates programs and services with other schools and agencies, and interacts with the superintendent's office. While a good principal involves staff, parents, and other members of the community in planning, decision making, evaluation, and a number of other aspects of school operation, in the final analysis, it is the principal who is responsible for what goes on in the school. The principal is in the best position to provide information, to answer questions, and to make changes.

Principals want to meet parents

Most principals welcome the opportunity to meet parents, and to discuss the school and its programs. It is not unusual for them to point with pride to the number of students and parents they personally know. They are aware of the value of maintaining communications with all parents, but often depend on feedback from a much smaller number with whom they have established a working relationship. If you are interested, it is usually possible to become one of these people.

Occasionally, principals cannot spend as much time as they would like with individual parents. This should not prevent you from having your conference and conducting your school survey. In most cases, a simple telephone call, a week or two in advance, is all that is necessary to schedule an appointment. Parents who take initiative have no difficulty in arranging meetings with school personnel.

Things to do before calling the school

Before you call the school, take these important steps.

- ✓ Become familiar with the School Survey Form.
- ✓ Delete and/or add questions to the School Survey Form.
- ✓ Decide what you wish to see during your tour of the school.
- ✓ Determine which staff members you want to meet.
- ✓ Plan the order of your school visit.
- ✓ Determine the amount of time to request for your visit.

Using the School Survey Form

The purpose of the School Survey Form is to help you, during your initial visit, to learn what you need to know about the school in as short a time as possible. It will guide your interview and ensure you do not overlook important questions. It also standardizes the information gathering process so you can make better comparisons between schools.

If you are relatively unfamiliar with the school you will be surveying, you should request about an hour for the interview. This is necessary if you want the person being interviewed to answer most of the questions on the School Survey Form. By doing this, you can feel confident you have covered the important aspects of the school's program.

You must realize that a comprehensive school evaluation would involve trained observers and take a substantial amount of time. This is not your purpose. You are interested in getting an overall impression of the school, with particular emphasis on those programs and services that could affect your child.

In the course of questioning the principal, you may find a recent comprehensive evaluation has been done by the school staff or an outside agency. If this is the case, it would be valuable information to have. By all means, request a copy of the study or summary of conclusions.

The School Survey Form has been designed to help you and the principal maintain your focus and save time. This will be the case if you can conduct the interview with little or no interruption. The questions are to the point, and most require only brief answers. It will be your responsibility to move promptly from one question to the next. You should note the principal's responses as this is the best way to ensure you do not forget an answer. If you anticipate difficulty in doing this, you may wish to ask if you can tape record the interview for later review. Finally, if after returning home you find you have not written down one or more important responses or other information, this should be done before it is forgotten.

Determining which questions apply in your situation

The School Survey Form should be used in its entirety if you are moving to a new community. This is also true if you think your child may require special services. By doing this, you can be confident you have learned about most of the things that might impact your child. You might begin by sitting down now, at home, and completing those survey questions you can answer using the information you have already acquired. Also, draw a single line through any question that is not applicable. It is a good idea to use pencil, so if necessary, you can make changes at a later date.

If you must schedule a short interview, or if you are somewhat familiar with the school, select ten or twelve questions that are most pertinent to your situation. You may even wish to write them on separate paper. This sheet can then be used for the interview rather than the complete School Survey Form. You can learn quite a bit in thirty minutes or less if you are organized. You should also find you can answer some questions by reviewing handout information that is available. Other questions can be answered from your observations the day of the visit.

Adding questions to the School Survey Form

Now is a good time to add questions to your School Survey Form. Space has been provided for this purpose on the last page. These questions should be based on your personal knowledge of your child and the need for specific information about the school. You may want to review your completed Parent Recommendation Summary, looking particularly for areas of concern about which you may wish to ask questions. For example, if you have determined your child could benefit from a particular teaching style, you may want to ask if a teacher with these qualities is available in your child's grade. If your Summary is complete, it should not be necessary, at this time, to review the supporting data in the Educational Records File or on the Child's Interest Interview Form or Know Your Child Worksheet.

Remember to include questions arising from discussions with family members, friends, business associates, or educators. When this has been done, you can feel confident you have customized your School Survey Form so it will be an effective instrument in obtaining the information you need to make informed decisions.

Planning your school visit

Most principals enjoy talking with parents and showing them around the school. As would be expected, they are disappointed if they cannot present either the building or the educational program at its best. The ideal time to visit is during the regular school day when classes are in session and you can get a general impression of the facility, students, staff, program, and services available under normal operating conditions. You will sense the interaction between children and adults and see the many ways teaching is being done.

Of course, circumstances may make it necessary to conduct your visit before or after the regular school day, on a weekend, or during a vacation. If this is the case, you may tour a dark building, or one with furniture and books piled in the corridors, fresh paint on the classroom walls, or cleaning equipment where the crews are working. While not an ideal time to visit, you might be able to see areas that would be inaccessible when school is in session. Also, you may be able to spend more time with the principal in a relaxed setting with fewer interruptions while conducting your survey.

There is a potential danger in not considering calendar and time differences when making comparisons between schools. For example, a building tour immediately before or after a vacation usually presents a somewhat different picture than a midweek tour on a regular school day. Also, you would not expect to observe the same things happening early in the morning as you would late in the afternoon. While it would be best to visit all schools during the same time of day, this is often impossible. It is entirely appropriate to revisit a school if you feel you need to see it at a different time in order to make better comparisons.

It is not uncommon for the principal to ask another staff member, a volunteer, or a student to conduct your tour of the building. Time constraints alone may make this necessary. If this is the case, by all means accept the offer. It would be wise to review with the principal and your guide, what you expect to see, so there are no misunderstandings. It is also a good idea to remind people that you plan to meet with the principal at a specific time, following the tour, to complete the School Survey Form. If these things are done, you can expect to meet the objectives of your visit.

Deciding what to see at the school

It is quite likely you have already decided what you want to see during your school visit. If not, you should make a list at this time. Include all areas that are particularly important to you and your child. For example, if you feel your son or daughter will require remediation or enrichment, you will certainly want to see areas where this instruction takes place.

If your child is interested in instrumental music, you might ask to look at individual and small group lesson rooms, practice facilities, instrument storage areas, and the auditorium. Unless your guide is a music teacher, you cannot expect answers to specific inquiries about music selection, the instrument loan program, concerts, or what is expected of students. These questions should be addressed to the teacher responsible for the program or if this is not possible, the principal or department supervisor.

Determining your visit sequence

You may wonder if it is better to tour the school before or after you interview the principal and complete the School Survey Form. I would suggest it is best to tour the building first, as you will gain information that will help you focus and frame your survey questions. Also, it will give the principal the opportunity to correct any inaccurate impressions you have as a result of your tour. Remember, there is usually only one opportunity to tour a school before you conduct your survey. You can return later as many times as you desire if there are additional things you wish to see.

Keep your observations in perspective

Your building tour will provide a snapshot glimpse of the school and a feeling for its overall climate. During this short time you may see or hear things either good or bad that are not typical of the school. If you have questions about any of these, ask your guide or the principal for clarification. It is important to keep your observations in perspective as you evaluate the school and its programs. This can only occur if you have accurate information.

On one occasion, while I was talking with parents who were considering sending their children to a school where I worked, the fire alarm sounded. There was a fire in a lavatory wastebasket. The building was quickly evacuated in an orderly fashion. A teacher extinguished the remaining embers well before the fire department arrived. It was only necessary for them to inspect the area and vent the smoke before everyone returned to the building. Fortunately, there was no damage. Later, the student who started the fire confessed to his actions and was disciplined. Everything went according to plan.

The visiting parents, who up to that point seemed very enthusiastic about the school, did not return to the building. It appeared from their demeanor that this incident was the primary basis for their decision to leave. If so, it was unfortunate, as there were thousands of excellent things going on in the school that day, including the school's response to the fire. I also imagine there were several dozen wastebasket fires in our nation's schools, all successfully extinguished.

What to expect on your tour
An initial tour of a school, when classes are in session, usually includes general-use areas, like the library/media center, gymnasium, auditorium, and special areas where students are actively engaged in learning. Keep in mind it is normal for your tour to focus on the "showplace" areas. There is nothing wrong with this, but it is a factor you should consider when drawing conclusions that might lead to later decisions. The presence of visitors in these rooms is least disruptive to the program. You may need to tell your guide if you wish to visit academic classrooms. When observing classes, try to be as unobtrusive as possible.

As you walk around the building, there is nothing wrong with stepping into a rest room or food preparation area to see its condition. You should also feel free to ask questions or to say a few words to students or staff members if it appears you will not interfere with what they are doing. It is important, though, to realize you are a guest, rather than a regular part of the school. If you are in doubt as to whether it is appropriate to say or do something, check with your guide.

Determining which staff members to meet
It may be necessary to talk with one or more specialists who might arrange for or provide special services for your child. Selection should be based on the principal's recommendations, and your knowledge of your child's past performance, interests, and present and future needs. It is to your advantage to limit the number and length of these meetings to those required to move ahead with your survey. You can easily schedule additional meetings after you have consulted with others and made some decisions about possibly pursuing your child's education at this school.

There are a number of ways to obtain accurate information regarding special education programs and enrichment opportunities without meeting individually with several teachers. Quite often, you can obtain the information you need from the school psychologist or a guidance counselor. You may even want to meet, at another time, with the special education committee or enrichment committee. Other staff members who usually have a good understanding of special education and enrichment programs are the curriculum coordinator and subject area chairpersons. If you have questions regarding any aspects of these programs, review them with the principal and ask for advice regarding additional meetings.

Determining how much time to request for your visit
By now, you should have a pretty good idea of the time your survey will require, as you have either added or deleted questions that might affect the one-hour estimate. Meetings with additional staff members, if necessary, will probably require a minimum of twenty to thirty minutes each. You will not be able to determine the exact amount of time to allow for your building tour as this will be the principal's responsibility. If school is in session, it will often take longer than if it is after school hours or during a vacation. The reason for this is

the added activity and a greater number of things to see. The principal or other person conducting your tour may also take the time to talk with an occasional teacher or student as the opportunity arises. This is good, but it does require time. Taking everything into consideration, you will probably want to allow at least thirty minutes for the tour.

As you can see, you should expect to spend about two hours at the school on your initial visit. If you are visiting schools close to home, it would be best not to schedule more than one or two visits each day. On the other hand, if you are investigating schools in an out-of-town location, you may need to schedule as many visits as possible while you are there. If this is the case, you should watch your time carefully, and make sufficient notes at each school, so that your observations do not seem to run together. It is frustrating to return home after visiting schools and not remember where you saw something you either liked or disliked. You may want to hold previsit or postvisit telephone conferences with school representatives if your time is very limited. This can work quite well, especially if information can be mailed or faxed to you at the conclusion of your telephone discussions.

On the following pages, you will find the School Survey Form. It should be reviewed, giving consideration to the information you have gained reading this chapter. Add items, delete items, and change questions to serve your purpose. When completed, you will have a survey form that should make it possible to obtain the information you need.

You are now ready to make an appointment for your school visit, tour, and interview with the principal. Chapter 7 includes a number of suggestions to help you make these arrangements. Once you have read this, you will be ready to conduct your interview and evaluate the results. This will complete the initial information gathering phase of obtaining educational excellence for your child. These steps will not need to be repeated. While you will want to recognize any new information and update your files accordingly, an annual review is all that should be necessary unless significant changes occur in either your child or the school.

SCHOOL SURVEY FORM

School name: _____ Grades in school: _____ Date of visit: _____

Address: _____

Principal's name: _____ Tel. No.: _____

This School Survey Form will help you learn about any school. It should be used in connection with a school tour and meeting with the principal and other staff members.

You will find some questions are more relevant to one grade level than another. This should be taken into consideration when conducting your interview. Do not hesitate to add or delete questions, or to develop a shorter survey, in order to best serve your purposes.

If you are familiar with the school, portions of Sections A-C and some other survey questions can be completed prior to your visit. This will save time during the interview.

In conducting your interview, it is best to phrase each question in your own words, rather than to read it as it appears on the survey form. This will create a more natural atmosphere and give you the opportunity to emphasize what you feel is important.

A. Initial Parent Impressions

When you telephoned the school was your call handled professionally? Y (yes) / N (no)

Were you successful in reaching the principal and making an appointment? Y / N

If not, did he or she return your call within a reasonable time? Y / N

Comments: _____

_____

B. Facility and Organization

Is the school located in a safe neighborhood? Y / N Is it easily accessible by walking? Y / N Bicycle? Y / N School bus? Y / N Is the location free of loud noises, heavy traffic, dust, and fumes? Y / N Have there been reports of asbestos, radiation, sick building syndrome or other harmful or potentially harmful effects? Y / N

Comments: _____

_____

Describe your impression of the building exterior, school grounds and nearby neighborhood. _____

_____

_____

_____

Is there evidence the school maintains adequate safeguards to protect students and staff from unauthorized persons coming on the school grounds or entering the building? Y / N Comments:_____
_____

Describe the condition, cleanliness, and lighting as you enter the building. _____
_____

Is there evidence of odor, temperature, bug, or rodent problems? Y / N _____
_____

Describe the condition of the rest rooms, lunch room, and kitchen. _____
_____

Does the building appear safe? Y / N _____
_____

Does the building seem to have adequate facilities for staff and students?

Classrooms	Y / N	Laboratories	Y / N	Playgrounds	Y / N
Gymnasiums	Y / N	Music practice rooms	Y / N	Athletic fields	Y / N
Auditorium	Y / N	Large group rooms	Y / N	Cafeteria	Y / N
Health room	Y / N	Library/Media Center	Y / N	School store	Y / N
Guidance	Y / N	Other: _____

Comments:_____
_____

Does the person interviewed seem comfortable with a school this size? Y / N Do you? Y / N Comments:_____
_____

If the school is large, does it use a house plan or other arrangement to simulate smallness? Y / N Comments:_____
_____

Does the school have a written philosophy? Y / N Mission statement? Y / N School improvement plan? Y / N
Comments:_____
_____
_____
_____

C. Students

Do students of different races, and with diverse ethnic, cultural, and religious backgrounds attend the school?   Y / N   If so, do they seem to get along well?   Y / N
Comments:_____
_____

What are some of the more common interests of students who are my child's age? For example, music, sports, technology, or the like. _____
_____

What aspects of student behavior create the greatest problems? _____
_____

How does the school deal with these problems? _____
_____

Is there evidence this plan is working?   Y / N   Comments: _____
_____

D. Staff

Does the school have adequate teaching, administrative, and support staff to do an excellent job of educating my child?   Y / N   What is the projected class size in my child's grade? _____ Is the principal satisfied with this number?   Y / N
Explain: _____
Does the school provide the professional services my child might need?

School nurse teacher	Y / N	Remedial specialists	Y / N
Guidance counselor	Y / N	Enrichment specialists	Y / N
Psychologist	Y / N	Speech therapist	Y / N
Social worker	Y / N	Limited-English-proficiency	
Law officer	Y / N	teacher	Y / N
Physical therapist	Y / N	Other:_____	

Comments:_____
_____

Has the school been able to attract and hold excellent teachers?   Y / N   _____
Comments:_____
_____
_____
_____
_____

What is the teacher attendance rate? _____% What percentage of the teachers have been faculty members for five or more years? _____% What percentage of the professional staff have advanced degrees? _____% Comments: _____
_____

Does the staff reflect the ethnic make-up of the school? Y / N
   Comments:_____
_____

Is the school experiencing staff problems? Y / N Describe: _____
_____

How is excellent teaching recognized? _____
Are all teachers assigned to subject areas in which they are certified? Y / N
   Comments:_____
How much individual planning time do teachers have? _____ Team planning? _____
Is this considered adequate? Y / N _____
Does the school have an effective in-service staff training program? Y / N
   Comments:_____
Does the school have written policies relative to staff recruiting, hiring, performance, and evaluation? Y / N Comments:_____
_____

Describe examples of staff enthusiasm and commitment to excellence. _____
_____

What factors are considered in assigning students to individual teachers? ____
_____

Who makes these assignments? _____
Does the school consider parent input or requests regarding a child's teacher or class placement? Y / N If this is the case, describe how this occurs. _____
_____

E. Curriculum

List any curriculum offerings that are in addition to the minimum program required by the state.

_____   _____   _____
_____   _____   _____

   Who can take these courses? _____
_____
_____

How is the curriculum determined, developed, and taught to children with different abilities? _____

In what grade are world languages introduced? _____ Computer education? _____ Health education? _____ Career education? _____

Does the school have written curriculum guides for all courses? Y / N Are these state? Y / N Local? Y / N Are curriculum guides available for parent review? Y / N

Describe any courses or programs that are particularly outstanding. _____
_____

F. Accountability

What standardized tests are used to measure student *aptitude*? _____
_____

How often are they administered? _____ What have the results indicated about children attending this school? _____

What standardized tests are used to measure academic *achievement*? _____
_____

How often are they administered? _____ Based on these tests, how does the *achievement* of children in this school compare with that of children in other schools in the district? _____ County? _____
State? _____ Nation? _____
Similar communities, i.e. city, rural, or suburban, throughout the state? _____
_____

What is the school district's student attendance rate? _____% Dropout rate? _____%

How many graduates go to four-year colleges? ___% two-year colleges? ___% Work? ___%

What is the district's history in regard to individual student honors and college scholarships? _____
_____

Describe any recognition the school has received for its programs during the past three years. _____
_____
_____
_____
_____
_____

Educational Excellence for Your Child

G. Cocurricular Program

Are the following activities available to all students?
    Special interest clubs? Y / N   Performing music? Y / N   Theater? Y / N

Sports:	Elementary	Middle	High
Intramural (within school, open to all)	Y / N	Y / N	Y / N
Extramural (with other schools, open to all)	Y / N*	Y / N	Y / N
Interscholastic (with other schools, selective)	Y / N*	Y / N*	Y / N

    *Often not offered at this level due to the limited maturity of the students.

Does the school have a newspaper? Y / N   Student-operated radio or television station? Y / N

List examples of the school's assembly programs and field trips: _____
_____
_____
_____

When are cocurricular activities held? _____
Is district transportation provided for activities? Y / N _____

H. Schedule

Is the school calendar available? Y / N Time school will open? _____ Close? _____
    Does the district have summer school or year round school? Y / N
    Comments:_____
_____

Is a sample schedule for a student in my child's grade available? Y / N
How much time do students spend with their academic teachers or teaching team?___
    Does the school serve lunch? Y / N   Cost? _____ Breakfast? Y / N   Cost? _____
Does the school offer supervised programs before or after school? Y / N
    Comments:_____
_____
_____

If bus transportation is provided, is the route schedule available? Y / N
    Comments:_____
_____
_____
_____
_____

I. Resources

Are the following resources available for student and teacher use?

Textbooks	Y / N	Computer software	Y / N
Audio and video equipment	Y / N	Library books	Y / N
Audio and video tapes/discs	Y / N	Directory of resource people	Y / N
Closed-circuit TV and studio	Y / N	Musical instruments to loan	Y / N
Films and film strips	Y / N	Health information	Y / N
Copy machines	Y / N	College and job information	Y / N
Computers/Internet access	Y / N	Classroom supplies	Y / N

Are there costs for using any of these resources? Y / N   Do these costs seem reasonable? Y / N   Comments: _____
_____
_____

J. Opportunities for Enrichment

List opportunities for enrichment:

_____   _____   _____

_____   _____   _____

Are high school courses offered in the middle school? Y / N   College courses in high school? Y / N   In what ways has the school been successful in providing an excellent education for gifted students? _____
_____
_____
_____

K. Opportunities for Remediation

If you anticipate your child will need special services due to physical or mental limitations, ask if they are available at the school. Special education? Y / N   Physical therapy? Y / N   Adaptive physical education? Y / N   Speech? Y / N   American Sign Language? Y / N   Interpreters? Y / N   Elevators? Y / N   Transportation? Y / N   Psychological services? Y / N   Job training? Y / N   Other: _____

In what ways has the school been successful in providing an excellent education for exceptional children? _____
_____
_____

Educational Excellence for Your Child

L. Use of Community Resources

Does the school utilize any of the following community resources? Adult volunteers? Y / N Business or industry? Y / N Government? Y / N Speaker's bureau? Y / N Nonprofit organizations? Y / N Upper-grade student tutors? Y / N Museums, zoos, parks? Y / N Comments: _____
_____
_____

M. Parent Organizations

Does the school have the following: Parent-Teachers Association (PTA)? Y / N Parent-Teacher Organization (PTO)? Y / N School committee or council? Y / N Music parents' group? Y / N Athletic boosters? Y / N Other? _____
Describe the services these groups perform. _____
_____
_____

N. Reporting System/Communications

How often does the school inform parents of student progress or lack of progress?
   Report Cards? _____ Interim Progress Reports? _____ Telephone?_____
   Parent Conferences? _____ Letters or Memos? _____ Other? _____
When are parent conferences held? _____ Open houses? _____
How does a parent schedule a conference? _____
What grading system (numbers, letters, statements, etc.) is used, why? _____
_____
_____

Is a sample report card available? Y / N
Does the school or school district have a newsletter? Y / N How often is it published?____
   Does the district publish an annual report on the status of the school and its students? Y / N

O. Additional Questions or Comments
_____
_____
_____
_____
_____

(Copyright © 1996 Kenneth R. Kimball, Jr.)

7

Visiting the School, Conducting the Survey, Reviewing the Results

You have become familiar with the School Survey Form and have a good idea of what you wish to see when visiting the school. You are now ready to do the following:

✓ schedule an appointment

✓ tour the school building

✓ conduct your school survey

✓ review and evaluate the results

✓ summarize your conclusions on the School Survey Balance Sheet

Scheduling an appointment

Scheduling an appointment should be easy, as most schools encourage parents to either call or come to the school if they have something on their minds. While it may be a little more difficult to arrange a one-hour appointment with a busy principal, calling well in advance should make this possible. If the principal will not be available during your time frame due to an out-of-town meeting, health problem or the like, an assistant principal, department supervisor, guidance counselor or teacher will be filling in. By all means schedule an appointment with this person. He or she will be able to provide much of the information you need and more than likely will be able to help you pursue your objectives.

There are, of course, a small number of school officials who, while voicing their interest in meeting with parents, really prefer to have education left to the "professionals." If you sense this is the case, you will want to thoroughly check out the school as you are already committed to achieving excellence through active participation in your child's education. This could be rather difficult if you don't have access to the necessary staff members.

Your visit, your agenda

The preparations you have made have given you a good idea of what you want to accomplish during your school visit. Keep in mind, it is "your visit" and "your agenda." You have a right to expect the school to respect what you are doing and to respond favorably to your request for a tour and conference. It should be realized, though, that it is beneficial to include the principal's suggestions if they do not conflict with the plans you have in mind.

During your telephone conversation, the principal might say, "I would like you to look at some of the things Mr. James and Ms. Romano, our sixth grade teachers, are doing," or "one of the people I want you to meet is our language-arts coordinator." The short- and long-term benefits of these meetings should not be underestimated. They can provide valuable information, additional contacts at the school, and the opportunity to demonstrate your receptivity to new ideas.

Appointment questions and answers

If you have previously been successful in scheduling appointments and holding meetings with school officials or community leaders, you may wish to use a similar approach this time. If you have not had this experience or are concerned you might forget something, it would be a good idea to be prepared to answer the following questions before phoning the school.

Q. Whom do you want to see?

A. You would like an appointment with the principal, but others might be included in the meeting at the suggestion of the principal.

Q. What do you want to do?

A. You expect to do two things: tour the building and interview the principal, giving him or her the opportunity to answer some survey questions about the school.

Q. Why do you want this appointment?

A. You are interested in learning more about the school your child attends if this is the case, or you are anticipating a change to a new school or community. You are very interested in having your child receive the best possible education. You have heard some positive things about the school and would like to know more about it.

Q. When would you like the appointment?

A. Look at your calendar before calling the school. Be prepared to suggest two or three times when you would be available. You should indicate the survey will require about an hour. Let the person taking your call estimate the length of the tour.

Remember, the best time to visit a school is when classes are in session. If this is not possible, you might ask for an early morning, late afternoon, or early evening appointment. While these times are less desirable in terms of your objectives and can create an inconvenience for the principal, conferences outside of school hours can usually be arranged.

Avoid Saturday or Sunday unless these are the only days you will be visiting an area. While principals perform school duties on weekends, most try to limit their involvement to previously scheduled events and emergencies. There is, of course, no harm in asking.

Q. Where do you want to meet?

A. Your first choice is the school. You may find that parent meetings are held in the district administrative office during vacations. If this is the case, you should still be able to complete the survey, but may not be able tour the school. It is entirely appropriate, though, to ask if someone could show you the school or if you could stop by on your own.

Telephoning the school for an appointment

Pick up the telephone and call the school if you feel you are ready to schedule an appointment. Ask to speak with the principal. Your call will quite likely be routed to the principal's secretary, especially if it is a large school. Introduce yourself and briefly state your purpose for calling. Ask to have your call returned or determine when you might call again if the principal is unavailable. Make sure you obtain the name of the person with whom you are speaking.

It would be a good idea to have the secretary schedule the visit if he or she offers. This is common practice, especially in larger schools. While this may eliminate the opportunity to talk with the principal before going to the school, arranging the meeting at this time will very likely hasten the date of your visit. Remember to state all of your whom-what-why-when-and-where information so that enough time can be allocated for all you wish to accomplish.

Ensuring a successful tour and school survey interview

The day of your school visit has arrived. You are well prepared and undoubtedly will be pleased with how well things go. Your personality and style will take over at this point. There is no need to take you through your visit step-by-step, but you may want to run through it on your own. Keep in mind that meeting parents is an every day occurrence for most principals. They especially enjoy conferences that are not stressful and those in which they feel they are helping parents and children.

There are a number of "do's" and "don'ts" you should consider in order to ensure your tour and interview go smoothly and to make them as productive as possible. They are based on experiences the author has had in helping parents do just what you are doing. While these suggestions have worked well for many, I am sure you understand there can be no assurance they will work in the same manner for you. Review the list. Determine which points you can use and adapt them to your particular situation.

Visit suggestions

Do:

- Schedule your visit well in advance.
- Confirm the appointment one day prior to your visit.
- Dress appropriately.
- Arrive at the principal's office at least ten minutes before your appointment.
- Introduce yourself, addressing the secretary or principal by name.
- Politely remind the secretary of your other commitments if there seems to be a noticeable delay.
- When meeting the principal, indicate your appreciation for the opportunity to talk.
- Briefly review the purpose of your visit, including your time frame.
- Relax and enjoy yourself. Your visit should be pleasant as well as productive.

Don't:

- Take your child with you on your first visit, unless suggested by the principal.
- Be critical of things you observe. At this point, your primary purpose is to learn, not judge.

Educational Excellence for Your Child

- Talk too much.
- Smoke or ask if you can smoke.
- Become upset by activity in the office.
- Assume that every program or course is open to or suitable for your child.
- Expect it to be like "when I was in school."

Tour suggestions
Do:
- Review what you want to see with the person conducting the tour.
- Be a good observer and listener.
- Ask questions.
- Let your guide set the tone in discussions with students and staff.
- Quietly indicate your satisfaction when you see something you like.
- Note relevant observations in writing.
- Express your appreciation for the tour.

Don't:
- Be surprised if the principal asks a staff member or students to conduct your tour.
- Talk louder than necessary.
- Expect an answer to every question.
- Delay the tour by asking too many questions or stopping too long in one place.

When you have completed your tour, you will probably return to the main office. Be sure to thank your guide, especially if you will not see this person again.

Survey suggestions
Do:
- Give the principal a clean copy of the School Survey Form if he or she requests one.
- Take brief notes while conducting your survey.
- Phrase questions in your own words.
- Ask for clarification when necessary.
- Move from one question to the next in an efficient manner.
- Remind the principal if answers are too detailed.
- Try to cover all material related to your child; omit irrelevant questions.
- If you run out of time, ask the the principal to complete the survey on a clean copy of the form and to mail it to you.

Don't:
- Be upset if the principal asks another staff member to respond to the survey.
- Try to make decisions at this time.
- Worry if some survey questions go unanswered.
- Try to write down too much detailed information.

Concluding your school visit

When you have completed the interview, ask any final questions you might have. Before leaving the school, tell the principal and secretary when they might hear from you. Allow time to review the information you have collected and to decide whether to schedule another appointment perhaps including your child. Finally, express your appreciation for the cooperation you have received.

When returning home

When returning home, you may realize there were one or two questions you forgot to ask. You may also think of additional things you would have liked to have seen on your tour. This is normal. If you have a question of great importance to your decision making, call the school and ask it. Less important questions can wait until you determine if you are seriously interested in a particular school. Rest assured you now have the vast majority of the information you will need to make informed decisions.

It is a good idea to write a short note of appreciation to the principal a day or two after your visit. No doubt, you will know what to say. If you don't have the time to do this or feel uncomfortable writing, pick up the telephone and deliver your message.

If you are considering several schools, you have probably scheduled additional appointments. The experience you have gained from visiting your first school and in using the School Survey Form should make your next visit much easier.

Identifying advantages and disadvantages on the Survey Form

You will return from your school visit with an abundance of information and will be anxious to do something with it. Information is wonderful, but to be of real value it must be evaluated. This can be done using a simple plus/minus method. In most cases, this will produce the information you need.

Review the completed School Survey Form. Mark in the margin those responses you feel indicate an advantage for your child with a plus (+) and the responses you consider a disadvantage with a minus (–). You could use two plusses (++) or two minuses (– –) or include brief notations to emphasize important items. It is not necessary to mark items that are either neutral or unimportant in your child's situation. Remember, your first thought is often your best thought. Thus, it is better to mark a questionable item lightly and move on to the next, rather than to dwell on it or leave it blank. If this is done, you can return to the item and make a decision more quickly. Keep in mind, that the results teachers are getting from teaching basic skills and their commitment to excellence are far more important factors than the exterior condition of the building or whether your child's friends attend the school.

As you are completing this process, I urge you to make use of as many resources as possible in determining whether items should receive pluses or minuses. This can be done by reviewing the common attributes of successful schools in Chapter 1 and referring to relevant sections of Chapters 4 and 5. Discuss remaining questions with the principal or appropriate people listed in a section of Chapter 18, "Where to get feedback." In most cases you will acquire the information you need.

At this point, you may feel you are dealing with more information than you would like. Also, you may not have enough space for your notations. If this is the case, you can summarize your data on the School Survey Balance Sheet.

Using the School Survey Balance Sheet to refine your data

The School Survey Balance Sheet makes it possible to further refine the information you have acquired. It can be used to make comparisons and to record factors that, in your opinion, are particularly important. It is easy to use, produces an unusually concise document, and is often quite revealing. In some ways it is similar to the mental process you may have followed when deciding whom to hire as a baby-sitter or whether or not to remodel the kitchen. It will be especially helpful if you are comparing several schools. The results of your analysis can be used along with other data to:

★ provide the best school situation for your child

★ select a new school

★ determine the situations in your child's present school that should be improved

★ develop an effective Education Action Plan for your child

Look at the sample completed Balance Sheet at the end of this chapter. You will see how simple it is to list advantages and disadvantages from your School Survey Form. Note that for some advantages, there are matching or related disadvantages. If this is not the case, you may see the word "none." While this pairing of entries is optional, it seems to work well, as it encourages full consideration of each item, often producing a clearer picture of the advantages and disadvantages of the school.

Sit down with a blank Balance Sheet and a pencil. Using your recently completed School Survey Form as a guide, record the school's key advantages in the left column and the key disadvantages in the right. You will save time if you only list the most positive (**++**) and most negative (**– –**) items from your School Survey Form.

When you have done this, you can easily see if one column on the Balance Sheet has more entries than the other. This is, though, a time to be very cautious as the number of items is only part of the picture. You have already learned that the importance of each item can vary considerably. Thus, the number of items should not be used to accept or reject a school or as a reason to become overly concerned about the school your child attends. You need to decide which factors are most important to your child and to you. This is a good time to discuss your thoughts with others. Often, they can help you narrow or broaden your perspective, whichever is necessary, in order to arrive at valid conclusions. After doing this, you may want to highlight the important factors or rank them from 1 to 10.

You will probably realize while completing the Balance Sheet that the process is nearly as beneficial as the results. It is often during this stage when it becomes apparent if a particular school is the one you want your child to attend. It is also a time when you might realize there are programs or services in your child's present school that you would like to either take advantage of or avoid.

Do a reality check

After completing your School Survey Balance Sheet, it is important to do a final reality check. This is especially true if you have been doing much of your analysis alone. You may have overlooked something important or misinterpreted a comment or observation. It is a good idea to ask a friend, relative, or your child, if he or she agrees with your conclusions. This will help you avoid decisions based on false assumptions or inaccurate information. You also might want to compare your findings with the information in the school's parent handbook, annual report, or other documents.

Still undecided, try this

Most parents will be able to identify, without further analysis, the school that best meets their expectations. A few people, though, may find this difficult. If this is your situation, it is time to focus on the two schools you consider best. This can be done by placing the School Survey Balance Sheets side by side, overlapping them so that only the advantages can be seen. Then do the same thing with the disadvantages. Think about the major advantages. Do they outweigh the disadvantages? Note your conclusions on another sheet of paper. Share this information with family or friends.

If, after going through this process, you still have not determined if one school stands above all others, and these are the only schools available, you can probably select either school. It is usually better to make a decision and move on rather than delay any longer. In this way, you can concentrate your efforts on the many things waiting to be done to improve your child's education at home and school.

Summary of your efforts to date

You have reached a milestone in your efforts to obtain an excellent education for your child. You have assembled a file of valuable information that may be second to none. You have a much better appreciation of your child's needs than you had just a short time ago. You know more about his or her school or potential school than the vast majority of parents. Of equal importance, the people at the school know you. They realize you are a concerned parent who has demonstrated an interest in your child's education. This combination should produce positive results as you move from the research to the action phase in obtaining an excellent education for your child.

Successful people realize the necessity of having sound goals. In Chapter 8, you will learn about the importance of establishing educational goals and how they can help your child. If you understand the information in this chapter, you may need only to scan it before moving on to Chapter 9 where you will develop an Education Action Plan. It will include long-, intermediate-, and short-term goals and appropriate strategies for reaching them. This plan will serve as a guide in your quest for excellence as your son or daughter moves from childhood to adulthood.

Educational Excellence for Your Child

SCHOOL SURVEY BALANCE SHEET

SAMPLE

School: _____*Any School USA*_____ Tel: _____ Date: _____

This balance sheet can be used to summarize the information on your completed School Survey Form. List only the most important advantages and disadvantages of this school, especially as they relate to your child. Limit each entry to four or five words as the back-up information is available on your School Survey Form. Do not assume items are of equal importance, as this is rarely the case. If you wish, the most important items can be ranked from 1 to 10, highlighted, or marked in some other way. Upon completion, you will have a profile of the school that should be very helpful in making educational decisions for your child.

Advantages	Disadvantages
Nice neighborhood	35 minute walk to the school
Basic skills are emphasized	Math and science textbooks are quite old
Active PTA & other parent groups	None
Very complete library / media center	None
Staff stability and enthusiasm	None
_____	No after school program
Standardized test results are excellent	None
_____	No summer school program
Vocal music program seems strong	Limited instrumental music program

Comments/Conclusions: __*Good solid curriculum. Consider this school and Oak Creek Elementary.*__

(Copyright © 1996 Kenneth R. Kimball, Jr.)

Visiting the School, Conducting the Survey, Reviewing the Results

SCHOOL SURVEY BALANCE SHEET

School: _____ Tel: _____ Date: _____

This balance sheet can be used to summarize the information on your completed School Survey Form. List only the most important advantages and disadvantages of this school, especially as they relate to your child. Limit each entry to four or five words as the back-up information is available on your School Survey Form. Do not assume items are of equal importance, as this is rarely the case. If you wish, the most important items can be ranked from 1 to 10, highlighted, or marked in some other way. Upon completion, you will have a profile of the school that should be very helpful in making educational decisions for your child.

Advantages	Disadvantages

Comments/Conclusions: _____
_____
_____

Continued on other side

Educational Excellence for Your Child

Advantages	Disadvantages

Comments/conclusions: _____

(Copyright © 1996 Kenneth R. Kimball, Jr.)

8

Background Information on Goals

Excellence seldom occurs by chance
You have learned that excellence seldom occurs by chance. It is only by setting high goals and doing the planning and work necessary to advance toward them that excellence can be achieved. While the process is not difficult, it does require some thought and, above all, commitment. You may only need to scan this chapter if you and your child are goal-oriented. If, on the other hand, you seldom set goals extending beyond a week or so, you will benefit from its contents. You can then feel confident moving to Chapter 9 where you will actually write goals while completing an Education Action Plan for your child.

Let's look at an example of an outstanding success in achieving excellence. In the early days of space exploration, President John F. Kennedy announced that the United States would place a man on the moon by the end of the decade. To most people, this seemed impossible. But that plan was developed, the work was carried out, and on July 20, 1969, the goal was accomplished. This feat could not have happened if any of these steps were omitted. You can help your child achieve success by making sure he or she has high goals, sound plans for achieving them, your support, and a willingness to work hard in carrying them out.

Excellence in education, excellence in life
In Chapter 1, excellence was described as the highest degree of good qualities, or "the best." The responsibility for ensuring your child receives an excellent education was placed primarily on you as the parent. It is important to emphasize that excellence in education goes hand in hand with excellence in life. We do not learn in isolation, but rather as part of our total life experiences. This must be kept in mind as you set goals and develop strategies for achieving them.

By working with your child in developing goals you are either directly or indirectly making the following important statements.

★ My child deserves the benefits of excellence.

★ The future is too important to be left to chance; it must be planned.

- ★ Developing clear and realistic goals is an essential part of effective planning.
- ★ My child is an individual and as such requires individualized goals and educational experiences.
- ★ I will play an active role in planning and obtaining an excellent education for my child.
- ★ I expect the school to help my child achieve his or her personal goals.
- ★ I will enrich my child's education in order to further his or her goals.
- ★ I will monitor my child's progress using the goals that have been developed and excellence, as the criteria.

The school will play a major role in helping your child reach the academic goals assigned to it by society. It can also help your son or daughter reach the broader goals of life. It is important, though, to remember the primary responsibility for the latter rests with you if your child is young, and with you and your child if he or she is older. Your ultimate goal should be to have your child assume full responsibility for his or her education and life by the time high school is completed.

Setting goals and communicating them to the school

As the principal of a large middle school, I often had the opportunity to discuss goals with children and parents. I found many had not given much thought to setting goals. Even those parents who seemed to have an idea of where their children were going, usually did not have a plan to get there. If they had one, it was often the school's plan, based on a short conference with the teacher or counselor or on an information sheet from the guidance department. This is not enough. Your child must have long-, intermediate-, and short-term goals if he or she is to have any hope of achieving excellence. These goals must be clear, realistic, and measurable. They should be summarized in writing and discussed with appropriate school personnel to gain their support and to avoid misunderstandings. The information you will need to carry out this process is included in Chapters 9 and 10.

> Aa Bb Cc Dd Ee Ff Gg Hh Ii Jj Kk Ll
>
> Planning ahead:
> People who do not plan ahead usually fall behind. They also may not know if they have arrived.

Teachers deal with goals every day. They also have ways to determine if goals have been met. While their overall effort must be to educate all children assigned to them, they are looking for ways to individualize the curriculum and their teaching methods. Most teachers would find it helpful to learn about your child's goals and the specific strategies you have developed to achieve them. They may also have suggestions for you that can make your job easier.

Heading in the right direction

You should realize that you will be doing most of the goal setting if your child is very young, while an older child should be included in the planning process. It is possible though, you may not be specific enough regarding where your child is going or the steps needed to get there. It has become all too common for young people to stray off course when their ultimate goals are not specific or continually kept in mind. I hope your child is never in a position similar to the overseas airline pilot who announced over the public address system. "This is the captain speaking. We have finally emerged from the storm. The good news is that we are an hour ahead of schedule. The bad news is that I just checked my flight plan and find that I have been flying directly away from our destination for the past ten hours. Please keep your seat belt fastened as you may experience some discomfort during the next couple of days."

One of the best ways for your child to avoid flying in the wrong direction is to have a written plan to follow; then to check it often to see if he or she remains on course. It is the long-term goals and strategies in a plan that guide a person on his or her voyage through life.

Some goals will change

Humans are influenced by an almost endless array of major and minor events that occur in their lives. They are continually evolving as unique individuals as a result of these events. Many people sense when change has occurred, is occurring, or might occur in the future. In response, they modify their goals and lives. Others are less aware of change and may not make the necessary adjustments.

As the person primarily responsible for your child, you may be the first to be aware of important changes in his or her life. If this is the case, and you feel they might affect your child's long-, intermediate-, or short-term goals, you will want to evaluate the situation. You can then decide if your child's goals or strategies need to be revised. It is best to avoid fads or whims. On the other hand, resist clinging to goals or using strategies that are no longer appropriate. You will be most effective if you remain focused, yet flexible, in guiding your son or daughter. Sit down and talk with your child whenever his or her interests seem to be changing. By doing this, you will be aware of factors that could affect your child's education.

Before writing your first goal

Before writing goals, you should begin to think about what you might want for your child. It is a good idea to review the documents that you have already completed. They contain some of the most important information you will consider when writing goals, and in developing ways to reach them. No doubt you have already begun to focus on two or three goals you wish to accomplish in order to ensure an excellent education for your child.

At this time, it should be helpful if you carefully consider several questions.

✓ Where do you expect your child to be in one, three, or ten years?

✓ What do you or your son or daughter want to accomplish through education?

✓ Are there positive aspects of the school that might benefit your child?

✓ Are there weaknesses in the school that you wish to avoid?

✓ What do you want the school's regular, remedial, and enrichment programs to do for your child?

✓ What are some of the things you can an do at home and in the community to help your child reach his or her goals?

Discussing goals with your child and others

While there are no fixed rules to follow when discussing goals with your child, there are a few suggestions that might help. Choose a relaxed setting. Be sure to allow sufficient time so that neither you nor your child will feel rushed. You might begin with a general discussion about the future. Ask your child to talk about what he or she might be doing in a few years or as an adult. You can then move from this to a more specific discussion about how to reach that point.

Introduce supporting data when you feel it will be helpful, but remember it is only necessary to share information that will be used in determining goals and strategies. This is especially true in the case of a younger child who might be confused or overwhelmed by what you are doing. As your child matures it is important to share more information and to get continuous feedback so that you are operating on the same wavelength.

You may want to talk about goals with someone other than your child. This would be a person whose judgment you respect in regard to educational matters. You could suggest your older child do the same. It might be a family member, friend, present or former teacher, or someone in the community who is familiar with your child. Talking with others will give each of you an opportunity to test ideas and pick up information and suggestions of value as you both continue to plan. You may wish to remind these people you are confiding in them as you respect their judgment on matters such as this and that you would appreciate it if this information would remain confidential.

You are now ready to use the information you have gained from reading this chapter to develop goals for your child. Using the Education Action Plan Worksheet that is included in Chapter 9 as a guide, you will develop long-, intermediate-, and short-term goals, and the strategies for reaching them. Samples of completed forms have been included so that you can see how this can be done.

9

Developing an Education Action Plan

An Education Action Plan is an itinerary for life

An Education Action Plan is somewhat similar to an itinerary for a journey. In fact, that is what it is, a plan for a journey through life. Thus, the planning process for each is quite similar. For example, when planning a trip, you might study travel brochures, historical data, and maps before establishing a route. You would include places you wished to visit and your means of transportation. You would establish beginning and ending times allowing for reasonable adjustments along the way. Similarly, an Education Action Plan uses the information that you have gathered to plan the future. This can be done when your child is any age and can extend as far into the future as you desire. If your son or daughter is young, you can begin by developing a plan consistent with your personal philosophy and understanding of your child. If your child is older, he or she should be involved in the process.

In addition to the obvious long-term advantages of having an Education Action Plan, it can also provide the following short-term benefits:

★ promote better communications between you, your child, and the school
★ demonstrate the importance you place on planning and education
★ help in the selection of a school, educational program, or specific courses
★ serve as an instrument to be used in negotiating the best possible educational situation for your child
★ remind you of ongoing and follow-up activities, necessary to ensure your child's goals are met
★ serve as a guide for selecting "out-of-school" educational experiences
★ serve as a foundation for the following year's plan

As in planning a journey, you must first determine the goals you wish to accomplish. This will be done using information from your child's Historical Records File, data from completed worksheets and forms included in previous chapters, and discussions with your child and others. Then, using the Education Action Plan Worksheet included in this chapter you will list long-term, intermediate-term and short-term goals and develop the specific strategies necessary to accomplish them.

For our purposes, a goal is the terminal point toward which you and your child are working, while a strategy is something that needs to be done to get there. An example of a goal might be, "to increase reading ability by one and one-half grade levels this year." Strategies to reach this goal might include receiving daily remedial instruction, bringing books home from the library, reading a book a week, subscribing to a special interest magazine, keeping a reading log, and holding regular parent/child reading discussions.

Goals can be reached in various lengths of time. The categories, long-term, intermediate-term, and short-term will work quite well when considering education goals. The primary reason for having intermediate- and short-term goals is to support long-term goals, the latter being established first.

Long-term goals are normally realized after four or five years

For our purpose, long-term goals are normally realized after four or five years. For preschool children, this could be as early as when they are seven or eight years old, while long-term goals for high school juniors or seniors might be realized when they are in their early twenties or even later in life. In the case of a young child, they are more likely established by the parent rather than the child. Long-term goals can be fairly broad but must lead in a direction you want to go. They should also give meaning to life.

Long-term goals should include vocational objectives

An older student's vocational objectives should be considered when establishing long-term goals. For example, an eighth-grade student with an interest in science and strong mechanical ability may have expressed an interest in preparing for a vocation that would make it possible to use these strengths while spending time outdoors. An additional long-term goal might be to obtain a position in a preferred geographic location. Long-term goals could include graduation from a technical school or college, then working in agriculture, forestry, or the construction business.

Another student might be particularly interested in collecting, processing, and disseminating information and like indoor work. Options might include working in a library, for a newspaper or magazine, or for a radio or television station. The completion of specialized training or college program would be necessary for most students.

There are, of course, challenging vocational opportunities not requiring a two- or four-year college degree. For many of these jobs, though, employers expect applicants to have specific high school and post-high-school courses and training before they will consider them for employment. If a student plans to go directly into the work force shortly after high school graduation, the completion of appropriate courses and other programs should definitely be included in a student's short- or intermediate-term goals.

Intermediate-term goals can be met in one to three years

For our purposes, intermediate-term goals cover a period from one to three years. They should be rather specific. For example, if a long-term goal is to obtain a college education in a particular field of study, then intermediate-term goals for an upper-grade student must include a rigorous college entrance program in high school and several cocurricular experiences. Emphasis would be placed on those subjects necessary for acceptance at an appropriate college. While the required high school courses will be quite similar for most college-bound students, there would be differences in electives depending on the field one chooses. Club and activity experiences would also vary.

Developing an Education Action Plan

An intermediate-term goal for a student pursuing a career in forestry would be to complete as many math and science courses as possible. Additional intermediate-term goals might include holding an office in the environmental club and attending conservation camp. A summer job working in a lumber yard or with a surveyor or urban landscape firm would provide valuable experience and should be included among the strategies to reach the goal.

The curricular and cocurricular preparation for a student entering the field of communications would include additional language arts, English, or humanities courses as well as club experiences in debate, school newspaper, or yearbook. Among the strategies helpful in entering this field would be experiences working part-time for a publisher, advertising agency, newspaper, or radio station.

Intermediate-term goals for all college-bound students should include visiting selected colleges, developing computer skills, and in many cases earning money for tuition and living expenses. If a young person does not plan to attend college, the out-of-school experiences one gains become very important. Intermediate-term goals must include carefully selected volunteer or paid work experiences in order to become more qualified for employment. Summer and part-time work experiences are particularly valuable. They should not be left to chance. You may know of cases where a part-time job in business or industry led to full-time employment. The benefits of this approach may include a greater choice of positions, higher starting wage, more opportunities for advancement, and the increased possibility of further education and training. It also cushions the overall transition from school to work.

Short-term goals can be reached within a year

Short-term goals are those that can be reached within a year. Some may even be completed in a few days. It is very important for them to be specific and measurable. In other words, you should know at the end of the "short-term" whether or not each goal has been reached.

To help achieve educational excellence, short-term goals must lead toward the accomplishment of intermediate- and long-term goals. This is not to say there is anything wrong with unrelated short-term goals. We establish and complete goals like this every day. It is important, though, to realize that unless the focus is kept on

> Aa Bb Cc Dd Ee Ff Gg Hh Ii Jj Kk Ll
>
> **Assigning students:**
> If parents were allowed to select their children's teachers, and teachers were allowed to select their students, some of each would never be chosen.

one's ultimate objectives, a short-term goal may detract from accomplishing a long-term goal. For example, a high school sophomore might have a short-term goal to earn enough money during the summer to buy a used beach buggy. This might be fine, unless this choice would prevent the student, who plans to become an archaeologist, from participating in an important archaeological dig or saving money for college. Giving preference to the beach buggy could make it more difficult to achieve the long-term goal, possibly limiting success.

Let's look at how a short term-goal can help achieve an overall objective of educational excellence for your child. The short-term goal might be to have your child develop the self-control necessary to pay better attention in class. While discussing this issue with your child and his or her guidance counselor, several strategies could be developed that your child could carry out in attempting to accomplish this goal. An additional strategy could be to have the principal assign your son or daughter to a teacher who has been successful in bringing about this change in other children. This would be a reasonable request, especially if the school has more than one teacher in your child's grade who meets this description. This placement could lead to improvements in the way your child behaves, thus paving the way for the accomplishment of intermediate- and long-term goals. You would know at the beginning of the school year if the placement had been made. You would also have a good indication by the end of the year if the teacher and your child had been successful in bringing about the desired changes in behavior.

The Education Action Plan Worksheet helps you write goals

The Education Action Plan Worksheet has been designed to help you organize, and record, your long-, intermediate- and short-term goals. If you look at the first sample form, you will see only one long-term goal is written on the page. This is because it takes only two lines to write, for example, the long-term goal "to be recommended for the high school college-entrance program." On the other hand, it takes a number of lines to record the numerous intermediate- and short-term goals necessary to achieve this long-term objective. Thus, most of your entries on a worksheet will be either intermediate- or short-term goals, and the strategies to reach them. These are also the goals that will be revised most often, thus requiring more space on the form.

A few clearly defined goals are best

It is best to limit the number of goals to those that are really necessary. It also helps to be as precise as possible in writing them. On the other hand, if your child is quite young, or establishing long-term goals seems difficult, it may help to begin by writing, "to receive an excellent education." This will allow you to start developing the more precise intermediate- and short-term goals and strategies necessary to achieve excellence for your child. It is better to have a limited number of goals and some ideas for achieving them than it is to have a shoe box full of goals and no idea of how they can be accomplished.

Writing goals and strategies

You are now ready to write long-, intermediate-, and short-term goals and the strategies for reaching them, using the Education Action Plan Worksheet as a guide. Your child's goals and strategies will be most helpful if they meet certain criteria.

Each goal should be:
- ✓ based on an analysis of the information you have compiled
- ✓ a high goal, but one that is achievable
- ✓ written in a clear, concise manner
- ✓ attainable by carrying out specific strategies
- ✓ measurable so that you and your child will know when the goal has been reached

Each strategy should be:
- ✓ related as closely as possible to accomplishing the goal
- ✓ an action that can be taken by you, your child, or someone else
- ✓ written in a clear, concise manner
- ✓ measurable so that you will know when it has been completed

Your child's Education Action Plan Worksheet provides an efficient way to organize your thoughts and a framework to outline your goals and strategies. It will save time if you write or print your entries clearly. Don't worry if they are not phrased as well as you would like. Also, do not be overly concerned if you have difficulty deciding whether something is a goal or a strategy. The fact is, the successful completion of a strategy could be a short-term goal. The important thing is to get the information down on paper so you can act on it. After all, this is a working document, subject to revision. If necessary, you can refine it later.

Before completing your first Education Action Plan Worksheet, look at the two samples at the end this chapter. While these are for fictitious students, they will give you a good idea of what you will be doing. The first worksheet represents a fourth grade child who, for the most part, has been doing average work but is having difficulty becoming a proficient reader. The child's parents, realizing he has this problem, want to make sure everything possible is done so that he will be recommended for the high school college-entrance program. The second plan is for a young woman in ninth grade who has done exceptionally well in elementary and middle school and who would like to become an Air Force pilot. After reviewing these examples, you will be ready to complete your first worksheet. Remember to involve your child whenever possible.

Completing additional Education Action Plan Worksheets

Having completed your first worksheet, you very likely sense the importance of what you are doing. Also, you should have a feeling of accomplishment and satisfaction. You are following through on a personal commitment and are one step closer to reaching your goal of educational excellence for your child. You may wonder why so many parents are willing to leave their children's education to chance. Perhaps, they don't realize the importance of their involvement or how satisfying the results can be.

Complete as many additional Education Action Plan Worksheets as necessary. Remember, your Education Action Plan Worksheets are primarily for your use. You will decide if they will be shared with school staff members or others who might be of help.

You might want to consider another use for the Educational Action Plan Worksheet. An example of this might be when an older child has been making poor decisions. You might decide it would be best if this child attended a different school. You could complete your own worksheet with a short-term goal to enroll your child in a new school. You could then develop the necessary strategies to gain acceptance and to get the teacher and program you desire. The completion of one Education Action Plan Worksheet, a conference at the school, and a couple of telephone calls are all that normally would be necessary to begin to reach this goal.

Thinking ahead

Now is a good time to mark your calendar so that you will remember to review your child's Education Action Plan Worksheet periodically. While this should be done whenever there is a significant change, it is best to establish two or three dates each year when you feel you will have enough information to take a more complete look at the plan.

One of your reviews should definitely be done in late winter or early spring so that you can complete it before student placements and schedules are made for the following year. By checking with the school, you can get a more accurate date as to when this occurs. It is much easier to have your requests approved if they can be considered right from the beginning rather than necessitating a change in work that has already been completed.

Educational Excellence for Your Child

EDUCATION ACTION PLAN WORKSHEET

SAMPLE #1

Name: __Bobby Bright_____ Age: __9__ Grade: __4__ Date: _____

Completion date

Long-term goal: _To be recommended for the high school college entrance program._ _____

Strategy: _Strengthen ability to learn by becoming an above average_ _____
Strategy: _reader as soon as possible._ _____
Strategy: _____ _____

Intermediate/Short-term goal #1: _Increase Bobby's interest in reading._ _____

Strategy: _Emphasize reading in elementary school._ _____
Strategy: _Emphasize reading at home._ _____
Strategy: _____ _____

Intermediate/**Short**-term goal #1: _Read 1 year above grade level by the end of this year._ _____

Strategy: _Make sure school is aware of Bobby's specific reading deficiencies._ _____
Strategy: _Ask the teacher to schedule Bobby for extra reading. Ensure that_ _____
Strategy: _periodic monitoring of reading skills takes place, and that I am informed regularly of the results._ _____

Intermediate/**Short**-term goal #2: _Develop a spontaneous interest in reading._ _____

Strategy: _Add high interest books and magazines to Bobby's daily reading._ _____
Strategy: _Make regular trips to library to read and select books._ _____
Strategy: _Set aside time, each day, for reading and writing at home._ _____

(continued on other side)

Developing an Education Action Plan

Completion date

Intermediate /**Short**-term goal #2: *#2 continued.* _____

Strategy: *Discuss, with Bobby, what he has read each day.* _____
Strategy: *Keep a reading log.* _____
Strategy: *Subscribe to a nature magazine.* _____

Intermediate/Short-term goal # __: _____ _____

Strategy: _____ _____
Strategy: _____ _____
Strategy: _____ _____

Intermediate/Short-term goal # __: _____ _____

Strategy: _____ _____
Strategy: _____ _____
Strategy: _____ _____

Intermediate/Short-term goal# __: _____ _____

Strategy: _____ _____
Strategy: _____ _____
Strategy: _____ _____

Intermediate/Short-term goal # __: _____ _____

Strategy: _____ _____
Strategy: _____ _____
Strategy: _____ _____

(Copyright © 1996 Kenneth R. Kimball, Jr.)

Educational Excellence for Your Child

EDUCATION ACTION PLAN WORKSHEET

SAMPLE #2

Name: _Mary Flyer_ Age: _14_ Grade: _9_ Date: _____

Completion date

Long term goal: _Become a commissioned officer (military pilot), preferably in the Air Force._

Strategy: _Attend and graduate from the Air Force Academy._
Strategy: _Alternative - enter Air Force through college ROTC._
Strategy: _Alternative - Naval Academy and enter flight school._
Strategy: _____

Intermediate/Short-term goal #1: _High school graduation in top 5% of class._

Strategy: _Take appropriate courses, especially advanced math and science._
Strategy: _Enroll in ROTC or attend military school._
Strategy: _Obtain high scores on SAT's, and other college entrance exams._

Intermediate/Short-term goal #2: _Strengthen qualifications with non-school experiences and strategies._

Strategy: _Visit Air Force and Naval Academies._
Strategy: _Attend summer program at service Academy._
Strategy: _Inquire about and seek congressional appointment._

Intermediate/**Short**-term goal #1: _Make sure high school courses are appropriate._

Strategy: _Obtain information from the Air Force and Naval Academies._
Strategy: _Talk with Academy representatives or graduates._
Strategy: _Talk with guidance counselor about courses for next year._

EDUCATION ACTION PLAN WORKSHEET

Name: _____ Age: _____ Grade: _____ Date: _____

                                                                                                              Completion date

Long-term goal: _____ _____

Strategy: _____ _____
Strategy: _____ _____
Strategy: _____ _____

Intermediate/Short-term goal #__: _____ _____

Strategy: _____ _____
Strategy: _____ _____
Strategy: _____ _____

Intermediate/Short-term goal #__: _____ _____

Strategy: _____ _____
Strategy: _____ _____
Strategy: _____ _____

Intermediate/Short-term goal #__: _____ _____

Strategy: _____ _____
Strategy: _____ _____
Strategy: _____ _____

(Continued on other side)

                                                                    Completion
                                                                       date

Intermediate/Short-term goal #___: _____   _____
_____   _____

Strategy: _____   _____
Strategy: _____   _____
Strategy: _____   _____

Intermediate/Short-term goal # ___: _____   _____
_____   _____

Strategy: _____   _____
Strategy: _____   _____
Strategy: _____   _____

Intermediate/Short-term goal # ___: _____   _____
_____   _____

Strategy: _____   _____
Strategy: _____   _____
Strategy: _____   _____

Intermediate/Short-term goal# ___: _____   _____
_____   _____

Strategy: _____   _____
Strategy: _____   _____
Strategy: _____   _____

Intermediate/Short-term goal # ___: _____   _____
_____   _____

Strategy: _____   _____
Strategy: _____   _____
Strategy: _____   _____

(Copyright © 1996 Kenneth R. Kimball, Jr.)

10

Getting Your Child's Education Action Plan Implemented

Working with the school to realize your child's goals
This chapter describes a number of steps you can take to bring about desirable changes in your child's formal education program. It is based on the understanding that you and the school are committed to providing the best possible education for your son or daughter while keeping in mind that the school has a legal and moral obligation to do the same for all children. This chapter will prepare you for a follow-up conference at the school aimed at bringing about specific changes that will benefit your child.

The courts have determined that schools must provide equal access to educational opportunity. In its simplest form, this means the school must offer your child an education that is, at a minimum, equal to that of other children. They have not said your child's education must be identical to that of other children. There is nothing to prevent the school from doing more for those who need additional services and can benefit from them. In fact, there are laws in some cases that mandate these services.

It would be a serious mistake to provide every child with a similar education without considering individual interests and ability. Likewise, it would be unrealistic to expect all students to reach the same level of academic achievement. The differences between children are, as you would expect, too great. While some states and school districts have minimum standards that all but a few students must meet in order to advance from one grade to the next and to graduate, these requirements tend to be just that, minimums. For your child to attain his or her fullest potential, it is necessary to establish high standards and then to do everything possible to reach them. If this is not done, opportunities to experience excellence will often be missed.

While all children in a given class may appear to be taught the same curriculum and in a similar fashion, I can assure you, this is not the case. Teachers are constantly making adjustments for individual children. This is done by spending more time with some children than others, varying the difficulty of the questions they ask, giving different assignments, pairing students so they can help one another, and using a number of other techniques. This customizing of education is one reason why it is so important to remind the teachers and others at school of your child's goals.

Unfortunately, the old saying, "If you don't do it, no one else will," is sometimes true in education. While most teachers are more than willing to provide the kind of attention conscientious parents desire for their children, their work load often makes this difficult if not impossible. At times, you may feel like you are the only person advocating for your child. If others are helping, you are fortunate; if they are not, it will be necessary to find ways to enlist their support.

It takes an entire village to raise a child

People live and function daily in a number of communities and subcommunities. Institutions within these communities provide the goods and services necessary for daily living. You have learned that the family and school are the primary institutions responsible for educating children. Thus, it is appropriate to consider the school an extension of your family in matters related to education.

> Aa Bb Cc Dd Ee Ff Gg Hh Ii Jj Kk Ll Mm
>
> Discussing problems:
> Many students find that there is only one teacher with whom they can discuss their problems. It is interesting to note that this is often one more person than they can find at home.

There is an African proverb that indicates it takes an entire village to raise a child. The process you are pursuing to ensure your child gets an excellent education is in keeping with this proverb. You are enlisting the support of family, friends, the school, and other organizations to help your child experience excellence. At the same time, you are quite likely bringing about changes in the school that should benefit all children in your community.

Let the school's organizational structure help you

In Chapter 6, you learned that most schools are organized in a hierarchy with the principal at the top. He or she provides leadership and makes many of the decisions that affect the education of children. Significant changes in your child's program, class assignment, or the like, are best discussed with this person.

If, on the other hand, your goals call for actions that can be taken by your child's teacher, guidance counselor, or another staff member, it is better to approach this person first. By doing this, you will give him or her the opportunity to help you reach your goals. This can lead to efficiency for you and the school. It can also help you gain an advocate who may be able to help your child at a later date.

You may not be sure who the decision makers are that can be of the greatest help to you. If this is the case, ask the principal, a guidance counselor, or the school secretary. The latter is usually very much aware of how things get done in the school. A friend who is knowledgeable about the school or a staff member with whom you are familiar is also an excellent resource.

Preparing for your follow-up conference

If you have developed one or more Education Action Plan Worksheets, very little additional preparation is needed prior to your follow-up conference. The information you will use during the conference should be available for easy reference, while backup materials can be kept in a envelope or briefcase. This will help keep you organized, thus reducing the need to shuffle through numerous papers during the conference in order to find the ones you want.

It is not necessary, or even a good idea, to take your child's complete Educational Records File into the school for your conference. It is better to determine ahead of time the papers you will need. If, on the other hand, you would feel more comfortable having the file nearby, you might want to lock it in your car. This way, you can easily retrieve one or more documents if necessary.

Copies and folders help establish credibility

You should make copies, ahead of time, of all information you plan to give to the principal or other person with whom you are meeting. While schools have copiers, it is to your advantage to avoid interrupting your conference to take care of this task. If you find it difficult to make copies, check with the school secretary to see if this can be done at the school prior to your meeting. Most schools will let you use their copier or will make copies for you at little or no cost.

If you plan to give the principal more than one or two pages of information, place them in a folder marked with your child's name and the date, for easy identification. Small details such as this coupled with the interest and sincerity you display will go a long way in helping you gain the credibility and cooperation necessary to accomplish your goals.

Conference attendees: Your child? Advocate? Staff member?

Before requesting a conference, you may wish to determine if it would be a good idea to have your child attend with you. If the principal or other person with whom you are meeting has not met your son or daughter, this is usually a good time. This does not mean your child should be present during the entire conference. An introduction, though, will help take your requests out of the theoretical and place them solidly in the real world. Also, it will give the person with whom you are meeting the opportunity to develop an initial relationship with your child.

If your conference concerns only one child, it is best to make alternative arrangements for any other children rather than have them accompany you to the school. All too often, the office secretary ends up serving as a baby-sitter while a parent is having a conference. This is a situation you should avoid.

It is a good idea to have your child take some interesting reading material, or a pencil and paper on which to draw or write, while at the school. A quiet activity ensures that something productive will be happening while he or she is sitting patiently in the conference or waiting in the outer office. An alternative would be to arrange to have your child spend the time in the library/media center or other suitable area of the school.

Normally, it is not necessary to have a friend, relative, or advocate attend a conference with you. It is an option, though, especially if you feel the presence of another person might help you achieve your objectives. If you decide to invite someone, make sure he or she is familiar with your agenda and goals and is agreeable to assuming certain responsibilities, even if it is just being a good listener. You should review this person's role well before arriving at the school for the conference.

Educational Excellence for Your Child

The principal may suggest including another staff member in the conference. This is generally a good idea, especially if the person chosen can help you in reaching your goals. If on the other hand, you feel the presence of this person would restrict conversation or in any way make it difficult to complete your agenda, it is important to say so. It is perfectly all right to tell the principal you wish to meet in private. After all, it is your conference. A graceful way to handle this suggestion is to express your interest in meeting the staff member before or after the conference, or at a later date, while indicating that this person need not be present at this time.

Making an appointment

The procedure for making an appointment for a follow-up conference with the principal or other staff member is similar to the one you followed in scheduling your school survey visit. If you did not conduct a survey, or if this is your first conference with a school official, you will find information on this subject in Chapter 7. When phoning the school, make sure you again state the purpose of the conference. Indicate who will attend, and be prepared to say about how much time you feel it will take.

Conducting a productive conference

This conference will be quite different from your earlier meetings with the principal and other school personnel. Previously you were seeking information about the school. Now you are requesting arrangements or changes that will benefit your child. The task becomes that of persuading the principal or others to accept your ideas, and to help you and your child in carrying them out. Therefore, your agenda and presentation will be somewhat different.

You have a clear idea of what you wish to accomplish, have prepared the necessary supporting materials, and have developed a number of strategies to meet your objectives. The primary flow of information, at least initially, will be from you to the other person. In other words, you will make a presentation. Remember, you requested the conference and developed the agenda. It is your responsibility to explain your request and to use the available time wisely. To do this, you must be prepared to convey your ideas in a well-thought-out, organized fashion.

Listen attentively to what is being said. It will help you understand the reasons why the other person feels certain things can or cannot be done. Careful listening can also result in questions you can ask, opportunities for agreement, strategies you can follow, or future actions you can take.

A productive conference would proceed in the following manner.

- Introduce or reintroduce yourself to the principal or other person with whom you are meeting.
- Initiate a very brief conversation to break the ice.
- Briefly outline your agenda for the meeting.
- Review background information.
- Present your goals and strategies, clarifying how they will benefit your child, and where applicable, the school.
- Provide oral and/or written supporting information.
- State the changes you desire. Be specific as to what you want done.
- Ask the principal what he or she can do to help you get these changes implemented.

Getting Your Child's Education Action Plan Implemented

- Reach agreement on as many issues as possible, compromising only when necessary.
- Discuss any options or additional actions.
- Summarize what the principal will do.
- Summarize what you will do.
- Jointly establish a time schedule for the actions to occur. Arrange for a written summary of this calendar.
- Agree to continue communicating, by telephone, or in future meetings.
- Express your appreciation for the conference and any help you have received.

Meeting with other staff members

One of the things the principal might suggest is that you discuss your goals and strategies with one or more other staff members. Unless this seems to be a stall or diversion, you should accept the opportunity. A meeting at that time, or within a few days, with a classroom teacher, guidance counselor, psychologist, special education teacher, school nurse, gifted program coordinator, or other specialist may be just what is needed to complete your agenda. As in the case of your conference with the principal, make sure this person clearly understands the reasons for meeting, and how the changes you are requesting might benefit your child.

Realize the school has options

Just as you considered several options before selecting specific actions to accomplish your goals, you should allow the principal to do the same. It is unlikely anyone knows and understands the school, its staff, and overall program better than this person. For best results, the principal, teacher, counselor, or other staff member should be given reasonable latitude in carrying out your requests.

There can be an added benefit from allowing school officials to use their judgment. By providing input, they are making a specific or inferred commitment to your plan. By doing this, they share considerable responsibility for the plan's, and thus your child's, success. They are, in fact, "buying into the change." What more can you ask?

Strengthening your commitment by offering to help

When trying to persuade others to see things your way or to get them to do what you want it often helps to reinforce your commitment with an offer of personal involvement. While this can be done with words, actions are usually much more convincing. One of the most effective things you can do is to indicate you want to assume responsibility for some of the steps that must be taken. You might begin by asking for suggestions of things you can do. While each situation is different and will require a varied level of participation, you might agree to monitor homework, phone the teacher biweekly, arrange for tutoring, reduce television viewing, or perhaps enroll your child in an out-of-school enrichment program. Steps you might take and examples of home and community activities that you might consider in fulfilling your commitment to your child and the school can be found in Chapters 14-17.

Persuasion can work for you

If you are like most people, you have spent a significant portion of your life persuading others or in being persuaded. While you may not have thought much about it, you are already familiar with the persuasion techniques that work best for you. These are the ones you will probably want to use in meeting with school administrators.

Schools do not operate in a vacuum, and administrators are influenced by a multitude of internal and external factors. Relevant facts, research reports, a quote from a book, a news story, the description of a personal experience or that of a friend, are often effectively used in persuasion. Quoting your child, a community leader, staff member, or school official can be helpful in making a point. It is important to be accurate. Also, these references should not be used in a threatening way unless you have exhausted all other means of bringing about the changes you desire. Choose your examples carefully, weigh the advantages and disadvantages of each, and be prepared to provide supporting data if they are challenged.

If you want to learn more about persuasion, most libraries have books on this subject. You might also want to look at one or more books on selling. These books will help you present your information in a logical, clear, and concise manner when attempting to convince others to accept your position. For best results, adopt only those ideas that fit your belief pattern and personality. It is best if what you do seems natural.

It is of utmost importance to avoid confrontation while at the same time not lessening your determination and expectations for excellence. It is better to agree to disagree on an issue rather than becoming upset or alienating the other person. The old adage about catching more flies with honey than with vinegar usually reigns in dealing with school administrators.

Knowing when to "back off"

Nearly as important as understanding the art of persuasion is knowing when to "back off." There is no magic formula to help you realize when you have pushed your request to the limit. You should be very sensitive to how the other person is acting, and to what he or she is saying. It is usually counterproductive to push your efforts to the point where the opposing position becomes set in concrete as this allows little or no room for movement at a later time.

It is important to close your conference in a cordial manner even if you have not accomplished any or all of your objectives. This will give you the opportunity to consult with others, to rethink your strategy, and possibly to try again. It will also permit the principal or other school administrator to further consider your requests and, perhaps upon reexamination, agree with your position and gracefully make the desired changes.

Change often takes time

The principal may not be able to make all the changes you desire. If this is the case, do not become discouraged as real change often takes time. The important thing is to get a commitment to act on certain requests, and the assurance that other requests will not be forgotten. You should check periodically to see that any requests on which you agreed have not been delayed or sidetracked. You have every right to expect changes to be made promptly. By agreeing on a time schedule before completing the conference, you can help ensure this happens.

Send a follow-up memorandum of understanding

Upon returning home from your conference, review and summarize the points on which you agree. Note who is responsible for implementing them. Within a day or two, write the principal expressing your feelings, hopefully positive, about the meeting. Include a summary of the items on which you agreed. This can be done by enclosing a list of items, or by including statements similar to these:

- "I was pleased to learn that Sam can attend Ocean Middle School next year. He will receive tutoring in seventh-grade French this summer so that his proficiency should be about the same as others in his eighth-grade class."
- "As a result of our discussions, it was agreed that Brenda will receive remedial reading three times a week for the balance of the year."
- "It is my understanding that you will assign Bill to Mr. Strict's class next year."
- "Your offer to change Melody's schedule so that she can take orchestra before lunch should solve the performing music problem."
- "While I was disappointed to learn Mr. Rivera's class is filled, I hope you will keep Mary in mind if a vacancy occurs before school opens."
- "I am pleased you agreed that Jeff does not need a second study hall. I trust you will be able to schedule him for Spanish I."
- "As we did not agree on the reasons for Ronald's lack of attention in class, I hope you will pursue your suggestion of having the school psychologist talk with him."

You should also state what you will do, and what your child's responsibility will be.

- "As you suggested, I will see that Harry watches less television and gets to bed by eight o'clock on school nights."
- "Sarah understands she will need to take additional math and science courses if she plans to pursue a career in environmental studies."
- "I have talked with Mike about the necessity of getting his homework done on time. Rest assured, his father and I will be monitoring this closely."
- "Ann now understands why it will be necessary to stay after school on Monday and Thursday for extra help."
- "Following our meeting on Tuesday, I talked with my supervisor. She suggested that Mark borrow our old office computer so that he can use the writing and algebra software programs from the school. We will be checking to see that he makes good use of this opportunity."

If you would like additional information on letter writing, several sample letters and a number of additional statements have been included in Appendix C. You may wish to consider customizing one or more of these samples for your use.

When concluding your letter include a statement asking the principal to contact you if he or she does not concur with your understanding. This should ensure that your verbal agreement is correctly interpreted. It will also serve as a reminder to the principal to take action if this is required. It is a good idea to include your telephone number at the end of the letter for ready reference.

What to do if you are not successful

Complete success is not always possible. Also, it tends to be relative. Only you can decide whether or not you have accomplished your objectives. If you feel you have not, you must decide whether to accept the unfavorable decision or to pursue it further. If you decide on the latter, there are a number of options available. Before proceeding, it would be a good idea to get additional input. Talk again with family members, friends, teachers, and others who have helped you in your efforts.

Based on the information you now have, you may decide to revise your original request and talk again with the principal, or abandon this procedure and go to a higher authority. In most cases, this would be the superintendent of schools or board of education.

There are also a number of organizations that may be able to advise or help you in achieving your goals. You may want to talk with someone who is active in the school's parent/teacher group, school advisory committee, or teacher's association. If your child has a mental or physical condition that makes it difficult to learn, or to function in school, you can request help from the building or district Special Education or IEP Committee. It would also be a good idea to contact one of the organizations in your community advocating for children with these problems.

There are a number of governmental agencies, including your state Department of Education, Health Department, and Children and Youth Services Department that may help in difficult situations. As a rule, it is best to try to resolve problems at the local level before contacting these agencies. You can expect each higher authority to ask you to exhaust all local resources before it acts on your request.

Legal action, a last resort

There are, of course, legal remedies to some educational problems. It is best to explore all alternatives first, as a legal resolution is often less than satisfactory to both parties. There is also the problem of expense and delay. All too often, a court does not consider a case and render a decision until after a child has moved on to another grade or school. There is little reason to pursue legal action if the outcome will not bring the results you want. Those would normally be achieving justice or educational excellence for your child or in some cases for many children.

More than one person has won a case in court, only to be disappointed in what was gained as a result of the litigation. Others have lost their cases. If you see this as a likely possibility, you may want to accept this disappointment and move on. Consider it a detour or delay in the journey of excellence and concentrate your efforts on alternative strategies and plans.

If, after careful consideration, litigation seems to be your only option, it will be necessary to determine your rights and your child's rights. A phone call to your family attorney, legal aid society, or bar association should produce the name of an attorney who specializes in education cases. If you have kept good records, you should be able to provide the documentation this person needs to advise you properly.

When going to a higher authority or initiating legal action, some parents are afraid the teacher, principal, or someone else at school will "take it out on their child." I can understand their apprehension. While I have heard of situations where this has occurred, I can assure you this is rarely the case. What happens most often is that staff members treat the child in the usual way or are extra careful to avoid anything that could be construed as unfair. Your objective should be to ensure there is no overreaction one way or the other. If you sense this is occurring, discuss it immediately with the appropriate school official, or in the case of litigation, with your attorney.

The importance of monitoring

You have reached the point where you can expect the school to make certain changes or arrange specific services they were not providing prior to your involvement. The real test, though, is if the agreements you have worked out with the principal or other staff members are carried out. You will also want to know if the desired results have been achieved. This can only be determined by carefully monitoring your child's program and progress.

There are a number of ways to determine if you are getting the desired results. These include feedback from your child or other children, your personal observations, and discussions with the teacher or other school staff. There are also report cards and interim progress reports that are sent home on a regular basis. Take the time to read them and to ask questions. If you do not understand any of these documents, additional information can be obtained by contacting the school.

Standardized tests are also useful indicators. Your child's test results should be sent to you for review, or made available during conferences with the teacher or guidance counselor. If you have not received this information within a month or six weeks after your child takes one of these tests, ask for it.

The following suggestions will help you monitor your child and the school in an effective and efficient manner.

- Discuss school often with your child.
- Ask your child questions, especially if you notice a change in attitude or behavior.
- Telephone the teacher or principal periodically or any time you suspect a problem.
- Request a conference if your concerns cannot be satisfied by phone conversation.
- Make notes of discussions with teachers and other school personnel.
- Keep a journal, especially if you suspect a problem.
- Write letters or memos to express your concerns.
- Keep copies of all correspondence.
- Visit the school periodically, or serve as a school volunteer on a regular basis.
- Increase your participation in the school's parent/teacher group.
- Attend scheduled parent conferences and other meetings.

You will find additional suggestions for monitoring in the next chapter.

Where do you go from here?

You have completed the initial phase of obtaining educational excellence for your son or daughter. While doing this, you have learned a lot about your child's interests and needs and have surveyed one or more schools. You know much more than most parents about how the school operates, what it has to offer and what it can realistically do. You have met several school staff members and quite likely have developed a working relationship with them. Additionally, you have a child who is quickly realizing the importance you place on education.

You have established realistic goals and strategies and have begun to implement them. You are committed to monitoring your child and the school. In short, you have become a wise consumer of education. The knowledge and skills you have gained during this process will serve you well as you continue your quest for excellence.

The value to you and your child of maintaining a close relationship with the school cannot be overemphasized. In the next chapter, you will learn how your participation in one or more aspects of the school program can benefit your child and other children. You will also see how it can add to your personal education and enjoyment.

11

Becoming Involved in Your Child's School

You should become involved in your child's school
There are many reasons why you should become involved in your child's school but the overriding one is to ensure that your son or daughter receives an excellent education. You learned in prior chapters this cannot be left to chance. If, for any reason, you still doubt the need to play a greater role, you might wish to consider the following questions.

- ✓ Am I uncomfortable leaving my child's education and future to the school?
- ✓ Do I need more than my child's report cards and one or two open houses a year to assure me that he or she is getting the best possible education?
- ✓ Would I like to have more to say about my child's education and school?
- ✓ Do I have the time, however limited, to invest in the improvement of my child's education and possibly the education of other children?
- ✓ Do I have any skills, or have I had experiences, that could benefit children?

If your answer to any of these questions is "yes," you should seriously consider becoming more involved in your child's school. In this chapter, you will learn about three effective ways to do this. These are:

- ✓ reading/phoning the school to keep abreast of information
- ✓ attending school events to observe what is going on
- ✓ participating in your child's school to obtain more information, and to be in a position to exert greater influence on his or her education

Each of these three levels of involvement will help you monitor your child and the school more closely. The first level, reading/phoning, can be done at home and requires the least commitment. While the information obtained at this level is limited, it can be very helpful in making decisions. The second and third levels, attending and participating, take more time and in all but a few cases require you to go to the school. As you can imagine, these levels provide much more information than merely reading or phoning. They also offer the greatest opportunity to influence change. By initiating all three levels of involvement, you will become aware of up-to-date information that can be used to guide your child's education to his or her greatest advantage. This degree of monitoring is essential if excellence is to be achieved.

Employers realize the importance of monitoring

The benefits of monitoring have long been apparent in educational and noneducational settings. You may have had the experience of employing someone to do a job, only to realize later that the results did not meet your expectations. Successful employers know they must monitor their employees in order to be sure work is done properly. They try to detect problems in the early stages and act quickly to correct them. They also gather information that can be used to avoid costly mistakes that might occur in the future. Why would any parent want to leave a child's education to chance when progress can be monitored continuously with a little additional effort?

A wise consumer monitors

It was pointed out earlier in this book that most people do a reasonable amount of investigation before purchasing an automobile. Unfortunately, their interest often wanes when it comes to monitoring the maintenance and repair work. All too often, the owners manual is placed in the glove compartment where it remains until the vehicle has a serious breakdown.

Let's look at an example of what might be considered adequate monitoring when automobile repairs are being performed in a shop. There are some lessons from this situation that can apply to education. From personal experience and discussions with others, I have concluded it is essential to know as much as possible about what is actually being done on my car when it goes in for repairs. Before work begins, I make it a point to read the owner's manual and other information that is available on my vehicle.

When the time comes for my vehicle to be repaired, I speak to the service manager and the mechanic who will work on my vehicle. I specify what I want done, the information I desire if decisions are necessary, and the results I expect. This does not seem to bother most mechanics or their service managers who, being aware of my interest, are cooperative.

When work begins, I try to locate myself where I can see what is being done. Often, I can tell whether parts are being replaced or just cleaned. I do not hesitate to ask questions or to volunteer information. While I cannot see everything, I have a pretty good idea if the requested maintenance is being performed. Perhaps, even more important, the mechanic is aware of my presence. This person knows I am monitoring.

As a result of my interest, I have been invited to look at worn parts during maintenance or repair, and have made replacement decisions on the spot. On more than one occasion, I have been able to have the work completed more economically and with less delay. I have also caught mistakes. I make it my job to ensure that excellent work is done.

Set aside time to monitor

Am I suggesting you should monitor your child all the time he or she is in school? Of course not. Even if you could do this, it would quite likely interfere with the normal development of your son or daughter. I would recommend though, that you become involved in the school to the degree necessary to have a good idea of how things are going. By doing this, you will be fulfilling your responsibility to your child, while protecting your interest and investment in the school.

The amount of time you spend at home or school dealing with education-related activities depends on your individual situation. It would be extremely rare though, if you could not devote some time to this important aspect of your child's life. As is often the case, some of the hardest working parents, or those who are on the job the greatest number of hours, make it a point to read memos, meet with teachers, attend school functions, serve as volunteers, or in some other way become a part of their child's education. If the desire is present, the time can usually be found.

> Aa Bb Cc Dd Ee Ff Gg Hh Ii Jj Kk Ll Mm Nn
>
> Checking information: Kindergarten teacher addressing parents: "If you promise to call me before believing what your child says happened in school today, I will check with you before believing what he or she says happened at home last night."

Becoming involved in your child's school educates you

Profound changes are occurring in society, which, of course, includes schools. Personal involvement in your child's school and overall education is the best way to learn about these changes. By observing, listening, and questioning, you can gain a wealth of information. You would not have this opportunity if you relied solely on memos from school, the morning newspaper, or what your child tells you at the end of the day.

Many parents have inaccurate, or incomplete information about their children's schools. Additionally, their benchmarks for education are usually based on a time in the past when they were attending classes a full generation earlier. While they should resist making decisions until they have complete, accurate, and up-to-date information, this is not always the case. The information you gain from personal involvement with the school is very likely to be more current, more reliable, and thus more useful than from any other source.

Choose your level of involvement

In order to help you determine the extent to which you might become more involved in your child's school, the three levels of involvement presented earlier; reading/phoning, attending, and participating are discussed in this chapter. It should be pointed out that it is sometimes difficult to separate the ways you might become involved in these three categories. Also, your initial involvement may lead to an increased level of participation, perhaps without your even realizing it.

It is important to be aware of all of the opportunities for greater involvement that exist in your child's school. Knowing this, you can choose those that will be most suitable for your situation. Your participation should be governed by your need for information, your interests and skills, and the time you have available. The following possibilities exist in most schools. Included are hints on how to make your school experiences as productive and enjoyable as possible.

First-level involvement—reading/phoning

First level involvement consists of carefully reading and understanding all items that are sent home from school. It requires a minimum amount of time, and should be considered

Educational Excellence for Your Child

essential by all parents, whether or not they are striving for excellence. Report cards, interim progress reports, standardized-test results, meeting announcements, and schedule and program information are items included in this category. An increasing number of schools have set up a home page and are providing information via the Internet. The school newsletter and your daily or weekly newspaper are also good sources of information. At this level of involvement, you will also want to seek information from your child. If there are things you don't understand or if you feel the need for more detailed information, you should phone your child's teacher, principal, or some other person at school who can answer your questions.

Make sure you receive notices and memos

You are certainly aware of the typical single-page memos that are sent home with children announcing meetings or providing information about the school. You will want to encourage your son or daughter to give them to you or place them in a visible location when arriving home from school. They are an important resource in your efforts to stay informed. Unfortunately, you might occasionally find one in your child's pocket, book bag, or backpack when you are sorting the laundry or packing the next day's sandwich at eleven o'clock at night. This can be a problem if the memo announces a meeting that was held earlier the same evening.

> Aa Bb Cc Dd Ee Ff Gg Hh Ii Jj Kk Ll Mm Nn
>
> The bulletin board:
> Early Americans realized the importance of the town bulletin board for exchanging information. An increasing number of computer users are realizing the same thing today. Check the Internet and see.

Teachers and administrators realize if they really want information delivered to a parent, it is more likely to get there if it is sent with a kindergarten student rather than a high school senior. This, of course, is not practical. There are, though, several things you can do to receive a greater number of these messages.

- Make your child aware of the importance you place on receiving information from school.
- Instruct your son or daughter to carry notices in a protected pocket, folder, or book bag, thus reducing the chances of loss.
- Help your child develop the habit of handing notices to you or putting them in an obvious place when arriving home from school.
- Insist that you are informed when there is a message.
- When asking your son or daughter questions about school, include a question as to whether he or she brought anything home for you.
- Express your disappointment and unhappiness if your child forgets to give you a message or to inform you of something happening at school.

- Suggest to the teacher and principal the value of using newsletters, weekly or monthly calendars, newspapers, and radio announcements, as well as the Internet, telephone and postal service to inform parents when things of importance are happening at school. Then, make sure you write these events on your calendar.

Use the phone to keep in touch

One of the most effective ways to become more involved in your child's education without leaving home is to phone the teacher on a biweekly basis. This should be often enough unless your child is having difficulty. When talking with the teacher at the beginning of the school year, explain that this is what you will be doing. Determine the best time to call, and assure the teacher you simply want to touch base regularly. Try to phone at a scheduled time. This will give the teacher the opportunity to think about your child, and perhaps gather information before you call.

Make sure you are organized before phoning the school in order to avoid overlooking something important. Try not to prolong the conversation unless it is obvious your child's teacher wishes to talk. It is also a good idea to keep an informal log of your conversations so there can be continuity in your discussions.

In addition to regular conversations with your child's teacher, it is a good idea to phone the principal occasionally, perhaps every month. Be sure to inquire about the kinds of things he or she has been trying to accomplish. Not only will your interest be appreciated, but your call will very likely prompt the principal to tell the teacher you called or to ask the teacher how your child is doing. Actions like these can provide dividends well beyond the obvious benefits occurring at the time.

It is unwise to carry on discussions about controversial issues or to argue on the telephone. Unfortunately, some people become overly bold when speaking to a person from a distance. As you cannot see the other person's facial expressions and body language, you will very likely be receiving incomplete feedback. This can lead to misunderstandings. If you find a phone conference is ineffective, it is time to have a meeting at the school. You may wish to include a staff member or friend who understands your position, and who can help resolve any differences.

When concluding a phone conversation with either the principal or teacher, make it a point to say something positive about the person or school and mention your continued availability and interest in your child's education.

Separated and divorced parents and the information loop

Separation and divorce present children, parents, and school staff members with unique challenges when it comes to the flow of information. It is often difficult for the parent who does not live in the same household as the child to obtain information or to stay in the communication loop. If you are in this situation and there is no legal reason prohibiting you from receiving information try to work out a satisfactory arrangement with your former spouse and your child. You may even be able to coordinate your parenting activities. If this seems impossible, or you are still having difficulty getting timely information, contact the school and ask to have duplicate copies of report cards, meeting announcements, and other school information mailed to you. By providing several self-addressed envelopes, or a fax number, you can often accelerate the flow of information. Be prepared to provide documents or written verification indicating you are entitled to receive information about your child.

Any system that you set up will need monitoring. If it begins to fail, remind the person responsible about your expectations. You may also want to make greater use of the telephone than is normally necessary to keep up-to-date on school activities, to ask questions, and to receive information about your child. I have known a number of divorced parents who called the teacher or guidance counselor each week and who felt this method was quite reassuring.

> Aa Bb Cc Dd Ee Ff Gg Hh Ii Jj
>
> Opportunities lost: A parent who fails to participate in child rearing misses the opportunity of a lifetime. Unfortunately, so does the child.

School activities can play a unique role in the lives of children and parents who are living with the disadvantages of alienation, separation, or divorce. While each situation is different, these events can provide an opportunity for a child's "other parent" to become better informed, assume additional responsibilities, and thus experience some of the satisfactions and frustrations of child rearing. They can even provide a common ground for solving some of the problems currently facing many families.

It is important that you receive information about your child's school activities if you are to attend or participate in them. Most teachers can and will work with either, or both, parents if they show an interest. It is extremely important that guidelines be clearly established by the parents and communicated to the advisor. They must also be receptive to the advisor's suggestions. This is necessary to prevent an otherwise positive experience from becoming a pulling match between parents that might harm the child, disrupt the activity, or embarrass the activity sponsor.

Understanding the school's reporting system

In order to participate fully in your child's education, you should learn as much as possible about the school's reporting system. You need to understand the information included on report cards and interim progress reports. You also must be able to interpret standardized test results and other evaluation reports. Your familiarity will help you ask probing questions, often leading to additional information from which you can draw valid conclusions. It will then be possible for you to more effectively monitor performance and progress and to make sound decisions.

It would take an entire book to describe the diverse reporting systems used by schools today. Schools use numerical grades, letter grades, no grades, teacher comments, levels of skill, parent conferences, handwritten report cards, computerized reports, quarterly or six-week-interim progress reports, and this is only a sampling. What does all this mean to you?

- While there may be common elements in reporting, it is unlikely the system used in your child's school is the same as you remember when you were a student.
- While you may feel the system you remember was better, this may not be the case.
- You should not be confused by, or fear, today's reporting systems. There is usually a simple answer to any question you might have.
- Even the best reporting systems provide only a small portion of the information you need about your child.
- If you want to learn more about the reporting system used by your child's school, the information should be available.

Deciphering report cards

There are a number of things you must know in order to understand the information on your child's report card. The card, or accompanying material, will often include an explanation of the marks or comments. Some schools include a page or two on this subject in their parent handbook.

If you can answer "yes" to the following questions, you should have no difficulty using school report information to make decisions. If not, you should ask for further clarification.

- If letter grades, numbers, or symbols are used on the report card, is there an explanation of what they mean? Do I understand this information?
- Are the grades reported on this card based on my child's actual performance, his or her effort, or a combination of the two? Has this been made clear?
- Does the information reported on the card indicate how well my child is doing in comparison to children of various abilities in the class or grade? Similar ability? Has this been made clear?
- Does the card indicate how my child measures up to the teacher's expectations? Is this clear?
- Do I know whether my child is passing or failing?
- Is it clear how the teacher will determine the final grade?
- Has my child's attendance and behavior been included?
- Are there comments indicating any steps the school might take if my child is having difficulty or is doing exceptionally well?
- Does the card indicate anything my child or I should do at this time?

If, after considering these questions, you feel a bit bewildered, do not become discouraged. Most parents need additional information before they are able to understand all of the data on a report card. In most cases, problems arise when the school has failed to provide an adequate explanation. Pick up the telephone, call the school, ask your questions, or arrange an appointment.

Second-level involvement—attending

The second level of involvement occurs at school where you will be attending orientation sessions, parent/teacher programs, open houses, conferences with your child's teachers, and meetings with guidance counselors. Demonstrations, spelling bees, science fairs, and other events in which your child is a participant and you are an observer could be included in this category. While this level of involvement requires more time than simply reading information or using the telephone, it will increase the knowledge you have to make decisions. It will also provide a greater opportunity for you to influence education. This level of involvement should be considered essential by parents who seek excellence for their children.

Attending functions will help you learn about the school

Many schools provide informal opportunities for parents to learn about the curricula and other programs. These include coffee klatches, afternoon teas, and meetings where teachers discuss curricula with parents. Most schools also hold annual orientation sessions for parents and children who are new, introducing them to the facility and educational program. Keep in mind that these meetings, as do open houses, provide information of value to a widely diverse audience. It is inappropriate and counterproductive to bring up, or dwell on, matters of interest only to you. These discussions should be held at another time.

Nearly all schools have parent/teacher groups. Most of these organizations hold regular monthly meetings and all parents are urged to attend. As many of their activities involve participating as well as attending, a complete explanation of parent/teacher groups, and the valuable role they play has been included in this chapter under "third-level involvement."

Most schools offer programs for parents of children who have remediation or enrichment needs. They encourage parents to get together and to share concerns about their children. Schools also work closely with support groups and other organizations within the community that have formed to deal with the problems created by various handicapping conditions.

Guidance counselors and school psychologists offer courses to help parents work with their children, for example, in developing responsibility and self-control. Some schools have formed single parent groups so these parents can discuss common problems. If you feel any of these programs might help you in your efforts to raise your child, you should investigate them. If your child's school does not already offer a program that you feel would be helpful, ask your contact person to organize a group or to assist you in getting one started. You might be surprised how many other parents share your interest.

Understanding open houses
Most schools hold at least two open houses a year, one in the fall, a short time after the beginning of the school year, and one in the spring. They are usually scheduled in the early evening and last about two hours. While each may bear the name "open house," they generally serve quite different purposes.

The fall open house is held to acquaint parents with the school and its programs. Often, there is a tour of the building and an opportunity to meet the teachers and other staff members in small or large group meetings. Individual teacher conferences are usually held at a different time. At this open house, your child's teachers will probably review the curricula and share their expectations for the year. Their presentations will include information about student behavior, homework policy, and the reporting system. You may be told how you can help, and be assured by the teachers of their availability, and desire to work with you in educating your child.

You should try to attend all open houses, but if you can attend only one major school event during the year, it should probably be the fall open house. Try to arrive early. Listen carefully, and ask general interest questions if you need further information or clarification. Make sure you introduce yourself to your child's teachers and assure them you are prepared to take part in his or her education. It is a good idea to give the classroom teacher or guidance counselor a small card or piece of paper with your name and telephone number. Include your child's name and indicate the times you can be reached. If you really want to be sure your child's teachers remember you, send brief notes the following day thanking them for their presentations.

In many schools, the spring open house gives teachers and students an opportunity to showcase some of the things they have accomplished during the year. Thus, it is an especially important event for them. Some principals use this opportunity to present valuable information regarding the year ahead. Often topics like the school schedule, course and program offerings, and class placement are discussed. You may also be provided with useful information regarding summer programs and activities offered by the school and community. You should consider all of these factors when deciding whether or not to attend.

A conference is a very effective way to communicate

An individual conference with the teacher is usually the best means of communication. Some teachers schedule a formal conference with each parent during a particular time of year. Others invite parents to call the school if they feel the need for an appointment. It is your obligation to take advantage of these opportunities. If the teacher requests the conference, attend! You need not worry about the agenda, as he or she will provide it. You should, though, consider any questions you would like to ask or comments you would like to offer.

If, on the other hand, you request a conference, you will already know what you wish to discuss. In order to make this meeting as productive as possible, it is usually a good idea to inform the teacher ahead of time of your questions or concerns.

While it is fairly common for children and parents to delay attending to problems, hoping they will resolve themselves, this is usually a bad idea. It is much better to pick up the phone, write a note, ask for a conference, or take some other action when you first become aware of a problem. As a rule, simple problems can be corrected with simple solutions. More complex problems, often resulting from inaction, will require more complex actions. Failure to act on the more serious problems may mean they will never be corrected.

Third-level involvement—participating

Third-level involvement offers you the opportunity to participate in your child's school. The most common form of parent participation usually involves activities sponsored by the school's parent/teacher group, or in some cases being a member of a board or committee. It can also include serving as a school volunteer in one of the many positions described in the next chapter. It requires the greatest commitment of time, but provides the best opportunity to learn about and monitor your child and the school. It can also add to your personal growth. If you are interested, and can set aside even a limited amount of time, this level of involvement can be most rewarding.

Parent/teacher groups help children and schools

Parent/teacher groups provide an opportunity for parents to participate in their children's education. They realize that parent support and involvement are necessary for the success of any child or school. Teachers and administrators realize they need the input and cooperation of parents to foster excellence. Parent groups, and especially parent/teacher groups, provide this medium. When parents and teachers, and in some cases students, get together, it is not long before they realize they have similar concerns. Additionally, they share many of the same ideas regarding solutions. By discussing these issues, in the presence of the principal and other staff members, plans are often developed that will benefit the entire school.

It is a rare teacher or administrator who does not see the value of responding to the concerns of even a small group of parents. When consensus exists and there is evidence of support, it is often quite easy for the administration to make changes. It is not unusual for a suggestion made by a parent group on a Monday evening to become a school policy or practice before the end of the week. This is the kind of input and response that benefits children.

Parent/teacher groups have been very effective in improving education through their support of legislation. It is common for these organizations to meet with legislators to discuss state aid, or to ask their school boards to provide additional services, library books, audio-visual equipment, or computers. While the time you spend attending meetings might seem to be significant, you can be assured that the results of your commitment will often outweigh the time expended.

Parent/teacher groups influence education

The National Congress of Parents and Teachers (PTA), working with its state and local affiliates, is the primary organization in the United States providing a means for parents to have a broad influence on education. This is one reason why many schools choose to have a PTA rather than a local nonaffiliated group, often called a Parent-Teacher Organization (PTO). While either group can be effective at the local level, the PTA with nearly seven million members stands above all others in its success in influencing education at the local, state and national levels. It is important to point out that membership in the National Congress of Parents and Teachers also opens the door to a wide array of information and assistance, some of which is available by computer on the World Wide Web. Information on these services and obtaining the National PTA magazine, *Our Children,* is included in Resources at the end of this book.

For one who is striving for excellence, there are personal advantages in belonging to your school's PTA, PTO, or other parent organization, and attending functions sponsored by the group. If you have not already been contacted by the organization, your school office can put you in touch with a member who will gladly provide information. Dues are usually minimal, but if this is a problem, you will still be welcome at programs sponsored by the group. In order to avoid missing an event, it is important to remind your child, the teacher, and someone on the board of directors that you wish to be informed when the organization's meetings and activities will occur.

If you have the time and are willing to spend a couple of hours a month serving as an officer or board member of your school's parent/teacher group, by all means make your availability known. Like most organizations, parent/teacher groups are continually seeking volunteers.

Serve on a study committee or board

The quality of the educational programs in any school or school district, is partially dependent on the work of various councils, study committees, task forces, and of course the school board. These groups hold meetings that are, in nearly all cases, open to the public. If you wish to learn more about education at this level or have a need to address any of these groups, I would urge you to contact your principal or superintendent. You may even want to consider joining one or more of these committees or boards.

Participate in educating your community

Every school needs community support to effectively carry out its mission. This support occurs when people who live and work in the area served by the school understand its philosophy, program and goals. Your child's school can become even more effective if you and other parents inform those who do not have children in school about the school and its needs.

Many communities have enthusiastically supported programs that might not have been possible if parents had not educated residents and enlisted their support. For example, parents of students involved in performing music groups have worked with cultural organizations and businesses to raise money for instruments, supplies, uniforms, and performance expenses. Industries have supported many aspects of the school program, including science and technology, by providing equipment, teacher training, and consultants. Parent groups have enlisted community support in building adventure playgrounds, exercise rooms, and swimming pools and have raised money for additional staff and equipment. In most communities, local businesses, usually led by the retail merchants, have a long tradition of supporting schools. It takes parent participation to generate this interest.

You can help the school meet its increasing responsibilities

Quite likely, your child's education and that of his or her peers has been adversely affected by social changes that have placed additional burdens on schools. Unfortunately, there is little reason to think this situation will improve very much in the immediate future. Also, the demands for what families consider the necessities of life, whether it is better housing, more conveniences, newer automobiles, or more expensive leisure activities, have curtailed the amount of money they are willing to spend on education. This has resulted in staff reductions, shortages of classroom supplies, outdated textbooks, and in some cases deteriorated facilities. Many schools offer very little incentive for America's most qualified graduates to become teachers. Until people place their priorities in order and become less self-centered, we will continue to have serious problems financing and providing education.

> Aa Bb Cc Dd Ee Ff Gg Hh Ii Jj Kk
>
> The cost of education:
> The real cost to society is not the cost of education, it is the cost when we fail to educate.

You can help alleviate these problems by supporting your schools. Insist that state and local financial effort is adequate to achieve excellence and that funds are allocated fairly. Monitor the schools in your community to see that all money and resources are used wisely. Your efforts need not stop here. Every time you issue a book as a library volunteer or do clerical work in an office, you are filling a position that might otherwise have cost the school money or, even worse, remained vacant. If you tutor students in your child's class who are having difficulty or supervise children working on a social studies project, you are quite likely giving the teacher more time to work with your child and others. These efforts can lead to excellence.

Participate in the school budget process

The budget has a significant effect on the resources and programs of every school and school district. Unfortunately, very few parents seem to care about the budget unless there are controversial issues under consideration, serious program cuts pending, or substantial tax increases anticipated.

Budget workshops and hearings can provide unique opportunities for you to learn more about school programs and to influence them. To do this effectively, you will need to see a copy of the budget and any supporting information that will be considered. Arrange ahead of time to review these documents. You may even be able to get your own copies.

Try to have as many of your questions as possible answered prior to the budget workshop or hearing. This can be done by calling the financial office, superintendent, principal, appropriate program director, or any school board member. By doing this, you will be better prepared to ask more specific questions or to suggest changes you would like to see made.

Some school districts form budget advisory committees to guide the board of education in reviewing the proposed budget. If your district follows this practice, and if this is one of your interests, by all means inquire about the possibility of becoming a member.

Take an interest in your child's cocurricular activities
Cocurricular activities give youngsters opportunities to learn new skills while doing something they enjoy. Your understanding of these programs can provide you with an expanded way to view your child, his or her peers, and the school.

The very nature of cocurricular activities makes parent interest and involvement important. Demonstrations, competitions and performances are events the entire family can share. Children are often very disappointed if their parents do not attend these events. You should use these opportunities to support your child in his or her efforts, and to gain a better understanding of the school's programs. When called upon to provide transportation, to purchase or rent equipment, or to help with supervision or the expenses of operating an activity, you will want to be as supportive as time and resources permit. Remember, your participation also provides an excellent opportunity to express your appreciation to those at school who may have spent many hours working with your child.

> Aa Bb Cc Dd Ee Ff Gg Hh Ii Jj Kk
>
> Society's problems: Governments that are more interested in building offices and ball parks than in solving society's problems will end up with offices and ball parks and society's problems.

Learn more about the school through volunteering
You have learned how the levels of involvement described in this chapter can help you become better informed about your child and his or her school. You are also aware of some of the more important ways you can increase your participation. A major activity that can provide some of the most interesting opportunities, and greatest rewards, is volunteering. In Chapter 12, you will become familiar with some of the most common volunteer positions existing in schools. You will also learn how volunteering can benefit you, your child, and other children and adults in the school and community.

12

Opportunities for School Volunteers

Volunteering can benefit you, your child, and the children and teachers in your child's school. In this chapter we will examine the major reasons for volunteering, discuss how you can become involved, and look at the most common volunteer positions that exist in today's schools.

What can volunteering do for my child?

The information you gain as a volunteer about school staff, structure, and program, can be very helpful in planning educational experiences for your child. Your volunteer experiences can also increase your communications with your child and the school. This combination can make it possible to take advantage of opportunities that could improve your child's education. It could also help you avoid situations that might not be in his or her best interest.

As a parent who has already made contact with the school, you realize the importance of having your child's teachers and principal know who you are. One of the benefits of volunteering is the opportunity it provides to establish fresh contacts and new friendships. This is very important as you strive for educational excellence. The school staff member or volunteer you work with today may become a valuable advocate for your child tomorrow.

What are the benefits of volunteering?

School volunteers receive satisfaction from being around children and in helping them become better educated. While they give their time and talent without receiving monetary reward, most report that they gain other benefits that are even more important. These range all the way from making new friends to acquiring and perfecting vocational skills that result in job offers.

Volunteering can provide a productive way for you to use your leisure time. What leisure time, you say? Busy people often find themselves thinking this way. Yet, busy people are the ones who most often say "yes," when asked to take on added tasks or responsibilities. Your decision to serve, or not serve, as a volunteer rests on establishing your own personal priorities. If you decide you want to volunteer, you can make it happen.

With few exceptions, volunteers report that helping at school is one of the most enjoyable things they do. This seems to be true whether they work directly with children, or behind the scenes in an office or library/ media center. Others display enthusiasm and indicate high levels of satisfaction while working with parents, teachers, and administrators in supporting school programs. You may feel that because you hold a full-time job or, for one reason or another are unavailable during the day, the school cannot use your services. This is usually not the case. There are a number of things that can be done at home, during the day, in the evening, or on weekends to benefit the school. These are listed later in this chapter.

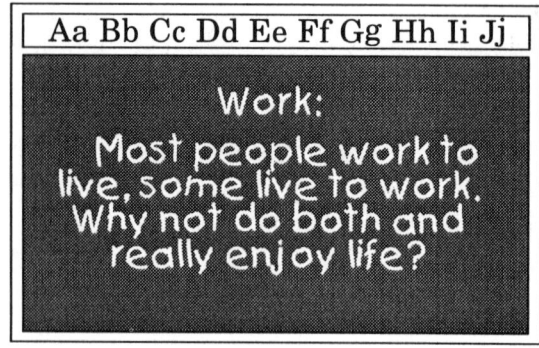

Develop new vocational skills as a volunteer

Serving as a volunteer can give you the opportunity to investigate new vocations. If you desire to enter the job market or are contemplating a change in careers, you can gain valuable experience, much of which might otherwise be difficult to obtain in any other way. Volunteering can provide you with an improved resume, letters of recommendation, and, perhaps most important, confidence. For some, it can lead directly to a paid position in the school where they are serving as a volunteer. For others it may be the best way to learn about vacancies in other schools or places of business. The direct and indirect benefits of becoming a school volunteer could be just what you need at this time in your life.

Volunteering can prepare you for greater responsibility

Your effectiveness in dealing with everyday problems depends on your ability to manage your life and, to a substantial degree, the world in which you live. Volunteering in a school can provide low-risk situations to develop leadership and interpersonal skills. Schools, by their very nature, offer opportunities for trial and error without fear of many of the adverse consequences found in other work settings. Make a minor error in front of twenty children and it will probably be missed or simply corrected without judgment. Make the same error in front of twenty adults in a work setting, and they may lose all confidence in your abilities. If your goal is to develop the skills necessary to be more effective in your home, at work, or in your community, serving as a school volunteer could provide the experiences you need.

What can volunteering do for my child's school?

Volunteers provide a wide variety of valuable services that schools find difficult to obtain from other sources. Time and budget constraints coupled with a desire to treat each child as an individual, drain the human resources of most schools. The vast majority of classrooms have only one adult, the teacher, in a room with twenty to thirty students. A volunteer can improve the adult to student ratio by 100 percent during the hour or two that he or she is helping. To a child who has a volunteer tutor, it can mean the difference between learning to read, write, or do math or struggling and not learning these essential skills.

How do I get involved?

You can inquire about volunteer opportunities simply by calling the school and asking to speak with the volunteer coordinator. In all but the largest schools, this will be a staff member or volunteer who makes these arrangements on a part-time basis. If this person is not available, ask that he or she return your call. Be prepared to discuss your interests, qualifications, and availability. In most cases your telephone conversation will be followed by an interview. This is particularly true of larger schools, where you may not be known. If this is the case, you should present yourself much as you would if you were applying for a paid position.

If your child's school is located nearby this can be a real convenience in terms of time and transportation in getting to and from your volunteer position. If, on the other hand, it is a little farther away, you may want to make arrangements to ride with another volunteer who lives in your neighborhood. I am familiar with cases where teachers have picked up volunteers at their homes in order to have them available to help in the classroom. In some districts volunteers ride school buses to and from their assignments. Discuss your transportation needs with the school's volunteer coordinator during your interview or any time you anticipate a problem that might prevent you from getting to school. In most cases, you will be pleasantly surprised with the suggestions and help you receive.

In addition to the many volunteer positions common to most schools, some schools have unique needs that expand the opportunities for volunteering. It is important to ask about all of the available assignments. Having this information, you can select a position for which you feel qualified, and that you will like. Another possibility is that you may possess one or more skills the school has not considered. If you think this might be the case, make sure the volunteer coordinator is aware of your unique qualifications, so these can be considered in assigning you to a position.

Of course, there is always the possibility you might be assigned to a volunteer position that does not seem to be just right for you. If you try a position for a reasonable time and it seems too difficult, or if you do not find it satisfying, ask for a different assignment. This is usually possible without changing your overall schedule or relationship with the school.

What volunteer opportunities exist in today's schools?

The following summary of positions, with accompanying notations, will give you an idea of some of the more common volunteer opportunities available in today's schools. They represent broad categories, and are listed in alphabetical order. To determine the specific kinds of help needed at the school where you would like to volunteer, it will be necessary to call the volunteer coordinator or principal. Most schools will promptly arrange an interview so that you can begin as soon as you desire.

Chaperone: Serve as a parent chaperone for school activities. Usually includes working with students, teachers, and other parents. May involve planning, arranging, and supervising after-school events. Accompanies teachers and students on field trips. The typical means of travel is by bus. Involves supervision of small groups visiting museums or other sites. Some personal expenses for incidentals may be incurred.

Clerical aide: Usually works in a school office under the direction of a secretary or office manager. Performs most functions of this support activity. Typing and computer skills are very desirable. Often, they can be developed or improved on the job. Other tasks include answering the telephone, sorting mail, operating the copier, preparing materials for distribution, and filing. May spend time serving students, teachers, or parents.

Cocurricular activity advisor: Uses personal knowledge and skills to sponsor activities. Examples include special interest clubs like computers, gourmet cooking, school store, aeronautics and space, photography, school newspaper, and child care. May also help with special events during or after the school day.

Counselor: Provides counseling to students in such diverse areas as self-control, improving attendance, health, homework skills, interpersonal relations, and college or vocation

Educational Excellence for Your Child

selection. Might work independently or with staff counselors. May also work with parents, either individually or in small groups. Credentials and professional experience comparable to those necessary for a paid position are normally required.

Instructor/coach: Helps individual students or small groups develop skills. Opportunities include music, drama, dance, sports, and public speaking. May require work outside regular school hours. Previous experience and demonstrated proficiency are very important.

Laboratory assistant: Helps the teacher set up experiments and demonstrations. Works directly with individual students and small groups. May conduct inventory, construct, maintain, and repair equipment, and order supplies. Often responsible, along with the students, for clean up. Important prerequisites include an interest in and knowledge of science and technology. Organizational skills and safety awareness are essential.

Library/media aide: Assists library/media staff. May work at the circulation desk checking materials in and out. Shelves books, supervises students, or works behind the scenes processing book and non-book materials. Often, there are opportunities to specialize in television or photography. Clerical, computer, and artistic skills can be helpful.

Mentor: Serves as a supportive adult figure for one or more students. Listens to concerns, stimulates thinking, discusses issues, and answers questions. May represent a particular vocation or profession. May discuss homework or other assignments. Helps students develop responsibility, self-confidence, and a vision of the future. Serves as a resource person and role model.

Monitor: Monitors students inside or outside the school. Possible assignments include cafeteria, corridors, playground, or school bus. Might oversee students while they are waiting for transportation, either outside the school, or at a neighborhood bus stop.

Receptionist: Welcomes visitors. Carries out school policy regarding who should or should not visit the school. Provides information, answers questions, and gives directions. Duties include receiving items dropped off at the school, using the telephone, issuing passes, and keeping a log of people entering and leaving the building. May escort visitors or conduct tours. Qualifications include friendliness, the ability to communicate effectively, interpersonal relations skills, and an interest in helping people.

Speaker: Speaks on topics of expertise. Audiences may include students, teachers, parents or other interested people. Group size can vary from a few people to large assemblies, depending on the topic and purpose. May work with students or teachers preparing for or following up on a presentation. May provide instructional materials or advise teachers regarding resources.

Teacher aide: Helps the teacher carry out daily routines, including the instructional program. Often works directly with individual children or small groups. May prepare materials, mark papers, and record grades. Opportunities usually exist in all grades and subject areas. Excellent experience for volunteers who are considering a career in teaching or becoming a paid teacher aide.

Telephone system operator: Answers the telephone and directs calls when the regular operator is not on duty. Needed most often in large schools with many telephones or with an older system. A clear, pleasant voice, a desire to help people, ability to communicate effectively in emergency situations, and a reasonable level of comfort with electronic equipment are important. Skills can be learned on the job. Often combined with clerical duties, especially during off-peak times. Quite likely to be employed as a paid substitute in the absence of the regular operator.

Tutor: Works directly with individual students. Helps those with limited proficiency develop reading, math, writing, spelling, world languages, English, and other academic or nonacademic skills. Previous teaching or tutoring experience, while not required, is helpful.

Volunteer in your child's future school

One of your primary reasons for volunteering is to have a positive effect on your son's or daughter's education. You will naturally think of serving as a volunteer in your child's school rather than in another building in the district. You might also consider looking ahead a few years. For example, if your child is now in elementary school, where will he or she attend middle school? Would you like to learn more about that school? Even more important, would you like to be involved in program planning and curriculum change taking place now that could benefit your son or daughter in the future? Volunteering in your child's future school could provide that opportunity.

Serve as a volunteer while at home or in the community

Most people like to volunteer during the regular school day. There are times, though, when this is not possible. Family responsibilities, physical limitations, appointments, or work schedules may prevent you from being at the school. These factors should not stop you from becoming a volunteer. You can help almost any time, day or night, by doing work for the school while at home. There are phone calls to make, newsletters to be published, and mailings to prepare. Perhaps you can imagine how valuable home volunteers, using their own telephones, can be when an emergency such as an early school closing due to inclement weather or an outbreak of a contagious disease makes it necessary to contact all parents within a relatively short period of time.

If you have a good mastery of basic skills, or a strong interest in a particular subject, your child's teacher can quite likely use your help in preparing materials or marking papers. Any task that is performed by you at home will give the teacher that much more time to work with students. You may also reduce the work that he or she must take home at the end of the day. This will provide the teacher with additional time to do other things outside school hours. As help like this is often difficult to obtain, interested teachers are anxious to provide the necessary training, materials, and instructions you might need. Some will even arrange to have the items delivered to and picked up at your home. Others may choose to work with you by computer or fax if you have these devices available.

There are a number of additional ways you can help your son or daughter and other students in your child's school while working in your home or community. This is a sample of some of the more common things you might consider.

- Become a homeroom representative.

- Obtain or construct items needed in the classroom.

- Write news releases or articles about your child's class or school.

- Serve on a school council, advisory committee or task force.

- Serve as a child advocate.

- Join others who are working to reduce the use of illegal drugs, alcohol, and tobacco or to deal more effectively with physical and mental abuse.
- Join a group concerned about better neighborhoods.
- Work to improve law enforcement and rehabilitation of youthful offenders.
- Work with scouting, YMCA, YWCA, 4-H, or recreation groups.
- Join a group committed to providing better services and opportunities for exceptional children and adults.
- Arrange work experiences for youth.
- Participate in "government day" or "career day."
- Plan and implement before- and after-school programs.
- Encourage people to vote on school issues.
- Support fund raising events (bake sales, craft fairs, auctions).
- Perform volunteer work in a museum, planetarium, aquarium, or nature center serving school groups.

Investigate school/business partnerships

You may wish to investigate the possibility of performing volunteer work for the school as a part of your regular job. Realizing education is at a critical stage, more and more businesses and industries are committing some of their resources to forming partnerships with schools. They recognize the need to expand their efforts beyond traditional activities like hosting field trips, donating money, and purchasing advertisements in school publications.

Partnerships can be cost effective for the school and private sector partners. Information sharing, the loan of staff members and equipment, internships, sponsoring workshops, awarding grants, and other direct involvement between private enterprise and the schools can result in program improvements. By doing these things, businesses can assist the school in producing job applicants who are better prepared with the skills, attitudes, and knowledge necessary to fill positions in the immediate area. This can lead to reductions in the training and retraining necessary when a business or industry hires local high school graduates.

A brief conference with your supervisor or the manager of the business or industry where you are employed might provide information about a role you could play in a school/business partnership. It is, of course, good to develop a few ideas of your own prior to the meeting.

13

Dealing Effectively With Change

Most parents realize that the world in which they live is continually changing. What they may not fully understand is how social changes affect their daily lives and that of their children. While it is possible to go through life with very little knowledge of social change, parents who are aware of what is going on in society are in a much better position to guide their children. We can only scratch the surface of this topic in a book of this length, but some aspects of change are so important they deserve attention.

In this chapter, we will look at some of the more significant changes affecting families and schools. We will also discuss steps you can take to help your child adapt to change, thus avoiding potential problems. While there are hundreds of things parents must do to successfully raise their children, the following suggestions have been chosen because of their importance and the ease by which they can be implemented. They also offer a great opportunity for parents to collaborate with one another in helping all children in the school and community. The ideas presented on the next few pages will help you do the following things.

★ Develop personal attributes in a supportive family setting.

★ Adopt positive family moral values.

★ Teach key skills to help your child adapt to change.

★ Help your child avoid exploitation.

★ Work with the parents of your child's friends.

Challenges facing families

A family in its simplest form usually consists of one or both parents and their children. A broader definition includes relatives or others who share a common interest, ancestry, language, or household. An extended family, a foster-care home, or a group home is often considered a family.

One of the primary roles of the family is to convey positive moral values and standards of behavior to the next generation. This is necessary for the continuation and improvement of society. The family is assisted by the church, school, civic organizations, and in some cases the government. While the support provided by these institutions is important, you as a key member of your family, must transmit positive morals if your child is to reach his or her fullest potential.

Each family is different from all other families and thus faces different challenges. An increasing number of parents are experiencing difficulty in meeting basic needs. In some families, there is only one parent in the home. It is very common for employment to remove the sole parent or both parents for long periods each day. An increasing number of parents have allowed their personal interests or desires to deprive their children of a supportive upbringing.

Many families have become separated from the support networks traditionally provided by relatives and close friends. Other families have found they must remain in communities where illegal activities have made the task of raising children all but impossible. While most children are not experiencing the more serious of these problems, the number is increasing. This has created a crisis as great as any the United States has faced, including some wars. If families cannot successfully raise and educate their children, the quality of life of most Americans will decline.

Challenges facing schools

An increasing number of children are arriving at school with physical and emotional burdens that interfere with their education. A lesser number don't attend school or classes on a regular basis. All too many children are uninterested in learning and do not mind preventing their peers from receiving an education. This has diverted the school's attention and resources from those students who are not having difficulty.

To deal with these situations, the school has found it necessary to change from an institution that focused primarily on education to one that not only educates but also deals with an increasing number of social problems. While some schools have been quite successful in carrying out these added responsibilities, others have not. As might be expected, the school can never replace a caring and nurturing family.

Some of the problems facing educators and others concerned about children include the following issues.

- Confusion over the degree to which schools should be involved in meeting what have historically been family responsibilities.
- Dealing with parents who believe they are not responsible for their children's education or behavior.
- Dealing with apathy, poor self-esteem, lack of respect for others, disorderliness and illegal activities within the school.
- Identifying where the money and other resources will come from to increase the services necessary to deal with problems resulting from the deterioration of families and society.

Fortunately, these problems need not prevent you from improving your child's education. If you are willing to make teaching and learning a personal and family responsibility, you can compensate for many of the inadequacies existing in today's schools and society. While this may require you and other members of your family to adjust the way you look at family life and education, the costs are minimal and the benefits great.

You can begin immediately to make positive changes. In this and the following chapters you will find hundreds of suggestions that can be used to improve your child's life. Most of these suggestions are easy to implement. The actions and activities they describe have already benefited millions of children and youth. They can do the same for your son or daughter.

Develop personal attributes in a supportive family setting

What we are and what we will become are dependent on our moral values, but also on the knowledge, skills, and attitudes we possess. These attributes are developed in both formal and informal settings throughout our entire lives. The family is one of these settings. As a parent, you realize that young children learn quickly. They imitate, they experiment, they create, they investigate, and they question. It is particularly important to capitalize on this natural phenomenon of learning during the preschool and early elementary school years if you want your child to develop positive attributes.

As children mature, they generally spend less time at home and more time in the company of nonfamily members. They are influenced less by their parents, and more by others, including teachers and peers. Ideally, they will also begin to assume greater responsibility for their actions and education. This does not mean you can cease your efforts to help your child learn as he or she matures. You can and should continue to play an important, yet changing role in your child's personal development.

Adopt positive family moral values

The adoption of, and adherence to, positive moral values is lacking in many families. If you, along with other family members, have not already devoted some time to this topic, you should do so without delay. Discuss things like respect, honesty, behavior, language, decision making, abuse, drugs, money, work, and use of free time with family members. Consider their input, but remember, you are primarily responsible for establishing high moral values for your family. Once you have established these values, you can further develop them into attitudes, behaviors, and skills that, if taught to your child, will contribute to his or her success.

Historically, the moral values of American society and institutions within it have been influenced by religion. These values have been the driving force in defining acceptable thought and behavior. This is still the case to a substantial degree. Religious institutions, along with families and character building organizations continue to do their part in translating moral values into attitudes and behaviors that children can understand and follow in everyday life.

The Scout Law is an excellent example of what one organization has done to guide its members. It states that a Scout is "trustworthy, loyal, helpful, friendly, courteous, kind, obedient, cheerful, thrifty, brave, clean, and reverent." Each of these twelve attributes is further described and defined in the *Boy Scout Handbook* so that it clearly conveys a very powerful message. Girl Scouts, 4-H, sports clubs, and other youth organizations also have pledges, oaths, codes of conduct, or laws to help participants become better members of the group, their families, and society.

Most parents would be more than pleased if their children adopted the moral values advanced by their religion, the Boy Scouts, or other youth organizations, and carried them on into later life. The problem is that this will not happen by chance. It is your responsibility to ensure that your child adopts the moral values necessary for success. This can best be done through your personal efforts and by enlisting the help of family members and others in the community.

Teach key skills to help your child adapt to change

Your child will need a number of key skills to succeed in a rapidly changing world. The skills your son or daughter possesses will define how well he or she is able to adapt. They also will affect, to a substantial degree, how much your child can give to and, in turn, benefit from society. The development of key skills is as much your responsibility as your child's or the school's. They cannot be left to chance. You must begin to teach these skills early, as every minute is important during the first few months and years of a child's life. These are a few of the key skills you will want your child to develop as he or she matures. You should be able to think of others.

analyzing	describing	questioning
appreciating	evaluating	reasoning
associating	explaining	relating
comparing	expressing	remembering
computing	implementing	solving
concentrating	listening	speaking
constructing	observing	synthesizing
cooperating	organizing	thinking
correcting	planning	understanding
creating		

As your son or daughter grows older, the school will play an increasing role in teaching these skills. As this occurs, your greatest contribution will be to provide the reinforcement necessary to help your child incorporate them in daily life. You may have found that you have difficulty remembering some of the simple skills you learned in elementary or middle school. Perhaps it is because you have not found it necessary to use them for a number of years. Similarly, your child may learn to solve complex problems, analyze writing samples, or to express appreciation, but unless these skills are practiced regularly, it is more than likely that some will be forgotten.

Help your child avoid exploitation

One of the most serious problems resulting from social change is the increasing number of children who are mentally and/or physically exploited each year. This subject deserves mention as it can be one of the most destructive things that can happen to a child. Exploitation can range from keeping a child away from school to work or to perform household chores, to blatant mental or physical abuse leading to serious emotional problems, injury, or death.

It is important to realize that your child is not immune to exploitation. Also, you may not be the first to recognize it if it occurs. Fortunately, there are things you and your child can do to reduce the chances of exploitation. A good way to begin is by recognizing some of the circumstances that might place your child in a vulnerable position. Some of the more obvious circumstances are when:

★ children have not been warned about exploitation and how it can be avoided.

★ parents do not establish and discuss behavior guidelines.

★ adults and older children do not adhere to high moral values.

★ children or adults have poor self-esteem.

★ unrelated people share living areas.

★ children are left unsupervised.

★ children have too much free time.

★ parents do not adequately investigate individuals and/or organizations before entrusting their children to them.

★ drugs and/or alcohol are present.

★ children are drawn into adult situations or acquire information intended for adults.

You are certainly aware of incidents where serious harm has been done to unwary children or youth. The person taking advantage of the child could have been any age. It might have been a stranger, but more likely someone he or she trusted. Most of these incidents occurred when supervision was inadequate or when the child's parent avoided taking action on the situation.

While child exploitation may seem infrequent and remote, it is not. Reports of exploitation, including sexual molestation of children while participating in school, religious, athletic, or other community activities, appear daily in the newspapers. Most incidents, especially those occurring in the home are not reported to authorities, and a far greater number are not covered by the press. You must remain vigilant and quite skeptical if you are to help your child avoid exploitation.

It is important to realize that some school situations place a child in a more vulnerable position than others. Cocurricular activities deserve special mention. While very important in the lives of many children, there are aspects of these programs that invite problems. Often, they are held in areas where supervision is more difficult than in a regular classroom setting. They may involve nonschool personnel. Some activities are held outside regular school hours, including evenings and weekends. On occasion, an activity requires individual attention as in the case of some music instruction, drama lessons, or sports coaching. It is important to know who is with your child and the level of oversight provided during these times.

Know who is supervising your child

You should maintain a heightened awareness of the motives and behaviors of those who are working with or supervising your child. Inquire about the background, qualifications, and experience of activity-sponsors or chaperones. Determine if they understand their responsibilities and take them seriously. It is a good idea for these people to know of your interest, expectations, and concerns.

You should teach your child to be alert to unsafe situations, or even the suggestion of an attempt to take advantage of him or her. Don't overlook the possibility of exploitation by family members or when playing or staying with other children. Stress the reasons for avoiding certain situations and how to act if they occur. Emphasize not being in a room, automobile, or other place alone or with only one other person unless you have indicated this person can be trusted.

Stress doing things in groups. Talk about how to stop an incident in its early stages, by screaming, resisting, feigning sickness, running, or using an emphatic, "No!" or "Stop!" Use role play to reinforce the use of these defenses. Finally, stress the necessity of informing you or another responsible adult as soon as possible if your child feels uncomfortable, suspects a problem, or if an incident has occurred.

Open communication between you and your child is very important, as is the need to report any incident or potential incident to the proper authorities. By doing the latter, you are fulfilling your responsibilities to your child as well as providing a much needed service to other children and their parents.

Meet your child promptly after activities

Another way to avoid potential problems is to ensure that your child is not left unsupervised at school before or after the regular session or cocurricular activities. This is also true of community activities your child might attend. It is your responsibility to see that he or she arrives and leaves at the proper time. Failure to assume this obligation can create a gap in supervision during which time your child is particularly vulnerable. The situation becomes even more serious after dark, in high-crime areas, or during inclement weather. Your child should not have to endure the experience of waiting outside a dark building, or even worse, walking home alone, accepting a questionable ride, or being taken to the police station to wait for you. The latter, of course, except for the embarrassment, is often the best solution.

You should always double check to determine when and where your child should arrive and be met following an activity. It is very frustrating for an event chaperone, teacher, or school principal who has worked all day and all evening, to "baby-sit" your child, or others, for even a short period of time. The situation becomes even more upsetting when it is obvious a parent who is arriving late has been shopping, participating in a recreational activity, or has just lost track of the time. You will want to avoid creating this situation.

By arriving a few minutes before the beginning or end of an event, you can avail yourself of the opportunity to see what is going on. Get out of the car. Go inside the building. Talk with the chaperones and other parents. They might provide information that could be useful in avoiding problems. You might even become interested enough to help supervise a future event.

Collaborate with the parents of your child's friends

You are well aware of the potential value of belonging to a parent/teacher group. There is, though, another group that can be very helpful in dealing with the changes that are occurring when you raise your child. It probably already exists to some degree and consists of you and the parents of your child's friends. Parent groups have been formed by parents who wish to agree on guidelines or rules that can be used in raising their children. If you have not already begun working with other parents in dealing with the situations affecting your child, you should seriously consider doing so.

Children often get their way because their parents make decisions, and reluctantly extend privileges without talking with other parents. You have probably been persuaded, against your better judgment, to let your child go someplace, or to do something, only to find later that other parents had reservations and would rather have said "no." If you and other parents take the time to discuss your concerns and establish rules or guidelines, you will be reasonably informed when making decisions.

Parent groups can be organized any time

Parent groups can be organized any time there is an interest or need. There are no limits as to how old your child and his or her friends should be before a parent group could be of benefit. Some groups have been established during the elementary or middle school years, others only after a serious problem has occurred involving young adults. It is advantageous to form a group even before children begin elementary school. It can provide the immediate assurances parents need when their children attend nursery school or begin kindergarten as well as provide ongoing benefits. Why wait until a couple of neighborhood teenagers

Dealing Effectively With Change

have died in an alcohol-related accident before discussing the use and misuse of the family car or attempting to gain control of an alcohol problem in a community? If you have not already formed or become involved in a parent group, you should do so now.

You might begin by contacting three or four of the parents of your child's friends. A small group often has advantages over a larger group as it is usually easier for parents in a small group to reach agreement. Your parent group does not need to be highly structured, as need and interest, and thus membership, will change from time to time. Some groups credit their success to not being formally organized as protocol can get in the way of action. They have found that after two or three meetings members rely almost entirely on the telephone. Often this is the only timely means of getting the information necessary to deal with emerging situations.

When considering a request from your son or daughter, you might hear the statement, "I'm the only one who has to be home by ten o'clock," or "All the kids are doing it!" If so, would you like to know if this is really the case? Fine, pick up the phone and call two or three members of your parent group, or, if time permits, include a thorough discussion of the topic at your next meeting. By considering issues with other parents and working with them, you can make decisions knowing others within your parent group share your feelings. This can be very reassuring. It is important, though, to make a conscious effort to keep all members in the communications loop so they do not feel left out when decisions are being made or when actions are taken. A phone tree will help ensure that everyone stays informed.

For a parent group to function smoothly, members must allow for the varying concerns, positions, and actions of other parents as each family situation is unique. Also, children mature at different rates. Occasionally a parent may have difficulty acting in unison with the group. You might even find you are in this position. Group members should be as understanding as possible when this occurs. If it happens fairly often, the problem may resolve itself as the parent who is out of synchronization with the decisions of the group will probably drop out.

The following concerns are typical of those your parent group may want to discuss. If there seems to be agreement, establish guidelines for your children.

- expected level of behavior
- appropriate dress for children of different ages and for various functions
- television program and video selection
- the amount of television that will be watched
- study hours
- telephone use
- acceptable language
- curfew times for weekdays and weekends
- boy/girl relations and dating
- adult supervision and chaperoning
- drugs, alcohol, and tobacco
- gang activities
- suggested allowance

- birthday parties
- automobile use
- chores
- sleep-overs, camping, overnight trips, etc.
- school parties and proms

It is entirely natural for children and young adults to attempt to expand the controls placed on them by their parents and society. They will continue to try to change the rules and guidelines through their actions and behaviors. Thus, there will never be a shortage of ideas and issues for parent groups to discuss.

An active parent group also can provide dividends that go well beyond establishing guidelines and rules. These are some of the more common benefits that you and other parents in your group might receive:

- increased availability of chaperones and supervisors who share similar expectations
- help in coordinating activities
- a reduction in unnecessary expenses
- ride sharing programs
- fewer disagreements when making decisions
- the assistance of a support group when requesting the school to make changes
- additional information regarding your children
- the assurance that you are not alone
- fewer disappointments and even saved lives
- the increased possibility of excellence for children and their families

As you can see, the discussions and decisions of your parent group can increase your ability to make the day-to-day decisions necessary to raise your child in a rapidly changing society. This should lead to improvements in the way you and your child relate to each other thus improving the overall atmosphere of your home.

A positive home atmosphere encourages learning

Children learn best when they grow up in an atmosphere that encourages learning. In Chapter 14, "Preparing Your Child for Optimal Learning," a number of guidelines and practices are presented to help you remove the obvious, and the not so obvious, stumbling blocks in your child's life. If you adopt even two or three new ideas and follow through on them, you will make a positive contribution to your child's future. It is this possibility that inspires many parents to make changes in their personal lives and in the quality of leadership they provide at home. For many parents and children, Chapter 14 could be the most important chapter in this book.

14

Preparing Your Child for Optimal Learning

Is it necessary for a child's physical and mental needs to be met before he or she can function at an optimal level? Can drinking enough water and getting adequate sleep affect learning? Is praise an effective tool in achieving excellence? Is it important for parents to serve as positive role models? Do these factors really make a difference? The answer to each of these questions is "yes." They represent just a few of the things you must consider if you want to ensure that your child is "tuned up" for serious learning.

Parent interest and guidance are keys to success

A child who spends too much time loafing, fooling around, or drifting from one thought or activity to another can benefit greatly from a parent taking greater interest in his or her life. This is not a suggestion that you become a part of every school and nonschool aspect of your child's routine. It is, though, an invitation to guide, to participate, and to lead when appropriate. The most effective parents are usually those who are able to offer guidance without their children being particularly aware of it. The more natural your efforts, the greater the possibility your son or daughter will mature as a self-motivated, confident individual, with the knowledge, skills, and attitudes necessary for success.

> Aa Bb Cc Dd Ee Ff Gg Hh Ii Jj Kk Ll
>
> **Feeling valued:**
> One of the primary factors in achieving success is that children feel valued. Interestingly enough, the same is true of parents and teachers.

Three lists of positive practices that will help you better prepare your child to learn and live have been included in this chapter. They are:
- ★ Ten "Super Things" to do immediately
- ★ Ten steps to physical excellence
- ★ Eight personal traits that can accelerate success

Educational Excellence for Your Child

I hope you are already following most of the practices described in these lists. It is quite likely, though, that you will find a couple of new suggestions. If this is the case, give them a try, or at least find out more about them so your child does not miss out on their benefits. Let's begin by looking at ten "Super Things" you can do immediately.

Ten "Super Things" to do immediately

There a number of things that you can do as a part of your daily life to provide direction and encouragement to your child. The ten practices discussed here do not require a great deal of work, are inexpensive, and can help prepare your child for optimal learning in a relatively short time.

1. *Emphasize learning at home.* Convey the fact that learning is important. Make sure your child understands that education does not stop at the end of the school day, the school year, or even at graduation, but rather, that it is an ongoing process. Emphasize that you are still learning and that you feel fortunate to have the opportunity to continually develop new knowledge and skills and to further your education. Include your child in some of your learning experiences. You might be pleasantly surprised with what follows.

2. *Teach by example, demonstrate excellence.* Much of the knowledge and many of the skills and attitudes children develop result from being with family members. This is especially true in their formative years. Parents who follow the old saying "do as I say, not as I do," will soon find they are not particularly effective in raising their children. The parent who tells a child not to smoke, or never to use profanity, but does otherwise, will have difficulty conveying the message or in bringing about a positive change in behavior. The same is true of work habits and the results they produce. Unsatisfactory performance at work and home sets a poor example. It should be avoided at all costs.

The examples you and other family members demonstrate in everyday situations will become part of your child's lifestyle. Teaching by example becomes essential for those seeking excellence. It is probably your most effective tool.

3. *Schedule and routine, especially for young children, are a parent's responsibility.* The way your child uses time is determining, to a substantial degree, his or her future. It is generally agreed that most children watch too much television, play too many video games, get too little sleep, and do not spend enough time in positive learning situations. If you have not recently done so, you will want to examine your child's time patterns, and those of other family members, to see if problems exist.

If you are not willing to establish mealtimes, bedtimes, study times, and deadlines for other events, your child will establish them for you. This can lead to chaos in any family and will more than likely have a negative effect on your child's education.

Work with your son or daughter in developing daily schedules and weekly calendars that establish a reasonable balance between work, school, sleep, recreation, and various other activities. Post them in a prominent location. See that the following day's schedule is reviewed the prior evening or at the beginning of the day. Once a schedule has been established it is important to stick to it. This requires self-discipline, an important quality you want your child to develop.

If, after careful analysis, you decide your son or daughter should spend more time on constructive activities, you will be able to use some of the enrichment suggestions offered in this book. If, on the other hand, your child is already involved in a number of positive social, educational, and recreational activities, you can feel comfortable knowing you are providing the kinds of experiences he or she needs.

4. *High standards for behavior are essential; they cannot be left to chance.* Yet, in many families they are. The average child watches television twenty-five to thirty hours a week, much of the time without adult supervision. Many programs include discussions, scenes, situations, advertising, and concepts that extend well beyond reasonable norms for children. Studies have indicated these vivid sound and sight experiences can become serious factors when children formulate their perceptions of what is considered acceptable thought and behavior.

Ask any teacher or monitor to describe how students behave in the cafeteria after seeing a television program that depicts a form of violence, or a segment on a meal time riot in a summer camp. Watch what happens in your family room if you allow your child and several friends to play out some of their television fantasies without reasonable supervision. You will probably find just what you might expect: unacceptable behavior.

You must help your child separate himself or herself from these influences and to develop self-control. This can best be done by taking an active role in deciding what is and is not acceptable and instilling high behavior standards right from the beginning.

5. *Patience and self-control are best taught by parents who demonstrate these characteristics.* There is no lower age limit when emotional situations and parent outbursts begin to affect a child. It is best to assume your child is going to be influenced by these negative situations whenever they occur.

As your son or daughter matures, he or she will have increased contact with the outside world, thus spending less time at home. Even then it is very important to personally demonstrate patience and self-control and to insist on it from other family members.

6. *Show a sincere interest in your child's activities.* Asking questions and listening to your child's answers are good ways to demonstrate interest. It is important to do this often and properly. You may already have found that asking, "How did school go today?" or "What did you do in school?" prompts a "Not much." or "Nothing." response. Be more specific. Ask questions like, "What was the best part of your day?" "How did the class react to your book report?" "Did your teacher go over the homework?" or, "What are the three things you are going to ask your guidance counselor when you see her?"

You need to know what your child is doing and to a degree, what he or she is thinking. An individual's interests, concerns, frustrations, and satisfactions can have a profound effect on his or her ability to learn, and in turn, success in life. If your child feels you are not concerned, he or she may develop an "I-don't-care attitude." This would be too bad, as it can easily be avoided by showing interest.

7. *Talk about excellence, and point out examples of this quality to your child.* All too often, parents assume children learn by magic from the many things going on around them. This does occur, but it is not always the case. Examples of excellence can be easily missed. This is why it is particularly important to make sure your child is aware of those things you admire or feel represent excellence.

8. *Positive educational activities are easy to identify if you watch and listen for them.* As a parent, you are aware of your child's interests and needs. Your commitment to educational excellence has raised your awareness of what might be positive educational experiences. Knowing this, you can arrange to have your son or daughter observe, investigate, or participate in one or more of these activities. They are often available at little or no expense.

Teachable moments occur at home as well as school. You are in an excellent position to recognize when a teachable moment occurs. A recent experience, a personal need, an above average interest in a topic, a positive physical or mental state, or any combination of these and other factors can create a teachable moment. You can capitalize on this phenomenon by introducing your child to appropriate learning experiences at this time.

9. *Encouragement is a powerful tool, yet one many parents fail to use.* Children, as do adults, have moments and even days, when they become discouraged. In some homes, children and parents talk less than ten minutes a day. Even worse, much of this conversation may be argumentative or critical.

Take the time to listen to your child and to offer help and encouragement. By doing this, you can make a substantial difference in your son's or daughter's success in dealing with educational challenges, interpersonal relationships, and day-to-day problems. A friendly smile, a hug, or a few helpful words at the right time can go a long way toward improving your child's outlook on life.

10. *Praise and rewards, when used sparingly, can be effective in helping your child achieve excellence.* By pointing out the good things he or she is doing, you may seldom need to mention the bad. Sincerity and timing are particularly important if you are to be effective. Praise is usually most appreciated when given close to the time the positive behavior occurs. If this is not possible, the "better late than never" rule is a good one to follow.

You must also decide whether to praise privately, or when others are present, and whether to respond verbally or to extend a privilege or reward. These are personal decisions that only you can make. In most cases, using your best judgment far outweighs fretting over the decision and adds to the pleasure of the moment.

Ten steps to physical excellence

A person's mental state and ability to function are directly affected by how one feels. Thus, your child's overall well-being and readiness to learn can be enhanced by ensuring that he or she does not suffer from physical problems that can be avoided or corrected. The following suggestions can lead to physical excellence.

1. *Annual physical examinations can provide important information regarding your child's physical status.* They may reveal conditions affecting how well he or she feels, learns, and functions. This information will help you take preventative measures before minor conditions become major problems.

Don't wait for the school to inform you that your son or daughter needs a dental checkup, eye exam, hearing test, or disease-preventing immunization. It is your responsibility to ensure that these things are done. If you find you have fallen behind, phone your child's physician for an appointment, or find out when and where the next clinic will be held.

2. *Exercise is necessary for proper physical and mental development.* Unfortunately, many children have become sedentary at a very early age. This inactivity may be affecting their readiness to learn. It can also cause physical problems that will follow them through life.

What can be done to solve this problem? The answer, of course, is exercise. To be effective, exercise must be proper and regular. If you have questions about the kinds or amount of exercise required, consult your child's physical education teacher, fitness or dance instructor, physical therapist, or physician. These people should be able to provide this information.

Preparing Your Child for Optimal Learning

A physician should be consulted if your child has physical problems that might be aggravated by exercise or if a strenuous regimen or activity is anticipated.

3. *Good posture is important.* The term "couch-potato" generates an image of poor posture while sitting in a near prone position, usually watching television. This is just one of the times when people are careless about their posture. Your child needs to be taught to sit, walk, run, bend, lift, reach, and lounge properly in order for all parts of the body to work in harmony. Don't overlook posture problems during the time your child is playing games or operating a computer. While the school may be able to help by promoting good posture, the primary responsibility rests with you and your child.

4. *Sleep is essential to human life.* It gives the body and mind the opportunity to rejuvenate. Sleep-robbing schedules and activities deprive many youngsters of the rest they need to function effectively at home, in the community, and at school. This can lead to dozing or daydreaming in class, slower and less precise mental and physical responses, and irritability. Any one of these behaviors can make learning and living difficult.

Lack of sleep can have an adverse effect on a child's interpersonal relations and can affect judgment and coordination in ways that endanger health and safety. Begin immediately to ensure that your child has adequate uninterrupted sleep. Establish a schedule with reasonable times when your child will be in bed. Insist that this schedule be followed with very few exceptions. This is often the easiest way to improve overall performance, and perhaps best of all, it's free.

5. *Adequate water intake is required for body systems to function properly.* Water aids digestion, dilutes harmful substances, flushes out waste and helps fend off disease. It also adds to body comfort. This is especially important to children as many of their activities and the environments in which they spend much of their time dehydrate their bodies. Don't encourage your child to depend on other drinks or food to meet daily water requirements. While some water needs can be met by these items, many do not perform the same functions as water. Some drinks even lead to fluid loss, creating a need for additional water.

A child sitting in class is better able to speak, listen, and think if he or she does not have dry throat and nasal passages or other discomforts caused by a lack of water. Make sure your child realizes the time to have a drink of water is before becoming thirsty.

6. *Proper nutrition is important in maintaining good health.* Eating the right foods in the correct amount is essential to achieve proper growth and development. The expression "we are what we eat" is just as true today as it ever was. Food choices for many are almost unlimited. Unfortunately, some of these foods are less than ideal for children. Become familiar with the most recent food-intake guidelines published by the government and plan meals that are nutritious and conducive to proper growth.

The eating habits we develop as children often remain with us throughout life. It is very important to teach your child about nutrition and to set a good example through your own food selection, preparation, and eating habits.

You must make sure your son or daughter has three adequate meals each day. It may also be necessary to supply snacks and drinks for the rapidly growing or more active child. It is difficult for a child who is participating in an educational or recreational activity to function at a high level if he or she is hungry.

If you have difficulty providing your child with a nutritious breakfast or in supplying an adequate lunch, contact the teacher, school nurse, or guidance counselor regarding meal programs offered by the school.

7. *Personal hygiene can have a significant effect on your child's health.* Good health habits, including personal cleanliness and wearing clean clothes help the body avoid disease and make a person more acceptable to others. Health often dictates the number of days a child is absent from school because of illness. It also contributes to how he or she feels while there.

As many diseases are transferred from the hands to the mouth, nose, eyes, and other parts of the body, and vice versa, you must teach your child to refrain from touching these areas except when necessary. You must also stress the importance of using soap and water to wash the hands whenever there is a likely chance of contamination.

The ease of transfer, and dangers of communicable diseases, including those which are sexually transmitted, should be adequately discussed at the appropriate times in your child's life. It is also important to remind your child to tell you of all injuries or illnesses, including those that might seem embarrassing. Emphasize doing this as soon as a potential problem is suspected. The lines of communication must be kept open so that your child feels comfortable discussing health-related subjects with you as he or she matures. Failure to do so can lead to lasting health problems or even death.

8. *Illegal drugs, alcohol, and tobacco have no place in the life of any child.* It is your responsibility to teach your son or daughter about the life-threatening, mind-damaging, financial, and legal problems created by using these substances. Equally as important, you must set a good example by the way you live. Many families are finding total abstinence for all family members is the simplest and best way to avoid the difficulties and tragedies that exposure to these substances can create.

For parents who do not feel confident dealing with drug, alcohol, or tobacco use and abuse, help is available in most communities. Information sessions are held by schools, religious organizations, and community agencies. There are books available on these subjects, and your physician, clinic, or hospital can usually be of assistance.

If, in spite of your efforts, you suspect your son or daughter is involved in substance abuse, or in any activity that might be injurious to his or her health, do not delay in getting professional help. These problems will not ordinarily go away by themselves. Prompt intervention can make the difference between overcoming the problem or many months or years of physical, mental, educational, legal, and financial anguish for you and your child.

9. *Many of our nation's children, like adults, have physical problems that affect them to one degree or another.* Fortunately, most of these problems are minor, and the human body and mind compensate with little or no help. Other conditions require minimal correction as in the case of most sight and hearing problems. Still others require major intervention in order to make it possible for a child to function effectively in the home, school, and community.

If you think your child might have a physical or mental condition that could make it difficult to carry out normal activities, it is important to have it investigated. The solution could be as simple as a schedule change, a different diet, instruction on how to do something a better way, or corrective exercises. In other cases wearing glasses, using a hearing aid, or undergoing therapy, or any one of a number of things might be all that is necessary to compensate for or to correct the problem.

While your child remains your responsibility, there are many competent professionals and community agencies, including the school and parent support groups available to help. Your job is to identify existing or emerging conditions and to deal with them promptly.

10. *Safety is of utmost importance.* It is your responsibility to provide a safe environment in and around your home and when operating your automobile. Home fire drills are essential. Smoke, heat, and carbon dioxide detectors; gun cabinets and locks; air bags and automobile seat belts; and approved helmets, are simple devices that have proven their worth over and over again. You will want to teach your child to behave in a safe manner and to avoid danger when he or she is with you as well as beyond your control.

Most accidents can be prevented if a little time is devoted to reviewing safe and unsafe situations. Become familiar with any safety or supervision problems that might lead to your child or others being injured. See that these conditions are corrected as soon as possible. Practice personal safety and help your child develop and practice safe habits at the earliest age.

Eight personal traits that can accelerate success

Just as your child's physical well being is important, so is his or her mental outlook and attitude. In fact, it is generally known that a child's emotional well-being can contribute to short- and long-term success. There are a number of personal traits that can help your son or daughter to be more receptive to learning. The following eight are especially important.

1. *A clear mind will give your son or daughter the best opportunity to learn.* Whenever possible, your child should arrive at school free of problems that might divert his or her attention from learning. By preventing or reducing confusion and conflict at home, you can play a significant role in seeing that this is the case.

If your child does leave home in an unusually distressed manner, it is a good idea to inform someone at school of the situation. Call your child's classroom teacher, the school nurse, guidance counselor, psychologist, principal, or other staff member with whom you have rapport.

Tell this person of your concerns. Educators have been trained to evaluate information such as this and are prepared to use it to help your child avoid more serious problems.

2. *An inquiring mind, open to new ideas and change, is essential.* Encourage your child to ask questions if he or she does not understand something. Emphasize the importance of obtaining all possible information before making decisions, arriving at conclusions, or taking actions. Involve your son or daughter in some of the creative thoughts, decision making, and ideas for change that interest you.

3. *The ability to focus on what is being taught is essential to your child's education.* Of equal importance is the length of time your child can remain attentive. Teachers realize children have rather short attention spans and have adjusted their lessons accordingly. They are less likely to know the reasons why a particular child is having difficulty focusing on a lesson.

If your child does not seem to take education seriously or is experiencing unusual difficulty learning, you will want to determine the reasons. Is the problem caused by a lack of understanding of the importance of school? Are the lessons too easy or too difficult? Could it be that your child's attention span is programmed to match the short segments between television commercials? Is it lack of sleep or exercise, the absence of self-discipline, or possibly the effects of improper foods or harmful substances?

Could it be that your child has the unrealistic expectation that teachers should present lessons on a daily basis that will entertain or stimulate interest at the same level as the expensive, commercially produced advertisements and television shows that most children watch? It is important to determine the causes of conditions that limit your child's ability to stay alert and maintain interest. Once these have been identified you can work with your child, school staff, and, if necessary, other professionals to increase his or her ability to focus on the lesson and, as teachers say, "spend more time on task."

4. *Receptivity to praise and criticism coupled with a willingness to act positively can accelerate learning.* These traits can be developed long before a child begins school by parents who are aware of their importance and who have the interest and desire to help their children. If criticism is necessary make sure your child understands that it is not directed at him or her as a person, but rather at correcting an unacceptable behavior. By keeping this in mind you can add to your child's self-esteem.

5. *Positive thinking, as demonstrated by a "can do" attitude, will help assure future success.* Many opportunities are available only to those who display a positive outlook when approaching problems. If a child mistakenly feels that his or her life is controlled only by external factors, it is all too easy to assume an "I'm-a-victim-of-circumstances," or "there's-nothing-I-can-do-about-it" attitude. This can be very limiting.

Children and adults must realize that they are responsible for their decisions and actions and, to a substantial degree, the outcomes that follow. They must be reminded that they control much of their lives. As most of your child's early attitudes are derived from observing and interacting with you and other family members, it is important for each of you to convey a positive outlook on life.

6. *Persistence in attempting to accomplish difficult tasks can lead to success.* While quitting may seem easier at the time, and there is always a chance of failure, the tangible and intangible benefits gained from sticking with a particular task will ultimately benefit your child. Your encouragement can make the difference between your child's quitting a difficult task or following through to completion.

7. *Emotional stability can add to mental and physical health, improve interpersonal relations, increase learning, and raise opportunities for success.* Children must be taught to deal with their emotions and to express them in constructive ways. It is not unusual for children to need guidance in handling love, anger, frustration, joy, sadness, success, failure, and the like. You can help your son or daughter develop emotionally in ways that are personally beneficial as well as acceptable to others.

8. *A pleasant demeanor can add greatly to acceptance by others.* It can also increase opportunities. A pleasant facial expression and eye contact when talking or listening can improve communications. Displaying positive body language and not being argumentative will normally increase one's opportunity to express a position. Try smiling more and teach your child to do the same. Think about the ways successful people carry themselves and behave. Then consider modeling some of these traits for your child.

Increase learning with a home learning center

Just as children need assistance in cultivating their personal traits, mental attitudes, and physical well being, every child needs a healthy place to learn. Unless your home is very crowded, it is more than likely that you have a place that can be set aside for your child to read, write, think, plan, and do homework. In Chapter 15, you will learn how to turn a small part of your home into an effective learning center. Many of the ideas presented can benefit your entire family.

15

Establishing a Home Learning Center

It is important for your child to have a suitable place and specific times to do homework and other projects requiring concentration. This area should be reasonably quiet so work can be done with as few distractions as possible. While most parents realize this, they may not be aware of some of the other factors that can increase the possibility real learning will take place at home.

The establishment of a home learning center for your child is one of the best ways to encourage learning. It can be as simple as an uncluttered space on a small table with a shoe box for school supplies or as complex as a mini-office with computer access to information sources around the world. If your child has his or her own bedroom, this is usually a good location for a learning center. If, on the other hand, all your rooms are shared, you will need to consider other locations and certainly be more innovative. In a small apartment, the kitchen table may be the only place to study. If this is the case, there are still a number of things you can do to optimize its use.

In this chapter you will find several lists that will help you in setting up and supplying your child's learning center. You should not be overly concerned if you cannot initially provide all of the suggested items. Children can usually bring home from school most of the information and materials needed to do their daily assignments. While other resources can be helpful, they may not be necessary. In fact, too much too soon can be confusing or distracting. I would suggest you begin with a rather modest learning center and add to it as the needs arise.

You have undoubtedly heard about very learned people who have educated themselves while working under extremely adverse conditions. They knew how to use their time effectively. How your child uses the time he or she spends in the learning center is much more important than most of the other resources that might be available.

Learning center environment

It is best if your child's learning center is reserved exclusively for his or her use. It should be an area everyone in the house identifies with learning. Location is paramount. If possible, it should be located away from areas where normal household activities occur. If this is done, interruptions by family members and friends and other unnecessary distractions, like television and telephone calls, can be kept to a minimum. Soft music or general background noise may not be a problem, as most children have become accustomed to studying with these sounds present.

A corner of your child's bedroom, space in an attic or basement, or even an alcove or closet can be an ideal learning center if temperature, ventilation, and other conditions are satisfactory. It is best to choose an area where study materials and projects can be left without being disturbed from one day to the next. If this is not possible, consider using a piece of rigid material like plywood or fiber board about the size of an open newspaper for a work surface. Uncompleted homework can then be left in place on the board for careful storage on top of a cabinet, on a closet shelf, or under a bed.

If you have a larger storage space, a heavy corrugated cardboard carton about the size of a newspaper with two adjacent long sides removed can serve as a study carrel. This will leave the two remaining long sides and smaller ends in place. When in use, it can be placed on a table with one open side toward your child and the other facing up. This will ensure some privacy, and provide a place to hang a calendar and to post notes or assignments. A piece of smooth plastic or hardboard can be placed over the cardboard in the bottom of the box to provide a hard writing surface. When not in use, this homemade carrel can be stored in a closet where it will protect ongoing work.

Adequate air circulation and temperatures that are not too warm or cool are important if your child is to remain comfortable and alert during the time he or she is studying. Look for signs of drowsiness or discomfort. Poor air circulation can usually be improved with the addition of a small portable fan. If temperature is a problem, it can often be compensated for by dressing differently, opening or closing a window, or by using an approved heater or small air conditioner.

Proper lighting will increase efficiency and reduce eye fatigue. Under ideal conditions, the area selected for the home learning center will have a reasonable level of natural or artificial background light. This should be supplemented with a desk lamp. It will fill in the shadows and allow your child to focus on the work being done.

Learning center furniture

- A desk or table with a drawer and smooth writing surface is one of the most desirable pieces of furniture a child can have in a home learning center. While activities like reading and large project construction may be done in other locations, most work will be performed at the desk or table.

- A chair that will allow your child to sit upright at a proper height in relation to the work surface is also important. Most homes already have a chair that meets this description. If you do not have one, place a cushion on the seat of an existing chair to raise a small child to a comfortable work level. You might also consider buying a new or used adjustable desk chair.

- A small bookcase or shelves, located within reach of the desk or table, will provide a place for books and other resource materials. A bookrack or bookends on the desk can serve as a satisfactory alternative.

- A file cabinet, plastic crate, or cardboard box will provide a place to store information and materials. If this is not feasible, consider using part of a cabinet, or space on a closet shelf.

- A wastebasket and box for recycling will round out the furniture requirements for a pleasant, efficient, and productive home learning center.

A folder, book bag, or backpack is essential

A home learning center will be of little value if assignments and the resource materials needed to complete them are left at school or are lost or damaged while being transported. Your son or daughter should have a folder, book bag, or pack that closes tightly to carry homework items to and from school. Before making a purchase, it is important to determine if there are any restrictions on the type of bag a child can carry. Some schools have found it necessary to establish security guidelines in an effort to control the items students bring to or remove from school.

Most children will choose a book bag or pack similar in style, but not necessarily color and detail, to those carried by other students. This is fine. The most important criterion in selecting a bag, assuming you have checked to determine if it meets school approval, is that your child feels comfortable carrying it. This is about the only way you can be assured it will be used regularly for its intended purpose.

Learning center supplies and equipment

Normally, children require a number of inexpensive supply items but very little equipment to do homework in a home learning center. By planning ahead, these items can be purchased in sufficient quantity and at reasonable prices. It is not necessary to provide more than the basic supplies and equipment until your child has had the opportunity to use the center for a few days, or even weeks. By that time, you will know what is really needed.

> Aa Bb Cc Dd Ee Ff Gg Hh Ii Jj
>
> Invest in the future: Invest in your child's education and you invest in the future.

Age, maturity, and dexterity should be considered when making purchases. For example, the scissors, glue, or instrument for drawing circles selected for use by a five year old would be quite different from those for an older student. Also, while it is good for a child to have his or her own supplies and equipment in the learning center, items used only occasionally can be shared with other family members. A stapler or pencil sharpener is a good example. Some items even make good individual or family gifts.

The following items will fill most of your child's needs. Later purchases can be made for major projects or for courses requiring specialized items.

cellophane tape	paper clips
colored pencils	pencil sharpener
crayons	pencils (No.2, with eraser)
envelopes	pens (ball point)
erasers	protractor for measuring angles
folders	punch (three hole)
glue (nontoxic)	rubber bands
index tabs	ruler (inch and metric)
markers	scissors (age appropriate)
notebooks	stapler with supply of staples
note cards (3x5, 4x6)	template, or compass for drawing circles
paper	

Educational Excellence for Your Child

Optional supplies and equipment:
- cassette recorder with spare batteries and blank cassettes
- electric or electronic typewriter or word processor with ribbon and supplies
- personal computer with keyboard, monitor, multimedia CD-ROM drive, printer, modem, word-processing program, extra discs, and educational software
- solar calculator

Before purchasing a typewriter, word processor, or computer, talk with your child's teachers and others who are familiar with the educational uses of this equipment. Not only can these items become quickly outdated, but in many cases, parents are foregoing the purchase of a typewriter or word processor in favor of a new or used computer. This would be my advice in nearly all cases. While more expensive, computers offer many more learning opportunities to the child and parent striving for excellence. For the occasional form, which needs to be typed, secretarial services are available at modest cost. As in the case of other major purchases, the wise consumer gets as much information as possible prior to making a purchase.

Learning center supplemental books and materials

Supplemental books and materials can be very helpful when working at home. Unfortunately, it is not always possible to anticipate everything needed to do a particular assignment. While most resources your child will need are available in the classroom or school library/media center, it may be difficult or impossible, to use them during the school day. Also, some reference books and resource materials are not available for loan. Consequently, you may wish to include some of these items in the home learning center.

The following list includes a number of resources that could be useful. While there has been no effort to rank their importance, every child should have a dictionary at home, and one at school. Older students should also have a thesaurus at each location. The need for other resources should be determined on an individual basis. As in the case of equipment and supplies, some supplemental books and materials make wonderful gifts and can benefit the entire family.

almanac	newspapers
atlas	reports
computer software	resource books
dictionary	tapes and discs
encyclopedia	thesaurus
globe	writer's handbook
magazines	

There has been an increase in the number, availability, and variety of commercial educational materials available for home and school use. Some are very good while others are of questionable value. They range from simple flash cards and workbooks to sophisticated computer software programs. Some materials have been designed to teach knowledge and skills at various levels, preschool through high school. Others provide opportunities for remediation or enrichment.

For less than seventy-five dollars, you can purchase a children's notebook size pre-computer with a variety of basic skills programs and several educational games. These devices are simple to operate and tend to be highly motivational. Available with programs for children in various grades and with several levels of difficulty, they provide wonderful reinforcement for classroom instruction.

For students who have the use of a personal computer, software programs on disk and CD-ROMs are available that have been designed specifically to prepare students for college entrance tests and trade and professional examinations. College courses are also available on a variety of subjects.

Start a home library/media center

Now is a good time to start a home library/media center if you don't already have one. Choosing books and other reference materials is an enjoyable task but it can be complicated. As a rule, you can never do too much research before making a purchase. This is especially true of books that are also available on much less expensive CD-ROM for use with computers. For example, a complete encyclopedia can be purchased on CD-ROM for about one hundred dollars. It is a good idea to begin by checking with your child's teachers, library/media specialist, and other professionals regarding their recommendations about any reference materials you might purchase.

> Aa Bb Cc Dd Ee Ff Gg Hh Ii Jj Kk
>
> Remembering:
> We remember about 1/5 of what we see and 1/5 of what we hear, but 3/5 of what we see and hear. Read this aloud three times.

If you are planning to buy a set of encyclopedias in book form, you will want to make the right choice. A good set requires a substantial investment, and is usually kept for a number of years. I have found it most helpful to spend a little time in the reference section of a library/media center. Look up two or three subjects in encyclopedias by several publishers. Include your son or daughter in this research. Consider your child's ability to read and comprehend the material presented, while keeping future growth in mind. By researching several topics in the books or on CD-ROM, you will begin to realize which encyclopedia is best for your child. The same procedure will work well if you are contemplating the purchase of an atlas, large dictionary, thesaurus, or other major reference book.

When shopping for books or computer software, ask lots of questions. If possible, preview each item before purchasing. Don't overlook the sets of books or software programs on subjects like science, art, geography, and history available at the supermarket or by mail. Some are of excellent quality and are reasonably priced. The idea of getting a volume each month appeals to some children and their parents. Receiving books at different times generates more interest in reading than might otherwise be the case while spacing out the cost. If you are ordering by mail, make sure the seller offers a trial period and a full refund if your are not satisfied.

You may wish to investigate used books. This is an inexpensive way to add to your home library/media center. It is a good idea to purchase only those books and other educational materials with recent copyright dates. The exception would be the classics, certain specialty books, or other books of particular interest to family members.

Computer information services

You probably will want to subscribe to an information service if you have a personal computer. These services can be accessed using a modem to connect your computer to a telephone or cable television jack. Modems are built into modern computers, but can be purchased inexpensively and added to most older models. It is also necessary to choose and subscribe to an information service offering the specific resources you want as well as providing an easy route to the Internet, and World Wide Web, or other networks. The most common services offer data banks containing a wide range of information. These include books, research reports, newspapers, magazines, and computer software programs. They also provide the opportunity to view home pages, to send messages by electronic mail, to hold on-line conversations, and to use bulletin boards to make announcements or reach others with similar interests.

> Aa Bb Cc Dd Ee Ff Gg Hh Ii Jj Kk Ll
>
> Making wise choices: Every choice has its consequences. A child's ability to make wise choices improves when given the opportunity to do so.

Some information services charge a modest initial fee to cover the costs of registration and start-up materials. There is a monthly service charge for a basic time allotment and a fee schedule for additional time and optional services. In some cases there may be toll charges if the network cannot be reached by a local call. You will probably find your child, or a friend is familiar with one or more of these services. If this is the case, you can obtain some of the information you will need before discussing the subject further with your child's teacher or an information service provider.

A word of caution; information services are extensive and open to all. As they are not regulated or monitored to the degree necessary to protect children, they are subject to many of the abuses that exist in today's society. You must carefully monitor your child's use of these services in order to avoid excessive costs, misuse, or exploitation.

Ten effective ways to use a home learning center
A home learning center is of value only if it is used, and used properly. There are a number of things you can do to ensure your child benefits from your efforts to provide the best possible environment for doing homework and leisure learning.

1. *Establish a time to do homework, and adhere to it unless there are extenuating circumstances.* One of the best times for most children to study is immediately following the evening meal as they are usually wide awake. If your child lets the homework go until later in the evening, it is more likely it will not be completed, or may not be done as well as it would have been at an earlier time.

In some situations, for example when a child is an early riser, homework can be done in the morning, but for most children, this time should be avoided.

Under ordinary circumstances, one of the least desirable times to do homework is immediately after school. This period should be reserved for more active pursuits as your child has been in classes all day. Exceptions might be when:

- doing homework can be substituted for nonproductive time
- this is the only time available
- it is part of an after-school child care or recreation program
- two students enjoy doing homework together
- a student or adult is tutoring the child

2. *Be prepared to help get the studying process started.* If necessary, remind your child that it is time to do homework, to read, or to be involved in some other learning activity. Make it clear that you are not going to be responsible for issuing daily reminders.

3. *Reduce noise and limit interruptions while your child is studying.* If the phone is used during this time, it should be only to clarify an assignment or to obtain information regarding homework.

4. *While soft background music may not be distracting, loud music, lyrics, talk shows, and entertainment on radio and television are much more invasive and should be avoided.* Television serves no useful purpose while doing homework except when the teacher has asked the students to watch a program. Therefore, it should be left off.

5. *It is important to show an interest in the work your son or daughter is doing in the home learning center.* Ask questions, and encourage your child to do the same, especially if he or she is experiencing difficulty. Remember what the previous day's assignments were. If you do this, you will be able to carry on relevant and helpful discussions. It is not necessary to fully understand a subject to help your child proceed with his or her homework. A few probing questions at the right time may be all that is needed. The greater awareness you have of what your child is doing in school and the learning center, the more effective you can be in helping him or her achieve excellence.

6. *Look at your young child's completed homework.* Some teachers ask you to do this daily and to initial the work. It is usually unnecessary to review homework each day for older children unless they are having difficulty. It is still a good idea to be aware of the assignments they are receiving and the quality of the work being done. Resist doing homework for your child, but offer suggestions and encouragement at appropriate times.

7. *Homework should be done while sitting at the desk or table designated for this purpose.* If an assignment includes extensive reading, a more comfortable chair might be more suitable. If this is the case, insist on good posture and lighting. Some large projects may require your child to work on the floor or other large surface. If this is the case you may want to suggest a suitable area.

The work surface and study materials should be kept clean and properly organized. Make sure your child's completed homework is neat and legible.

8. *It is important for your child to have positive feelings about homework and the learning center.* It should not be used as a general discipline area. The exception might be if the punishment is directly related to your child's failure to do homework or to use the area properly.

9. *The learning center and study materials should always be ready for use.* An older student should be responsible to see that all supplies necessary to do homework are on hand. A younger child should be reminded to tell you well before he or she runs out of something. If this is done, the item can be replaced at a convenient time and at a reasonable price.

You should not accept excuses like, "I can't find any paper, my pen is dry, or I thought I had another notebook," at seven o'clock Sunday evening. If this occurs, it is probably best, after expressing your displeasure, to hand your child a similar or substitute item, if you have it. Then, say, "Now you can do your homework."

10. *It is a good idea to have your child develop the habit of using the learning center daily even if there is not a specific homework assignment.* By having a book to read, a letter to write, a journal to update, or an ongoing project to complete, your son or daughter will begin to appreciate the importance of learning. The self-esteem, discipline, and confidence, so necessary for success will become part of everyday life.

In Chapter 16 you will find dozens of exciting educational activities that can be carried out at home. Some have gained popularity only recently, while most have been favorites of children and youth for a number of years. Each has been chosen as it provides an interesting way to increase learning while offering satisfaction and enjoyment. Many of these activities will enrich the lives of everyone in your family as well as lead to increased learning for your child.

16

Home Activities that Increase Learning

Activities can enhance your child's formal education
It is important to realize the benefits of having positive educational experiences outside regular school hours. You have learned that while the school plays an important role in educating children, it is limited in what it can provide. Carefully selected activities can fill many of the inevitable voids in your child's formal education. Also, they can provide enrichment experiences that can be of great benefit as he or she moves through life.

Home is one of the easiest places to pursue additional activities. Your child can choose from an almost endless number of interesting and challenging experiences, any one of which can increase learning. As a parent committed to excellence, you should be looking for ways to involve your child in one or more home activities.

Educational activities can be fun and inexpensive
You may recall some very interesting nonschool educational activities that you enjoyed when you were young. Many were aimed at your age group, while others were suitable for any age. Some of these experiences captured your interest for only a short time. Other activities may have evolved into hobbies or work that you pursued over an extended period, even into adulthood. With few exceptions, the activities were satisfying, and more often than not, inexpensive or free. These are the kinds of activities we will review in this chapter.

Every experience can be a learning experience
Keeping in mind that every experience can be a learning experience, you should be on the lookout for opportunities to enhance your child's education. Carefully selected home activities can be just as educational as those provided by the school. If you have ever pursued a hobby to the point where you became "an expert," you probably realized you had learned as much, or even more than you might have learned in an advanced high school or college course. There is also a high probability you increased your ability to learn on your own and to make independent decisions, thus better preparing yourself for lifelong learning. This is what you want your child to be able to do.

Selecting activities

Your child's interest, ability to plan and work alone, skill level, and persistence are factors that should be considered in selecting activities. Your availability to encourage and support your child is also important. Many activities can be adapted to any age level. Thus, your child's age should not rule out an activity if you are willing to be involved. It is important, though, to resist steering a child toward activities that are more appropriate for much younger or older children. Either case can lead to a lack of interest in a relatively short period of time. If your child is elementary school age or younger, you will quite likely be the one who determines whether an activity is suitable. If you have questions on this subject, consult someone who is directly involved with the activity, your child's teacher or other appropriate professional.

Before beginning a new activity or substantially increasing the time and effort devoted to an existing activity, step back and assess your child's overall use of time. It is important to ensure that he or she does not have too much responsibility or too many things to do. Often, this can be seen in the way a child feels and behaves. If your son or daughter is experiencing physical problems, is showing signs of fatigue, no longer looks forward to an activity or school, or has difficulty carrying out personal responsibilities, it is usually time to put on the brakes. As your child may not be fully aware of the overscheduling or how to gracefully lighten the load, your help will be needed to restore balance in his or her daily routine.

Some activities have limited lives

It is important to realize that some activities satisfy a person's interest only during a particular span of time. You might say these activities have limited lives. It is normal for children and youth to want to try new things. Often, this is their only way of deciding if a particular activity is right for them. Do not become discouraged if your young child, after seriously trying an activity, does not pursue it as long as you might expect. If, though, he or she seems to jump from one activity to another without serious participation, delay the introduction of similar activities until your child is more mature.

Your interest and enthusiasm are important

Your interest and enthusiasm can be pivotal to your child's success in investigating or pursuing an activity. Begin gradually if the activity lends itself to this approach. Resist the urge to purchase all the equipment and supplies at one time except when it is essential to getting started or when safety is involved. If your son or daughter seems to be progressing well, you can usually play a passive role. If this does not occur, offer encouragement and support. If, after a reasonable time, this does not work, it may be best to drop the activity. There is usually very little lost, and the next opportunity is often nearby, waiting to be tried.

Getting your child started on a home activity

The activities presented in this chapter have been selected for their educational value and, in many cases, continued popularity. While most activities can be carried out at home, some

---

Aa Bb Cc Dd Ee Ff Gg Hh Ii Jj Kk

Making mistakes: Children who venture into new areas of learning usually make mistakes; children who don't, make the greatest mistake.

will tap community resources, a topic that receives further review in Chapter 17. In this chapter and the next, the information listed under "Educational benefits" will help you realize the value to your child of pursuing each activity. Precautions and other information are included under "Important information." These suggestions should help you decide if an activity is suitable for your child and worthy of further investigation. Under "Ideas for pursuing this activity," you will find steps you and your child can take to get started and to follow through.

As you might imagine one the best sources of information on an activity is someone who is already involved in it. This is especially true of hobbies. Most hobbyists are anxious to talk about their pursuits. They can provide current information on where to obtain further information and how to get started. It is not unusual for a hobbyist to share the necessary items to begin to pursue a hobby. Library/media centers and computer information services are, of course, also excellent sources of information on nearly any activity.

As an interested parent, you are in the best position to know if your child has an interest in an activity that is not included in this chapter. If this is the case, add additional activities that might be especially interesting or valuable to your child.

When you have completed your review of this list, you will be ready to move on to Chapter 17. It describes a number of interesting educational community activities for children and youth. These activities can be found in most cities and towns, and in many rural areas throughout the country. Many can serve as extensions of the activities your child may already be enjoying at home.

HIGH INTEREST HOME ACTIVITIES LIST

The following list includes dozens of interesting educational activities your child can pursue at home. For easy reference, and because of their academic importance; reading, writing, mathematics and science activities have been listed first; others follow in alphabetical order. As you review this list you may find your son or daughter has already expressed interest in a particular activity. It may even be that he or she is participating in one or more at this time. If this is the case, you already have some idea of the types of activities your child might enjoy.

Activity: Reading:
Educational benefits
- The ability to read continues to be absolutely essential to obtaining an education and success in life.

Important information
- Reading is inexpensive.
- Reading skills must be reinforced and perfected at home.
- Reading often leads to interest in other activities.
- Your child should see you and other family members reading.

Ideas for pursuing this activity
- Make sure there are books, magazines, and other reading material in your home.
- Read daily to your young child.
- Have your older child read to you.
- Use a computer to teach or reinforce reading skills.
- Give books to family members as gifts.
- Subscribe to a daily newspaper.
- Have your child talk about the things he or she is reading.
- Subscribe to magazines of interest to your child and other family members.
- Be on the lookout for lists of recommended books.
- Keep a log of books read.
- Make regular trips to the library and newsstand.
- Read signs and labels.
- Use a dictionary.
- Read aloud to others.
- Learn the meaning and use of a new word each day.
- Do crossword puzzles.
- Play word games.

Activity: Writing
Educational benefits
- Writing is a primary means of communication.
- Writing goes hand-in-hand with reading, one supporting the other.

Important information
- Remember, the only way to learn to write, is to write.

Ideas for pursuing this activity
- Have your child write something each day.
- Keep a daily journal or diary.
- Write messages or notes; post them where they can easily be seen.
- Write personal letters to relatives and friends.
- Write business letters to companies, governmental agencies and elected officials.
- Request free or inexpensive materials.
- Write a pen pal in another community or country.
- Write short stories, articles, plays, and poems.
- Write news releases for clubs and organizations.
- Write letters to the editor and classified ads.
- Make suggestions to improve your child's writing.
- Submit an essay your child has written to a newspaper or magazine.
- Make lists of things that are important.
- Hold spelling bees or other competitions.
- Develop codes and word puzzles.
- Use a new word in a writing exercise each day.
- Use the computer or typewriter as a writing tool.

Activity: Mathematics
Educational benefits
- Provides reinforcement for computational skills.
- Serves as a practical way to use math concepts.
- Introduces new skills and concepts before they are taught in school.
- Makes math more enjoyable.

Important information
- Math is essential for all children and adults.
- Avoid transferring negative stereotypes about math to your child.
- Many times children do not even realize they are doing math when they are pursuing math activities.

Educational Excellence for Your Child

Ideas for pursuing this activity
- Utilize mathematics in the kitchen, workshop, garden, and other places in or around the home.
- Use paper and pencil, flash cards, worksheets, calculator, child's precomputer, or personal computer to learn, understand, and reinforce math concepts and computational skills.
- Develop a budget reflecting anticipated income from allowance, gifts, or work and projected expenditures for purchases, entertainment, and savings.
- Open a savings account.
- Contribute a percentage of income, or savings, to a nonprofit organization.
- Solve mathematics puzzles.
- Play games involving real estate, the stock market, or business decisions.
- Work out the odds for carnival games, lotteries, contests, and other activities involving chance.
- Keep records of rainfall, plant growth, bicycle or automobile mileage, purchases, energy use, sports records, time, distance, exercise, height and weight, and the like.
- Read, draw, and interpret graphs.
- Keep records for a small home business.
- Do magic tricks involving numbers.
- Design math puzzles or games.

Activity: Science
Educational benefits
- Helps one understand scientific method.
- Can increase reading comprehension.
- Provides an opportunity to use math skills.
- Increases vocabulary.

Important information
- Science can be taught as a part of many activities; baking, cleaning, astronomy, recycling and the like.
- Parent supervision and emphasis on safety are of utmost importance.
- Science kits and related items make wonderful gifts.
- Can be a high interest area for most children.

Ideas for pursuing this activity
- Plan and conduct a scientific investigation; become familiar with background information, develop a hypothesis, design a study to test the hypothesis, conduct the study, collect data, analyze results, draw conclusions, and report the results.
- Read about science and scientists.
- Watch science programs on television.
- Add science books and other reference books to your home library/media center.

- Subscribe to an age-appropriate science magazine.
- Visit a laboratory.
- Interview a scientist.

Activity: Air/space
Educational benefits
- Can reinforce nearly all academic and nonacademic subjects.
- A high interest area for all ages.

Important information
- The National Aeronautics and Space Administration (NASA) is an excellent source for information on this subject.

Ideas for pursuing this activity
- Design, construct and fly kites, model planes, or rockets.
- Read about flying, famous aviators, and astronauts.
- Learn about commercial and military aircraft.
- Read science fiction books and magazines.
- View air and space programs on television.
- Learn about weather and aviation.
- Set up a home weather station.
- Monitor aviation radio bands.
- Plan a trip to an airport or space museum.
- Subscribe to an aviation magazine.
- Attend an air show or fly-in.
- Learn about experimental aircraft, hang gliders, parachutes, and lighter-than-air craft.
- Join a flying club, the Civil Air Patrol, or an Explorer Scout unit.
- Take a balloon or airplane ride; operate the controls.
- Take flying lessons.
- Visit someone who is building or restoring an airplane.

Activity: Animals
Educational benefits
- Caring for a pet encourages responsibility and sensitivity.
- Can reinforce concepts learned in science and other academic subjects, life skills, industrial technology, and agriculture.

Important information
- Good health habits and safety awareness are very important when raising animals.
- Become familiar with federal and state regulations regarding wild and exotic animals.
- Check local ordinances; and subdivision and building covenants for restrictions regarding animals.

Educational Excellence for Your Child

- Check with several experts before accepting or purchasing birds, fish, reptiles or other animals.

Ideas for pursuing this activity
- Raise tropical fish, or a small domestic animal if permitted.
- Raise larger pets and farm animals in a rural setting.
- Train and show animals.
- Ride and care for horses.
- Observe a veterinarian at work.
- Work part time for a veterinarian.
- Observe and record animal activities.
- Add animal books and videos to your home library/media center.
- Subscribe to an animal magazine.
- Join an animal club or society.
- Keep bird and animal counts.
- Construct animal cages and containment areas.
- Design, build and erect bird houses and feeders.
- Plan a trip to a farm or agricultural exhibition.
- Plan a trip to a zoo or natural history museum.
- Attend an Audubon Society meeting.

Activity: Art
Educational benefits
- Promotes creativity.
- Raises self-esteem.
- Helps develop manual skills.
- Develops an appreciation for the work of others.

Important information
- The proper use of sharp and pointed tools must be taught.
- Carefully read labels. Some paints, glues, and other art materials are toxic. They should be avoided or used with caution.

Ideas for pursuing this activity
- Take art lessons.
- Sketch, draw, paint and construct art work.
- Sculpt with clay capable of being fired in a kitchen oven or small kiln.
- Assist in selecting artwork for display at home.
- Plan and decorate a bedroom or family room.
- Create computer art.

- Paint a mural.
- Read about art and artists.
- Visit art museums and galleries.
- Enter art contests.
- Study art from different periods.
- Meet artists.

Activity: Assembling
Educational benefits
- Helps develop manual skills.
- Encourages planning and organization.
- Can strengthen reading skills.
- Develops consumer awareness.

Important information
- Select items for assembly that are within your child's skill range.
- Can save money.
- Stress safety in handling materials and using tools.

Ideas for pursuing this activity
- Select and purchase a do-it-yourself kit.
- Read directions carefully.
- Learn to use simple hand tools.
- Assemble furniture, toys, bicycles, and other equipment.
- Discuss engineering, design, and safety regarding the project.
- Submit warranty card.

Activity: Astronomy
Educational benefits
- Increases understanding of math, science, history, literature, and technology.

Important information
- The unaided eye is all that is needed to locate and view the moon, milky way, constellations, several planets, meteors, comets, aurora borealis, and other natural phenomena.
- Some satellites are visible without equipment.
- Binoculars or a low power telescope will add to your knowledge and enjoyment.
- Never look at the sun as it can seriously damage the eyes or cause blindness.

Ideas for pursuing this activity
- Learn to use a star chart.
- Identify stars and constellations.
- Check the weather page of the newspaper for information on astronomy.
- Read about astronomy.

Educational Excellence for Your Child

- Learn about the relationship of the sun, earth and moon.
- Learn about tides.
- Study Greek and Roman mythology.
- Watch astronomy programs on television.
- Plan a trip to a planetarium or observatory.
- Join an astronomy club.
- Purchase or construct a telescope.
- Set up a home planetarium.

Activity: Automobiles
Educational benefits
- Can provide opportunities to use math, science, reading, art, industrial technology, and research skills.
- Maintenance and repair activities help develop manual skills.
- Can help teach consumer education.

Important information
- Emphasize safety. Include pedestrian and bicycle safety, especially for young children.
- Include the study of other modes of land, air, and water transportation.

Ideas for pursuing this activity
- Study the history of automobiles.
- Subscribe to an automobile magazine.
- Read the automobile section of the newspaper.
- Start an automobile library.
- Keep maintenance and trip records.
- Learn about the mechanical aspects of the automobile.
- Visit an automobile maintenance facility or repair shop.
- Perform automobile maintenance and repairs.
- Attend a car show or automobile race.
- Compare models and equipment.
- Learn about purchasing, leasing, financing, and insuring a car.
- Take driver education when old enough to drive.

Activity: Baking and cooking
Educational benefits
- Support life skills courses.
- Develop the ability to follow directions and measure accurately.
- Strengthen reading, science and math skills.

- Promote praise from family members.
- Can increase knowledge of other cultures.
- Increase self-esteem.

Important information
- Excellent parent/child activities.
- Stress safety in handling food and using equipment.
- Can save money.

Ideas for pursuing this activity
- Learn about nutrition.
- Shop for ingredients.
- Read package and container labels, and use this information in planning menus.
- Review and follow recipes, measure and mix ingredients, cook or bake.
- Learn about kitchen chemistry, economics, and safety.
- Prepare meals.
- Conduct proper cleanup.

Activity: Business

Educational benefits
- Can support most curriculum areas.
- Teaches the importance of planning and organizing.
- Money earned from a business can be used for other educational purposes.

Important information
- A number of young people have started and operated successful small businesses while still in school.
- Business ventures and the children operating them should be carefully monitored.
- Initial customers might be family, friends, and neighbors.

Ideas for pursuing this activity
- Start an age-appropriate home business.
- Investigate license, insurance, and tax requirements.
- Consider providing a service like cleaning houses, washing windows, caring for lawns, cleaning cars, providing child care, or performing tasks for elderly neighbors.
- Manufacture and distribute a needed product.
- Sell items traditionally marketed by young people: newspapers, items prepared or constructed at home, produce, and seasonal merchandise.
- Have a yard sale.
- Make items to sell or donate to a worthy cause.
- Advertise, keep records, utilize banking services.

Activity: Calendar
Educational benefits
- Increases understanding of time, seasons, holidays.
- Supports math and science.
- Helps a child become better organized.
- Develops responsibility.

Important information
- Some computer programs include calendars.

Ideas for pursuing this activity
- Read about the history of calendars.
- Keep an up-to-date calendar of personal and family activities.
- Set up a book or file listing birthdays and important events.
- Send greeting cards on holidays, birthdays, and anniversaries.
- Record homework assignment due dates.
- Keep a diary or journal.
- Learn about time and the solar system.

Activity: Chemistry
Educational benefits
- Reinforces understanding of science, life skills, and industrial technology.
- Promotes accuracy in measuring.
- Teaches safety.

Important information
- Select appropriate and safe chemistry set for age level.
- Parent supervision is essential.

Ideas for pursuing this activity
- Learn about the composition of common household items.
- Read labels.
- Discuss environmental problems and dangers.
- Read books on kitchen chemistry or home chemistry.
- Perform and keep records of simple experiments.
- Visit a laboratory or manufacturing plant that uses or produces chemicals.
- Interview a pharmacist or chemist.

Activity: Child care
Educational benefits
- Reinforces knowledge and skills learned in life skills courses.
- Develops responsibility.
- Provides an opportunity to learn about and practice health and safety.

Important information
- Can be a way to earn money.
- Provides a valuable service.

Ideas for pursuing this activity
- Learn child care skills from parent, community program, or at school.
- Read about children and child care.
- Help care for a younger brother or sister.
- When older, provide child care services for relatives or neighbors.

Activity: Chores
Educational benefits
- Teach and strengthen life skills.
- Reinforce the concept that all members should accept responsibility for the operation and success of the family unit.
- Help develop new skills.
- Can introduce the child to the relationship between work and leisure.

Important information
- Avoid assigning too many chores, especially to young children.
- Children need to be taught to do chores properly.
- Expect regularly assigned chores to be done without remuneration as a family responsibility.
- Pay child as an incentive to perform extra work.

Ideas for pursuing this activity
- Have regularly assigned chores: wash dishes, take care of clothing, do laundry, pick up toys, organize desk and dresser, recycle items, take care of trash, and the like.
- Hold spring and fall work days. Do additional jobs around the house and yard as requested by parent.

Activity: Collecting
Educational benefits
- Supports most subject areas.
- Helps develop knowledge and skills in researching, locating, appraising, trading, bartering, buying, reconditioning, categorizing, displaying, advertising, and selling items.

Important information
- Items collected are limited only by a child's interest, imagination, financial resources, and in some cases storage space.
- Parent supervision is essential when collecting items that might be breakable, valuable, rare, or possibly dangerous if not handled, stored, displayed, or disposed of properly.

Educational Excellence for Your Child

Ideas for pursuing this activity
- Collect coins, stamps, baseball cards, miniatures, shells, insects, leaves, minerals, dolls, models, autographs, photographs, books, arrow heads, old documents, comics, antique toys, or the like.
- Catalog items.
- Learn to appraise items.
- Trade items.
- Construct display boxes, shelves, or cabinets.
- Arrange displays, prepare written or oral descriptions.
- Read books, magazines, and newsletters on collecting.
- Join a collector's club.
- Attend garage sales, flea markets, and conventions.

Activity: Communications
Educational benefits
- Increases language, reading, and writing skills.
- Promotes planning and organizing.
- Communicating on the Internet is an excellent way to increase computer and communicating skills.

Important information
- Success in pursuing this activity is often dependent on parent interest and communication skills, as well as a willingness to devote time to the activity.

Ideas for pursuing this activity
- Conduct family show and tell.
- Learn to answer the telephone properly.
- Request information, order items, make reservations.
- Call a radio talk show.
- Prepare announcements and speeches, rehearse using a cassette recorder, and deliver to groups.
- Produce a video.
- Design, make, and display signs.
- Learn or develop a communications code.
- Learn about radio, television, facsimile, print media, and electronic mail.
- Communicate with others with like interests using the Internet.

Activity: Computers
Educational benefits
- Motivate children and adults to learn.
- Tutorial software programs teach or reinforce basic academic skills.

- Can be used for either remediation or enrichment.
- Will support hobbies and other educational activities.

Important information
- Computers are becoming a key to education.
- Computer use can begin before elementary school.
- Professional advice is essential in selecting equipment and programs.
- Parent interest and supervision are necessary.

Ideas for pursuing this activity
- Investigate simple precomputers designed for young children.
- Do homework on a computer.
- Use programmed learning materials.
- Write letters.
- Publish a newspaper or newsletter.
- Learn a world language.
- Keep financial records.
- Make greeting cards and signs on the computer.
- Subscribe to and use an information service for access to the Internet and the World Wide Web.
- Research topics.
- Play educational games.

Activity: Conservation

Educational benefits
- Can support and enrich most subject areas.
- Raises self-esteem.

Important information
- Provides opportunities for family members to do things together.
- Saves resources, including money.

Ideas for pursuing this activity
- Read conservation articles.
- Develop a folder of information on conservation.
- Conduct a home energy audit; look for poor insulation, air leaks, and excessive use of water, electricity, fuel oil, gas or other energy.
- Conduct a survey of unnecessary packaging material entering the home.
- Write letters to legislators, editors, and corporate executives about conservation issues.
- Serve as a volunteer on a reforestation project.
- Plan and develop a low-water-use landscaped area.
- Compost lawn and garden waste.

Educational Excellence for Your Child

- Assume responsibility for your family's recycling program. Keep records and make trips to the recycling center, transfer station, or landfill.
- Select products made from recycled or recyclable materials.

Activity: Constructing
Educational benefits
- Reinforces reading, math, science, and industrial technology knowledge and skills.
- Develops planning and organizing ability.
- Encourages development of manual dexterity.

Important information
- Can save money.
- Be sure to emphasize safety.

Ideas for pursuing this activity
- Set up a toolbox or workbench with tool holders.
- Construct small items for personal or family use.
- Make items for gifts or charitable purposes. Items like bird houses and feeders, dog houses, bookcases, and simple furniture make good projects.
- Subscribe to a "build-it-yourself" magazine.
- View construction and home repair programs on television.
- Read about house construction.
- Visit a building construction site.
- Plan a trip to a cabinet shop.

Activity: Contests
Educational benefits
- Help develop critical reading ability, thinking skills, accuracy, neatness, and meeting deadlines.
- Can help a child understand statistics.
- Can help a child experience winning and losing.

Important information
- Careful parent supervision is necessary, especially if money or physical participation is required.
- Contests should be selected on the basis of age and maturity.

Ideas for pursuing this activity
- Enter contests at school or those sponsored by local businesses or civic organizations.
- Look for contest information in newspapers and other publications.
- Learn to identify good and bad contests.
- Read the disclaimers and other fine print on contest announcement, forms, and contracts, and explain what they mean.
- Keep records of contests entered.

Activity: Coupon clipping
Educational benefits
- Provides a way to use reading, math, and life skills.
- Reinforces the importance of following directions and meeting deadlines.
- Teaches consumer education.
- Helps develop organizational skills.

Important information
- Good parent/child activity.
- Saves money.

Ideas for pursuing this activity
- Clip and organize coupons.
- Keep records.
- Read fine print.
- Trade coupons.
- Shop using coupons.
- Integrate with comparison shopping.
- Fill out forms and mail for refunds.

Activity: Crafts
Educational benefits
- Develop an appreciation for handmade work.
- Can help in understanding history.
- Promote creativity and boost self-esteem.
- Improve manual dexterity.

Important information
- There are craft projects to fit most budgets.
- Provide opportunities for unified family efforts.
- Can provide part-time income.

Ideas for pursuing this activity
- Discuss craft work with friends and family.
- Plan projects.
- Purchase materials or kits.
- Construct craft items.
- Recycle common household items.
- Teach others to make craft items.
- Join a craft group.
- Develop a craft library.
- Subscribe to one or more craft magazines.
- Sell or donate completed items, or use them as gifts.

Activity: Educational games
Educational benefits
- Increase general knowledge.
- Develop and improve problem solving ability and decision making skills.
- Develop critical and abstract thinking skills.
- Can improve eye-to-hand coordination.
- Can help develop fairness, patience, and respect.
- Promote reading and following directions.
- Can improve spelling and vocabulary.
- Reinforce math skills by keeping score.
- Can aid in developing confidence.

Important information
- Carefully consider age recommendations when purchasing games.
- Select only those games that instill positive values.
- Preview computer and video games carefully, looking for inappropriate material, including violence.
- Watch for signs of eye strain when playing computer games.
- Discourage games that promote gambling.

Ideas for pursuing this activity
- Learn about, select, purchase, and trade games.
- Read directions and explain them to others.
- Play games and hold competitions.
- Keep score and list records.
- Invent new games; develop written rules, teach others to play.

Activity: Educational toys
Educational benefits
- Support life skills education.
- Can reinforce general knowledge and skills, especially in younger children.
- Can be used to teach safety, and respect for people and things.

Important information
- Ask yourself and others, "How is this toy educational?"
- Consider age recommendations, cost, safety, and durability.
- There are a few toys that encourage a child to conserve and/or improvise.
- Make excellent gifts.

Ideas for pursuing this activity
- Involve child in selection, purchase, or construction.
- Compare the value and durability of various toys.
- Teach your child to use toys properly.
- Invent and construct educational toys.

Activity: Electricity and electronics
Educational benefits
- Reinforce math, science, industrial technology, and reading skills.
- Reinforce the need to follow directions.

Important information
- Parent supervision is essential.
- Select only "low voltage" electronic and physics kits for young children.
- Household voltage kits for youth or adults must be used with caution.

Ideas for pursuing this activity
- Establish an electrical/electronics library.
- Subscribe to an electrical/electronics magazine.
- Build buzzers and bells, shortwave radios, alarm systems, motors, solar-operated items, remote-control devices, and a variety of other useful items.
- Learn to use measuring devices.
- Install entertainment-center components.
- Install telephone and cable television extensions.
- Select, install, and maintain alarm systems.
- Demonstrate electric and electronic principles to others.
- Use completed electrical and electronic devices in the home or use as gifts.
- Teach others about electricity and electronics.
- Inform others about electrical safety.

Activity: Entertaining guests
Educational benefits
- Helps develop planning and organizational skills.
- Reinforces knowledge, skills, and attitudes learned in life-skills courses.
- Provides an opportunity to develop interpersonal skills.
- Is an excellent way to learn about people and places.
- Can aid in developing good manners and a sense of sharing.

Important information
- A parent or other knowledgeable person should teach these skills to the child.
- Supervision is important at all stages.

Ideas for pursuing this activity
- Read about and practice proper etiquette.
- Plan a party for friends or relatives.
- Prepare house, patio, or yard for a picnic or party.
- Shop for and prepare food.
- Decorate for an event.

Educational Excellence for Your Child

- Learn to greet guests, introduce people, conduct meaningful conversations, assign seating, arrange table settings, announce dinner, seat guests, serve food, and handle minor incidents.
- Host visitors who are on vacation.

Activity: Gardening
Educational benefits
- Can increase knowledge of science including weather, insects, plant nutrition, cultivation, growth, and survival.
- Supports life skills.
- Can help develop self-esteem.

Important information
- Can contribute to family nutrition.
- Can save money.

Ideas for pursuing this activity
- Read about gardening.
- Listen to gardening programs on radio, or watch on television.
- Plan and lay out a garden.
- Select gardening supplies and equipment.
- Prepare seedbeds, pots, boxes, or garden soil.
- Purchase seeds and plants.
- Develop and maintain a compost system.
- Learn about conserving water and fertilizing.
- Care for the garden.
- Study and record weather conditions and plant growth.
- Sell produce, or give items to friends and neighbors.
- Keep accounts.
- Plan a visit to a farm or farmers' market.

Activity: Language
Educational benefits
- English skills often improve while learning another language.
- Complements study of history, geography, economics, and culture.
- Proficiency in two or more languages can expand opportunities for employment.

Important information
- Consider learning a world language that can be used at home, in the community, or while traveling.
- Consult a language teacher regarding appropriate teaching methods and programs.
- Programmed learning materials are available for computers and tape and video players.

Ideas for pursuing this activity
- Select a world language and learning materials.
- Involve the entire family if there is interest.
- Check community access and public radio and television station schedules for possible courses.
- Take regular lessons from an instructor.
- Practice daily.
- Use the language while talking with others.
- Learn about countries or areas where a language is spoken.
- Read books, magazines, and newspapers printed in other languages.
- Write letters or use the Internet or the World Wide Web to correspond with a pen pal in another country.
- Prepare ethnic food.
- Listen to selected language programs on television, and broadcast or short wave radio, for instruction and reinforcement.
- Host a visitor who would like to practice English language skills.
- Visit an area in the United States or another country where the selected language is spoken.

Activity: Library/media center
Educational benefits
- Can support all subject areas.
- Having and using a home library/media center can make a major contribution to experiencing educational excellence.

Important information
- The establishment of a home library/media center can benefit the entire family.
- Books and multimedia resources are more likely to be used if they are kept where they can be easily seen and are readily available.
- Consider appointing your child "head librarian" or "library/media specialist."

Ideas for pursuing this activity
- Plan and discuss the layout of a home library/media center.
- Begin with the books and other resources you presently have.
- Discuss resources that family members would like to add.
- Install shelves, cabinets, or files if you do not already have them.
- Purchase resource materials at book stores, auctions, or garage sales.
- Give books and other materials as family gifts.
- Include maps, charts, posters, pamphlets, video tapes, and reports.
- Catalog materials for ready reference.

Activity: Magic
Educational benefits
- Can develop problem-solving ability, manual dexterity, and quick thinking.
- Can help develop public speaking and performing skills.
- Can build self-esteem.

Important information
- Inexpensive initial investment.
- One age-appropriate book is all that is needed to get started.
- Very good parent/child activity.
- Provides an opportunity to entertain as a volunteer, or to earn money performing while still in school.

Ideas for pursuing this activity
- Read about magic and magicians.
- Go to magic shows and meet magicians.
- Write for catalogs and information.
- Learn age-appropriate magic tricks.
- Construct magic items and build equipment.
- Entertain family, relatives, classmates and friends.
- Arrange, publicize, and present magic shows.

Activity: Model building
Educational benefits
- Develops reading skills and manual dexterity.
- Reinforces the need to follow directions.
- Promotes organization and neatness.
- Can stimulate interest in history, science, art, industrial technology and math.

Important information
- Resist selecting kits that might be too difficult.
- It is necessary to set aside an area where partially completed models can remain undisturbed while being built.
- Adequate ventilation is necessary when using some glues, paints and solvents.

Ideas for pursuing this activity
- Visit a model store.
- Write for catalogs and information.
- Select and build models.
- Join a model club.
- Fly, sail, race, demonstrate or display completed models.
- Participate in model shows or conventions.

Activity: Music
Educational benefits
- Can complement the study of history, language, literature, science, and mathematics.
- Can help in understanding various cultures.
- Can enhance self-discipline and creativity by taking voice lessons or playing an instrument.
- Can improve self-esteem.

Important information
- Consult a music teacher or other accomplished musician before selecting an instrument or learning method.
- Resist decisions based primarily on statements by lay people or the availability of a used instrument.
- Keyboard, piano, or organ instruction can benefit all musicians.
- Don't overlook the recorder, harmonica, xylophone, guitar, drums, and other basic wind, percussion, and string instruments for personal enjoyment.
- It is often better to initially borrow or rent an instrument rather than to purchase one.

Ideas for pursuing this activity
- Meet with a music instructor to discuss options.
- Determine whether to study vocal music, instrumental music, or both.
- Discuss instrument and lesson availability with the instructor.
- Select an instrument and case, maintenance supplies, spare parts, and music stand.
- Purchase lesson books and music.
- Set up a practice area and schedule.
- Attend concerts and recitals.
- Perform individually and/or in a group.
- Select and purchase tapes, videos, and compact discs.
- Organize a family music group.
- Read about famous composers.
- Learn about the characteristics of sound.
- Learn about the relationship of music to math.
- Compose musical selections.

Activity: Photography
Educational benefits
- Teaches one about composition, color, and lighting.
- Reinforces physics, and chemistry if darkroom work is done.
- Stimulates creativity.
- Can improve self-image.

Educational Excellence for Your Child

Important information
- Appropriate for all but very young children.
- Wonderful family activity.
- Can reinforce the feeling of a family unit.
- Can use a disposable camera.

Ideas for pursuing this activity
- Read about photography.
- Subscribe to a photography magazine.
- Research available equipment.
- Learn to take various types of photographs.
- Plan and set up a home darkroom.
- Develop film and print pictures.
- Join a photography club.
- Mount and display photos.
- Keep a photo album.
- Make, edit, and show home movies and/or videos.
- Organize slides and present shows.
- Submit photographs to local newspapers.
- Enter photo contests.
- Earn money taking pictures or doing darkroom work.
- Interview a photographer and/or photographic technician.

Activity: Physical fitness/athletics/recreation (home and community)
Important information
- As many physical fitness, athletic, and recreation activities can be pursued either at home or in the community, you will find educational benefits, important information, and ideas for pursuing these activities under this heading in Chapter 17.

Activity: Puzzles
Educational benefits
- Develop problem solving skills.
- Can increase ability to visualize spatial relationships.
- Can help improve memory.
- Word puzzles increase vocabulary and spelling ability.

Important information
- Maturity and age are important factors to consider in selecting puzzles.
- Look for age recommendations on package.

Ideas for pursuing this activity
- Visit toy stores or newsstands to select puzzles.
- Subscribe to a puzzle magazine.

- Enter contests.
- Make puzzles for peers or younger children.

Activity: Radio/television
Educational benefits
- Can supplement all subject areas.
- Can introduce new useful information.
- Can serve as an incentive to read about a topic.

Important information
- It is a parent's responsibility to determine the amount of time a child will be allowed to listen to the radio, watch television, or play video games.
- Think twice before putting a television in your child's bedroom.
- Too much television or the wrong kinds of programs can adversely affect a child's behavior and sense of reality.
- Parents should carefully supervise program selection.
- Stress educational listening and viewing.
- Limit entertainment viewing to a small portion of total viewing.
- If after beginning to view a program it seems unsuitable, discontinue watching it.
- A parent's listening or viewing habits may become a child's habits.

Ideas for pursuing this activity
- Read television reviews, discuss options, decide on programs to watch.
- Establish a weekly schedule of educational programs to be viewed. Include documentaries, news and current events, curricula-related programs, cultural programs, "how-to" programs, and the like.
- Encourage and conduct follow-up discussions of programs viewed.
- Watch programs with your child.
- Make videos of family activities and events.
- Submit audio tapes or news videos and other original material to local radio and television stations.
- Call talk shows.

Activity: Recycling
Educational benefits
- Increases environmental awareness.
- Instills an understanding of the need for conservation.
- Develops responsibility.
- Increases understanding of math, science, life skills, and economics.

Important information
- A good way to save or earn money.

Educational Excellence for Your Child

- Caution your child about the need for cleanliness in handling recyclables.
- Discuss the dangers of breakable, sharp, poisonous, flammable, and toxic materials.

Ideas for pursuing this activity
- Set up and maintain a home recycling center.
- Subscribe to a recycling or environmental magazine.
- Conduct studies and keep records.
- Make regular trips to a recycling center, transfer station, or waste disposal facility.
- Visit a factory that uses waste paper, metal, glass or plastic to produce new products.
- Redeem cans and bottles for refund of deposit.
- Hold a flea market or garage sale.
- Use recycled items to make things.
- Write a newspaper article or letter to the editor urging readers to recycle.
- Support recycling legislation.

Activity: Repairing and maintaining
Educational benefits
- Can help develop responsibility.
- Should increase manual dexterity.
- Repairing an item, or doing something to prolong its life, can be very satisfying and can build self-esteem.

Important information
- Can make it possible to own items that might not otherwise be affordable.
- Tools make good gifts.
- Can save money.

Ideas for pursuing this activity
- Select tools and learn to use them properly.
- Set up a shop or work area.
- Work on items.
- Read instruction sheets and service manuals.
- Keep maintenance and repair records.
- Set up a library/media center of books, videos, and other reference materials on maintenance and repair.
- Subscribe to a "do-it-yourself" magazine.
- Listen to or watch home, outdoor equipment, and automobile maintenance programs on radio and television.
- Attend free programs, workshops, and demonstration at stores, schools, and various other locations.
- Instruct family and friends how to properly use and maintain items and equipment.

Activity: Scrapbooks and family records
Educational benefits
- Will increase historical knowledge and put past events in perspective.
- Provide an opportunity to increase writing skills.
- Can help in developing organizational skills.

Important information
- Help create a family record.
- Can involve parents, grandparents, and other relatives.
- Can add to a sense of belonging.

Ideas for pursuing this activity
- Discuss and review genealogy with family members.
- Acquire photographs and other records from parents and relatives.
- Research documents housed in library/media centers, newspaper offices, court houses, cemetery files, churches, or synagogues.
- Interview relatives.
- Write a biography or autobiography.
- Write portions of the family genealogy.
- Select scrapbook, photo album, or other display materials.
- Inventory and organize materials.
- Prepare captions.
- Mount and display photographs and other memorabilia.

Activity: Sewing
Educational benefits
- Develops reading, math, science, and life skills.
- Develops manual dexterity.
- Provides an opportunity for creativity.
- Leads to pride and self-esteem.
- Reinforces the importance of following directions.

Important information
- Promotes efficient use of materials.
- Supervision is important when a young child is using a sewing machine, sharp instruments, or hot iron.
- Can save money.

Ideas for pursuing this activity
- Learn basic stitches.
- Do needlecraft, cross-stitching and braiding.
- Learn to use a sewing machine.
- Learn about fasteners and alternatives to sewing.

Educational Excellence for Your Child

- Learn about clothing care.
- Repair clothing, knapsacks, belts, shoes and the like.
- Select patterns, purchase materials, and construct clothing or other items.
- Learn about the history of fibers, spinning, and weaving.
- Learn to crochet, knit, or use a knitting machine.
- Visit a Colonial America demonstration.
- Learn to spin fibers or weave.

Activity: Shortwave radio
Educational benefits
- Radio listening supports social studies. It can lead to a better understanding of people, politics, geography, economics, history, religion, and current events at home and abroad.
- Reinforces listening skills.
- Provides a practical use for math and science knowledge.
- Develops and reinforces time and distance concepts.
- Can help when learning a world language.

Important information
- Can lead to amateur-radio hobby involving two-way communication.
- Can provide additional uses for a personal computer.
- Safety in using electrical items, and in erecting antennas is of utmost importance. It must be taught and reinforced.

Ideas for pursuing this activity
- Use an existing family radio, or acquire new or used equipment.
- Purchase a list of radio stations throughout the world.
- Study the effects of nature on radio reception.
- Visit an electronics store.
- Visit commercial and amateur radio stations.
- Learn about, and experiment with, antennas and tuners.
- Keep a reception log. Record station call letters, date, time, conditions, signal strength and other pertinent information.
- Report signal reception to transmitting stations and receive confirmations.
- Start a library of radio and electronics information.
- Attend a radio club meeting, emergency drill, field day, or convention.
- Construct radios or associated equipment.

Activity: Show and tell
Educational benefits
- Develops communication skills, including public speaking and acting ability.
- Builds respect and promotes positive family relationships.

- Stimulates planning and thought.
- Can improve self-esteem.

Important information
- Conduct family show and tell sessions two or three times a week, preferably when all family members can be present.
- Ask questions, resist criticizing.

Ideas for pursuing this activity
- Describe a recent experience.
- Bring examples of work.
- Rotate host.
- Plan future programs.
- Record or video tape presentations.

Activity: Weather
Educational benefits
- Recording weather conditions at regular times develops responsibility, and reinforces the importance of accuracy.
- Increases understanding of science; provides an opportunity to use scientific method in observations and predictions.
- Utilizes statistics and other math skills.

Important information
- A weather radio, or home weather station, is a useful gift.
- Parent assistance and supervision are necessary in locating and installing weather monitoring equipment.
- Stress safety.
- Consider appointing your child as the meteorologist, or "Disaster Preparedness Coordinator" for your family.

Ideas for pursuing this activity
- Develop a weather shelf in your home library/media center.
- Learn how weather has affected important world events.
- Read about weather, watch the "Weather Channel."
- Listen to NOAA weather radio broadcasts.
- Learn to identify cloud types and other weather indicators.
- Learn to use instruments like the rain gauge, thermometer, weather vane, compass, barometer, hygrometer, and wind speed and direction indicator.
- Construct simple weather instruments.
- Set up a home weather station.
- Monitor the weather.
- Keep a log of weather conditions.
- Predict the weather.

Educational Excellence for Your Child

- Report weather conditions to a local radio or television station (equipment is often available free or on a loan basis).
- Attend weather seminars.
- Learn about disaster preparedness.

Additional home activities suggested by parent or child

The format used for this list is a good one to follow when considering additional activities. By listing educational benefits, important information, and ideas for pursuing an activity, you should be able to get an indication if a particular activity might be worthwhile for your child.

(Copyright © 1996, Kenneth R. Kimball, Jr.)

17

Community Activities and Resources that Increase Learning

Most communities offer activities that can enrich a child's education and increase learning. Some are designed to meet the interests and educational needs of a particular age or interest group, while others have universal appeal. You will probably find a number of activities in your community that can be considered extensions of those that your child is already involved in at home. Many are available at little or no cost. It is only necessary for you or your child to search out these activities. Determine the ones that you feel would be beneficial and interesting and make arrangements for your child to participate.

Obtaining information about community activities

One of your best sources of information about community activities is the newspaper. Most papers include calendars listing the hours of operation of library/media centers, museums, historic buildings, and other facilities. They announce the places and times when courses or special events will take place. You can also obtain information from friends, bulletin boards, brochures, flyers, radio, television, and your child's school.

It is wise to telephone a day or two before you plan to visit a facility or attend an activity to confirm its location and hours of operation. If necessary, you can also inquire about the best route to get there, where to park, or the best time to arrive for a special event, tour, or demonstration.

Determining if a program or activity is appropriate

In addition to knowing about the educational activities offered in your community, you must have adequate information to decide whether a particular program or course is appropriate for your child. A brief conversation with the person responsible for an activity or program will usually provide the details you need to make a decision. This will also give you the opportunity to learn about any unusual circumstances, to personalize your relationship with someone familiar with the activity, and, if necessary, to enroll your child. You may recall the good feelings you had when a person operating an activity welcomed you by name and indicated he or she was looking forward to your participation.

Depending on the maturity of your son or daughter and the nature of the activity, you may wish to spend time observing what takes place during the first session. This is particularly important if you have questions about the scope and quality of the program, or the adequacy of supervision. You might even consider serving as a volunteer if help is needed or if you would like to know more about the program.

Selecting activities

You will find many educational enrichment opportunities for your child if you live in or near a metropolitan area. You may want to keep a folder of information on programs that might serve your child's present or future needs. On the other hand, if you live in an area with limited opportunities, you may wish to suggest to other parents or community leaders that certain programs be offered. Just mentioning the subject might prompt others to help you start an activity.

Involve your son or daughter in reviewing community activities. This will help you gain a better understanding of his or her interests. Select one that you agree might be good to pursue. If you find it is suitable for your child's age group, is not too expensive, and does not require too great a commitment, give it a try. If enthusiasm runs high, you may not need to do much more than be a good listener, offer support, and monitor your child's progress. If, on the other hand, your child does not seem to relate to the activity within a reasonable time or enthusiasm begins to wane, you may need to become more involved. In some situations, it may be best to drop the activity, perhaps considering it again some time in the future.

The following activities have been selected for their educational value and high interest to children. They are listed in alphabetical order and are examples of what is available in many communities. As in the case of home activities, the information under "Educational benefits" points out some of the ways your child can benefit by participating. "Important information" will help you investigate the activity. In some cases, it also includes precautions you can take to avoid some of the potential problems associated with the activity. Listed under "Ideas for pursuing this activity," you will find specific things you can do prior to, during, and after, your child becomes a participant.

When you have completed your review of this list of community activities and resources, you will be ready to move on to the final chapter in *Educational Excellence For Your Child*. Chapter 18, "Assessing Progress and Moving On," will help you determine the extent to which you have been successful in achieving increased excellence for your son or daughter and, to a degree, the school. There are ideas on how to get feedback and indicators you can use to look at your child and the school. There are also suggestions to help you use the information you have gained and the techniques you have developed, to continue to pursue the best possible education for your child and other children in your family and community.

HIGH INTEREST COMMUNITY ACTIVITIES AND RESOURCES LIST

The following list presents a number of interesting educational activities your son or daughter might pursue in your community. For easy reference, the activities have been placed in alphabetical order. As you review the list, you may find your child has already expressed interest in a particular activity. It may even be that he or she is participating in one or more at this time. If this is the case, you already have a good idea of the experiences your child might enjoy.

Activity: Auctions
Educational benefits
- Require one to think fast, and use math skills.
- Can provide an opportunity to see and handle historic items.
- Provide the opportunity to observe people, and to study human nature.

Important information
- May be a good place to purchase books and other items for your home library/media center.
- Parent supervision is essential for young children.

Ideas for pursuing this activity
- Check the newspapers and bulletin boards for auction announcements.
- Learn to evaluate items.
- Become familiar with the bidding process.
- Participate in bidding.
- Recondition purchased items if necessary.
- Hold a real or mock auction.

Activity: Camping (day or sleep-over)
Educational benefits
- Provides almost unlimited educational and recreational experiences.
- Provides a chance to meet and live with other children, some with quite different backgrounds.
- Develops independence.
- Includes opportunities for leadership.
- May provide tutoring or other assistance to increase competencies.
- Usually promotes physical fitness.

Important information
- Begin investigation during the fall or early winter as some programs quickly fill.
- Determine if the camp you are considering is properly licensed and certified by the appropriate governmental agencies and associations.

Educational Excellence for Your Child

- Carefully check program offerings, qualifications of staff, level of supervision, and health and safety record.
- Submit application, physical exam report, and other required information on time.

Ideas for pursuing this activity
- Investigate the availability of camp programs offered by recreation departments, schools, religious groups, scouts, clubs, and private organizations. Consider day camps and sleep-over camps.
- Compare camp program offerings with the interests and needs of your child.
- If possible, obtain the names of several parents who have sent their children to the camps you are seriously considering. Contact them regarding their impressions of the camp.
- Ask about financial help, part-time work, or a scholarship, if needed.
- Carefully read all materials provided by the camp before and after your child is accepted.
- Begin to gather the recommended clothing, equipment, and supplies and place them in one location.

Activity: Clubs/community groups/religious organizations
Educational benefits
- Can provide reinforcement for academic and nonacademic areas.
- Offer opportunities to develop leadership skills.
- Can help develop positive moral values.

Important information
- Provide time with others with similar interests.
- Can lead to enjoyable experiences.
- Parent involvement is desired and, in some cases, required.

Ideas for pursuing this activity
- Investigate clubs available in the community.
- Consider religious organizations, school clubs, community service groups and programs like YMCA, YWCA, sports, 4-H, scout programs, boys and girls clubs, and the like.
- Carefully check out programs. Who will supervise the participants? Where does the activity take place? What is the expected level of parent involvement? What are the costs of membership? Are there ongoing expenses?
- Determine if the organization has proper insurance.

Activity: Concerts and performances
Educational benefits
- Develop an understanding of, and appreciation for, the arts.
- Can stimulate interest in becoming a regular observer.

- May prompt your child to participate in, or increase his or her involvement in the arts.

Important information
- Provide excellent opportunities for parents and children to do things together.
- Early reservations are often important.

Ideas for pursuing this activity
- Determine the availability of concerts and programs.
- Prepare your child for what he or she might see and hear at performances.
- Attend or participate in orchestra, band, theater, vocal, and dance performances.
- Don't overlook folk, regional, and ethnic music demonstrations, workshops, and concerts.
- Inquire about the possibility of attending dress rehearsals and matinees as a way to avoid crowds and save money.
- Meet performers and ask questions.
- Purchase sheet music, tapes, compact discs, or videos.
- Conduct follow-up discussions and activities.

Activity: Enrichment programs
Educational benefits
- Provide an immediate route to excellence.
- Are offered by schools and other community organizations.

Important information
- Should be age appropriate.
- Child should express significant interest in participating.
- Will require a commitment of time and energy.
- May require a registration fee and the purchase of equipment and/or supplies.

Ideas for pursuing this activity
- Check with the school, other parents, and community organizations regarding opportunities and useful information.
- Read local newspapers and listen for radio and television announcements.
- Enroll as early as possible, as openings may be limited.

Activity: Fairs/expositions
Educational benefits
- Provide an opportunity to learn more about specific areas of interest like agriculture, arts, business, industry, science, hobbies, books, or computers.

Important information
- The first day of a multiple day event is often the most crowded and hectic.
- Exhibitors often run out of printed information and begin to disassemble their displays early on the last day of a fair or exposition.
- When feasible, attending two half-days will usually result in more learning and enjoyment than one full-day.

Educational Excellence for Your Child

- Take the time to rest periodically.
- College and job fairs are a must for all high school students.

Ideas for pursuing this activity
- Read newspapers, magazines, and bulletin boards to learn about fairs and expositions.
- Determine those areas where you will concentrate your time.
- Conduct preparation and follow-up activities.
- Talk with exhibitors and obtain information.
- Gather materials to take home for later review.
- Urge your child to display projects, demonstrate a skill, or participate in some way.

Activity: Field trips
Educational benefits
- Support all subject areas and make learning more relevant.
- Can be very helpful in choosing a vocation.

Important information
- Can be arranged for your child or a group.
- Discuss protocol, behavior, and safety.
- Request permission before taking photographs, videotaping, or recording the visit.

Ideas for pursuing this activity
- Determine, with your child, the places he or she would like to visit.
- Possible field trips include:

bakery	hospital	prison or jail
city hall	industrial plant	radio station
college	long-term care facility	recycling center
computer center	military installation	television station
farm or nursery	office	warehouse
fire station	parent's workplace	wastewater plant
generating station	police station	water plant

- Involve your child in arranging the visit.
- List things to see and questions to ask.
- Make notes for later reference.
- Summarize observations.
- Describe the field trip to family members, small group, or school class.
- Write a letter of appreciation.

Activity: Hobby shows and conventions
Educational benefits
- Provide an opportunity to talk with experts.
- Supplement things taught in school and make curriculum areas more relevant.
- Antique shows can increase knowledge of art, history, and technology.

Community Activities and Resources that Increase Learning

- Coin shows help in understanding mathematics and history.
- Automobile, boat and air shows can help teach science, mathematics, art, drafting, social studies, technology, and driver education.
- Computer exhibitions help teach language arts, mathematics, science, technology, business, and history.
- Fashion shows reinforce life skills, art, design, and mathematics.
- Health fairs and sports shows help in understanding the value of physical fitness.
- Outdoor shows can add to one's appreciation of the environment.

Important information
- Accompany younger children.
- Limit attendance time for maximum benefit.

Ideas for pursuing this activity
- Watch newspapers for announcements.
- Check with club members and friends for program information, including when and where shows and conventions will be held.
- Check club newsletters and trade publications.
- Listen for radio and television announcements.
- Call or write for a convention program and details.
- Plan a trip to a show or convention.
- Attend seminars.
- Consult with experts.
- Collect and read information.

Activity: Lessons and courses
Educational benefits
- Help the learner obtain additional knowledge and skills.
- Help perfect existing skills.
- Can improve physical fitness, mental alertness, and self-esteem.

Important information
- Selection is highly dependent on interest, age, and maturity.
- May require parent involvement, including transportation.
- Expenses may be incurred.

Ideas for pursuing this activity
- Review your child's interests.
- Investigate the availability of individual or group lessons in your area. Offerings often include the following:

art	firearm safety	martial arts
boating and sailing	first aid	music
computers	fishing	photography
CPR	gardening	sewing
dance	golf	skating

199

Educational Excellence for Your Child

    drama   horseback riding   swimming
    driver education   jewelry making   tennis

- Investigate curriculum, instructor qualifications, costs, time requirements, health and safety record.
- Select teacher and program suited to your child.
- Provide parent support.

Activity: Library/media centers
Educational benefits
- Support all aspects of school curriculum.
- Reinforce research skills.
- Help children develop library/media habits early in life.

Important information
- Provide an excellent place to review books, magazines, encyclopedias, and audio-video materials prior to purchase.
- Parent should demonstrate and emphasize proper behavior as one negative incident can discourage a child from using this resource.
- Pleasant place to be during adverse weather.
- Many library/media centers need student and adult volunteers.

Ideas for pursuing this activity
- Do leisure reading, research, and homework in a library/media center.
- Attend book reviews, story times, and lectures.
- Listen to records and tapes.
- Use audio/visual devices, microfilm reader, and the copier.
- Use computers to access the Internet, World Wide Web, and Global Library.
- Obtain library/media cards for all family members.
- Sign-up for the library/media center newsletter.
- Join library/media center friends group.
- See that your child receives instruction on how to locate items using the catalog system.
- Plan regular trips to select and return books.
- Attend used book sales.
- Utilize the library/media specialist as a resource person.

Activity: Museums/zoos/preserves
Educational benefits
- Support and enrich the school curriculum.
- Stimulate an interest to learn more about subjects.
- Can add an educational component to holiday and vacation plans.

Community Activities and Resources that Increase Learning

Important information
- Limit visit to no more than two or three hours, when possible.
- Teach your child how to behave in various facilities and outdoor environments.

Ideas for pursuing this activity
- Determine the resources available in your area or areas where you might travel.
- Don't overlook historic buildings, battle fields, parks, and nature centers.
- A conducted tour or self-guided tour with an instruction sheet or audio program can provide a good introduction to a facility.
- Investigate special events, after-school, weekend, and vacation programs.
- Sign up for the newsletter.
- Obtain books on the subject.
- Increase learning with previsit orientation and follow-up discussions.
- Inquire about becoming a volunteer.

Activity: Open houses
Educational benefits
- Provide the opportunity to visit and learn about businesses, industries and institutions that might not otherwise be open to the public.
- Can help in choosing a career.
- Add to one's knowledge of the community.

Important information
- College and vocational or trade school open houses are of utmost importance to students who are planning post-high-school education.

Ideas for pursuing this activity
- Check newspapers, radio, and television for announcements.
- Call businesses and industries regarding unannounced opportunities.
- Make the necessary arrangements to attend.
- Follow through on any ideas gained at an open house.

Activity: Physical fitness/athletics/recreation (home and community)
Educational benefits
- Exercise the body and mind.
- Reinforce the necessity of following directions.
- Encourage quick decision making.
- Help develop proper breathing and coordination.
- Develop skills: balancing, running, jumping, throwing, catching, dodging, climbing.
- Teach fair play.
- Provide opportunities for leadership.
- Develop interests that can be pursued throughout life.
- Can increase confidence and boost self-esteem.
- Could lead to possible scholarship help for future education.

Educational Excellence for Your Child

Important information
- Check with your child's physician as well as a trainer, physical therapist, or physical education teacher before beginning a strenuous exercise program. This is especially important if your son or daughter has physical problems.
- Lessons are important for skill development, safety and maximum enjoyment.
- Lessons from certified instructors are required for some activities.
- Thoroughly investigate activities that have high accident rates before deciding whether or not to participate.
- Check with several experts before making equipment purchases.

Ideas for pursuing this activity
- Exercise daily, or several times a week.
- Participate in dance or martial arts classes.
- Play sidewalk games.
- Participate in individual or small group sports like:

bicycling	juggling	skiing
bowling	jump-roping	snorkeling
canoeing	kayaking	spelunking
climbing	racquetball	surfing
diving	rowing	swimming
fishing	running	tennis
golf	sailing	walking
hunting	scuba diving	windsurfing
in-line skating	skating	wrestling
jogging		

- Participate in team sports like:

baseball	football	soccer
basketball	hockey and field hockey	track and field
cross-country running	lacrosse	volleyball

- Work out at home or in a gym.
- Listen to sports events on radio or watch on television.
- Read books, magazines, and the sports section of the newspaper.
- Keep records; memorize sport trivia.

Activity: Politics
Educational benefits
- Supplements citizenship education.
- Helps develop interpersonal skills.
- Early participation can continue through adulthood.

Important information
- Parent participation with younger children is advised.

Ideas for pursuing this activity
- Read about candidates and issues.
- Watch candidates and political programs on C-Span and other television stations.
- Analyze political advertisements.
- Write and call candidates.
- Lobby representatives and officials.
- Attend forums and rallies.
- Work with parents or others on campaigns.
- Collect political buttons, cartoons, stickers, brochures, posters, and banners.

Activity: Safety/survival skills
Educational benefits
- Accident avoidance information, personal safety techniques and age-appropriate information regarding drugs, alcohol, tobacco, and communicable diseases are an essential part of every child's basic education.
- Safety and survival skills go hand in hand with nearly all occupations and leisure time activities.

Important information
- You cannot assume that others will teach your child safety/survival skills. You must be sure the proper instruction is provided.
- Safety/survival skills should be taught well in advance of their need.
- Most safety/survival skills require continual reinforcement and periodic updating.

Ideas for pursuing this activity
- Determine which safety/survival skills are necessary and appropriate for your child. These can cover the full range from avoiding burns and moving objects, in the case of a young child, to reducing fatigue and practicing defensive driving for the young adult.
- Read about and discuss safety/survival skills.
- Look for announcements of helpful programs on bulletin boards and in newspapers and school memos.
- Don't overlook radio, television, and community calendars as good sources of information.
- Many youth organizations and summer camps emphasize or teach safety/survival skills.
- Investigate the availability of the following workshops, demonstrations, and courses:

abdominal thrust technique	health/first aid
bicycle safety	hurricane preparedness
boating safety	lifesaving
CPR	outdoor survival skills
decision-making	pedestrian safety
disaster preparedness	rescue breathing

driver education
electrical precautions
firearm/hunter safety
fire safety

self-defense
swimming
weather protection

Activity: Shopping
Educational benefits
- Can increase mental math skills.
- Provides an opportunity to make comparisons.
- Can be used to develop self-control.
- Helps in understanding the importance, and relationship of climate, location, and the availability of natural and human resources to finished products.
- Demonstrates the interdependence of people throughout the world.
- Provides a way to understand the value of money and its relationship to work and lifestyle.
- Reinforces the importance of reading the fine print on labels.
- Can help one appreciate the value of do-it-yourself projects like clothing construction, woodworking, and crafts.

Important information
- Adult supervision and guidance are necessary for young children.

Ideas for pursuing this activity
- Read about products, write for catalogs and information.
- Check newspapers and fliers for sales.
- Compare products and prices.
- Learn to plan purchases.
- Subscribe to a consumer magazine.
- Read and evaluate label information, i.e. content and/or ingredients, nutritional value, expiration date, and place of manufacture.
- Learn about product care, trouble shooting, repairs, and warranties.
- Look for similarities and differences in the various languages used on labels and in directions.
- Consider second-hand items, attend garage sales and flea markets.
- Look for items made of recycled materials, or materials that can be reused.

Activity: Summer school
Educational benefits
- Can help a child avoid repeating a course or an entire grade during the regular school year.
- Often includes enrichment courses, some of which may only be offered during the summer.
- Usually includes remedial programs for academic subjects.

Important information
- Consult with your child's teacher or guidance counselor regarding course recommendations.
- Obtain prior written confirmation indicating a course will be accepted for credit in lieu of a regular or failed course.
- Arrive early at registration to assure place in class.
- Be prepared to pay registration fees or tuition.

Ideas for pursuing this activity
- Check fliers from school and newspaper announcements for course offerings at your child's school or other schools in the area.
- Don't take more classes than you can do a commendable job of completing.
- Arrive promptly for classes.
- Set aside time each day to use the library/media center.
- Be prepared to spend sufficient time on homework, which is often quite intensive.

Activity: Theater
Educational benefits
- Develops an appreciation for the arts.
- Can improve speaking ability.
- Performing can increase self-image.
- Teaches the importance of team work.
- Provides a medium for creativity and expression.

Important information
- Offers many opportunities other than acting.
- Is a very good family activity.

Ideas for pursuing this activity
- Check arts section of newspapers for information on performances.
- Contact local arts council or representatives of community theater groups for information.
- Attend plays and dress rehearsals.
- Become involved in acting, set construction, costuming, collecting props, sound production, publicity, ticket sales, or other tasks.
- Young children can often work with a parent.

Activity: Travel
Educational benefits
- Can supplement nearly all subject areas.
- Planning can be as educational as the trip.

Important information
- Involve your child in pretrip planning and posttrip activities.

- Free or reasonably priced information is available about most places where you might travel.
- Early planning and reservations are necessary to avoid delays and disappointments.

Ideas for pursuing this activity
- Seek family input in selecting and planning day trips, longer journeys, and vacations.
- Talk with a travel agent. Write or call the Chamber of Commerce, or Department of Tourism for travel brochures and other information about possible areas to visit.
- Obtain information from your local library/media center, the Internet, or the World Wide Web.
- Develop an itinerary for the trip including routes, travel times, places to stay, and what to see.
- Assign specific responsibilities to each family member (selecting routes, budgeting, making reservations, preparing vehicle, packing, keeping a log or journal, taking photographs).
- Conduct follow-up discussions and activities.

Activity: Tutoring
Educational benefits
- Can improve knowledge, skills, and ability.
- Develops confidence and self-esteem.
- Makes it possible to move to the next level of learning with a better foundation than might otherwise be the case.

Important information
- Can reduce or eliminate the need to repeat a course or grade.
- May be available free through the school, community center, religious organization, friend, or college.
- Parent interest and commitment to a positive tutoring experience can be almost as important to achieving success as the work done by the tutor and child.
- Could include your child being tutored, or serving as an academic or nonacademic subject tutor for a family member, classmate, or friend. Could also include participation in a peer or cross-age teaching program dealing with drugs, alcohol, depression or the like.

Ideas for pursuing this activity
- With the help of your child, the teacher, guidance counselor, or tutoring center, determine the type of tutoring needed.
- Check with the school on the availability of tutors in your area.
- Determine when the tutoring can be done, the cost, the materials needed, and the transportation requirements.
- Arrange for tutoring.
- Set aside sufficient time in your child's schedule to complete assigned work.

- Provide encouragement and support for your child as he or she will be assuming additional responsibilities.

Activity: Volunteering
Educational benefits
- Improves the self-esteem and skills of the volunteer while providing a needed service to others.
- Adds to a better understanding of people.
- Provides an introduction to vocations and leisure time activities.

Important information
- Could lead to a paid position.
- Some of the information included in Chapter 12, "Opportunities for School Volunteers," applies to young people.

Ideas for pursuing this activity
- Young children need parent direction and help in selecting a position and becoming a volunteer.
- Young adults can contact organizations directly or go through the school or local volunteer bureau.
- Parent monitoring is important to avoid possible exploitation.
- Include your child in your volunteer activities.
- Young adults can volunteer in day-care facilities, and in remedial, enrichment, recreation center, and summer-camp programs.
- Coordinate activities with the school for possible credit.
- Serve as a volunteer in a particular position only as long as it remains interesting, productive, and satisfying.

Activity: Work
Educational benefits
- Develops responsibility.
- Reinforces skills taught in school.
- Provides opportunities to investigate vocations.
- Can provide income for future education.
- Can provide practical experiences in obtaining work: i.e. locating available positions, completing applications, obtaining recommendations, interviewing, accepting conditions, signing papers, and the like.
- Introduces the young adult to the world of work: i.e. experiencing sign-in sheets/time clocks, being supervised and evaluated, adjusting to work place protocol, getting along with others, paying taxes, and gracefully leaving a job.
- Demonstrates the value of networking.

Important information
- Inquire in the school guidance office or call the Labor Department about state and federal work regulations before pursuing employment. There are restrictions on hours and type of work for children and youth of various ages.

- Work must not interfere with education. While each student is different, most can handle up to ten hours a week without much difficulty. It has been found that twenty or more hours a week will have an adverse effect on the grades of most students.

Ideas for pursuing this activity
- Read about various vocations.
- Locate available positions by talking with friends, relatives, school guidance counselors, reading classified advertisements, making telephone inquiries, and visiting employers.
- Go through the process of applying for a position.
- Hold a mock interview.
- Organize daily schedule to allow for work and work-related activities; i.e. sleeping, doing homework, dressing and grooming, preparing lunch, eating, and commuting.
- Establish a budget.
- Set up a savings account.

Additional community activities suggested by parent or child

The format used for this list is a good one to follow when considering additional activities. By listing educational benefits, important information, and ideas for pursuing an activity, you should be able to get an indication if a particular activity might be worthwhile for your child.

(Copyright © 1996, Kenneth R. Kimball, Jr.)

18

Assessing Progress and Moving On

Continuous monitoring of a continuing journey

By now, it should be entirely clear that education is the continuing journey one takes through life, rather than the destination at the end. It is the day-to-day experiences along the route that determine if the trip has been a success. This is why continuous monitoring is so important. Good teachers monitor daily. They ask questions, evaluate work, give tests, and look for progress or lack of progress in each of their students. Good parents do the same. They do not leave learning to chance. While they may only receive reports from the school several times a year, they check their children's progress much more often. There does come a time, though, when it is a good idea to look back over several months or a year to determine if the progress you expected has been made.

You have already begun to determine progress

How can you evaluate the progress you have made in obtaining educational excellence for your child? The answer lies in understanding what you have been doing since you began using this book: collecting and organizing information, investigating schools, asking questions, establishing goals, developing an Education Action Plan, suggesting ideas, persuading the school to help, making changes at home, and of course monitoring your child's progress. By becoming more involved in your child's education, you have more than likely already received a number of indications that you have increased his or her exposure to excellence. You may even be aware of changes the school has made, at your suggestion, that have benefited your child or other children in your child's class, grade, or school.

There are many indicators you can use to help you recognize excellence. Some are evident while they are occurring while others may not become apparent for some time, even after a number of years. Unfortunately, it is not possible to determine if you have been totally successful. To even begin to approach this point would require the information contained in a full-length book and a lot more monitoring and research than most parents are prepared to do. You should, though, be aware of some of the more obvious indicators. In this chapter, you will learn where to look and what to look for when assessing the impact of your efforts on your child's education and school.

Review your child's Education Action Plan

As part of your evaluation of progress, you should review your child's Education Action Plan. It will remind you of what you expected to accomplish within a specific time frame. Try to determine if you, your child, and the school have stayed on track in carrying out your original or revised goals and strategies. It is especially important to review all short-term goals as they may already be completed. If this is the case, you can mark them appropriately. Be sure to write the date of completion next to your notation. If this has not occurred, these goals may need to be further refined and will undoubtedly require new strategies and additional attention in the future.

Next, look at the intermediate- and long-term goals. Are they still relevant? Has success or failure to reach any short-term goal made it necessary to reconsider or revise longer-term goals? If so, this should be done at this time. It is important though to resist modifying goals without adequate convincing information indicating they need to be changed. You may want to make notations in the margin of your child's Education Action Plan or on a separate sheet of paper indicating your preliminary conclusions about each of these goals and strategies. They can then be reconsidered at a later date if more information becomes available. This will be of help as you move on to a new school year and another phase of your child's education.

Where to get feedback

Your efforts to increase educational excellence have brought you and your child in contact with a number of school and nonschool people, some of whom can be good sources of feedback. To make things easier, their opinions are usually available just for the asking. Now is a good time to inquire if they have noticed specific changes in your child or the school. As in your previous investigations, it is best to avoid asking broad questions as they tend to encourage a general response that may not be particularly helpful. Relate your questions to what you have been trying to accomplish and you will more than likely get useful answers. The following people can provide information:

advisory committee members	parent/teacher group members
children, including your child	principals and assistant principals
classroom teachers	psychologists
college or university staff	school board members
curriculum specialists	school nurses
family members	social workers
friends	special-area teachers
guidance counselors	special-education teachers
neighbors	State Education Department staff
parents	

Tests as indicators of success

Schools use standardized tests to measure individual, group, and total school achievement. Except for individual test results for children other than your own, this information should be available to you. If you have not already seen this data, you can begin by asking your child's teacher, guidance counselor, or principal when it will be ready for your review. When it is presented, be sure to ask for any help you might need in interpreting the data. Some of it can be complicated if it is not presented properly. Also, people involved in testing, like other professionals, use language and techniques that might be unfamiliar to you.

While a careful review of test results can be helpful in making educational decisions, it is important to realize that most of the things that happen at school are not measured or tested. The same is true of things that happen at home. Even if they were, the resultant data might have little or no use. Fortunately, achievement tests are usually good indicators of educational progress. As such, they can be helpful in determining the degree to which your child has mastered the essential knowledge and skills tested. By looking at the test results for the entire school and comparing them with the data from previous years, you should also be able to sense whether the school is making headway in obtaining educational excellence for all.

Indicators to look for in your child

You will have a good indication your child is moving toward excellence if the following things are occurring. As it would be very difficult, if not impossible to prioritize these indicators, they have not been listed in any order.

Child Success Indicators

- improved report card grades
- more favorable comments from teachers
- standardized achievement tests indicate your child has progressed more than expected in all, or most, categories when compared with test results from the previous year
- has very few behavior problems at home or school
- looks forward to school
- rarely misses school or class
- likes the teachers
- discusses school with you
- brings things home to show you
- likes the curricula
- attends school functions outside regular hours
- gets along well with others at home and school
- has increased leisure reading
- does not spend excessive time watching television or playing video games
- begins homework and other tasks without being asked
- completes assignments accurately, neatly, and on time
- often does more than is expected
- asks questions at home and in class
- participates in class discussions
- has gained increased confidence and self-esteem
- demonstrates a willingness to accept responsibility
- persists in doing things until completed
- participates in optional school and community activities
- has friends who value education

Educational Excellence for Your Child

You do not need to complete your own personal report card to know if progress has been made. Your review of each of the goals and strategies on your child's Education Action Plan, and the other activities you have conducted should make this apparent. The Plan, with notations, does in fact serve much the same purpose as a report card. It would be a good idea, though, to add any additional comments you might have to your child's Educational Records File, perhaps on a separate sheet of paper. Again, be sure to date everything.

Indicators to look for in the school

You realize that your efforts in obtaining increased excellence for your child may very likely result in positive changes in your child's classroom or school. You may already have seen evidence of this. One of the most satisfying things you can experience is having others realize your suggestions or efforts have made a difference. Educational excellence at the school level usually results from many people working together but often it is one person who begins the process or sees it through to completion. You may sense your commitment to excellence has made a difference if one or more of the following things has occurred as a result of your efforts. Like the child success indicators, these have not been listed in any order.

> Aa Bb Cc Dd Ee Ff Gg Hh Ii Jj Kk Ll Mm
>
> Formula for school improvement: One of the quickest ways to improve a troubled school is to assign the best teachers to the school. It also helps to have the best principal and the best support staff on the job before the children arrive.

School Success Indicators

★ positive changes in philosophy, policy, organization, or curricula resulting from your suggestions

★ improved standardized test scores

★ increased information being provided by the school

★ more meaningful conferences, and discussions with school personnel

★ increased receptivity to new ideas

★ people recognizing and supporting your suggestions

★ a reduction in discipline problems

★ better attendance rate

★ reduced drop out rate

★ students and teachers working harder

★ recognition for outstanding programs

★ better teachers attracted to school

★ school taking action where problems exist

Assessing Progress and Moving On

- ★ board of education allocating more resources to the school
- ★ increased parent participation
- ★ increased number of students exhibiting "Child-Success Indicators"
- ★ teachers and other staff members feeling more valued
- ★ improved student and staff morale
- ★ community support for programs and budget
- ★ more positive press coverage
- ★ improved graduation rate
- ★ families with children moving to the area to take advantage of the schools
- ★ an increased number of awards and scholarships

Moving toward increased excellence

There comes a time when it is best to stop evaluating the past and to move on to the future. You will be ready to do this when you feel you have a reasonably good idea of your child's accomplishments to date. This is when you will update your child's Education Action Plan and take other steps necessary to ensure he or she experiences excellence the following year. As mentioned in Chapter 9, late winter or early spring is usually the best time for this review. If possible, complete your work before class placements and student scheduling begin. Check with the school to determine when this occurs. It is usually much easier to have your requests approved if they can be considered right from the beginning rather than necessitating a change in work that has already been completed.

As you have carried out one complete cycle in helping your child achieve educational excellence, you will be able to save a lot of time in gearing up for the next year. Review the earlier chapters of this book. Determine those steps you can omit and those you will need to repeat. At a minimum, you will want to do the following things.

- ✓ Make sure your child's Educational Records File is up to date.
- ✓ Confer with your child to determine if his or her current or future needs or goals have changed.
- ✓ Review goals and strategies on your child's Education Action Plan Worksheet. Identify those that should be revised or dropped.
- ✓ Develop new goals and strategies, as necessary, and add them to your child's Education Action Plan.
- ✓ Discuss your plans for educational excellence with others who can be of help.
- ✓ Confer with school personnel to ensure arrangements will be made to implement your plans.

Helping others achieve excellence

It is never too early, or too late, to use the ideas and methods described in this book to seek educational excellence on behalf of other children. If you have not already done so, now is a good time to begin. You are very much aware of the techniques that have worked. You must remember though, there is no assurance they will work in a similar manner or as well in other cases. Each child and every situation is different. Therefore you must be prepared to modify your approach as conditions warrant. Your past accomplishments, though, should help assure future success.

The future prospects for excellence

The desire and challenge of every school, every community, every parent, and every American must be to substantially improve the quality of education in the United States. It has been and continues to be a key building block in the foundation of our democracy. As such, our very existence depends on it. Most of the serious social, health, and economic problems we face can only be solved by having an educated populous. As the solutions to these and other problems are needed immediately, educational excellence for all our nation's children must not be delayed.

> Aa Bb Cc Dd Ee Ff Gg Hh Ii Jj Kk
>
> Schools and society: The real question is not what kind of schools we want, but what kind of society we want. If we neglect the first, we will be very disappointed in the second.

Our goal must be to make every school an excellent school. When this is accomplished, educational excellence should be available to every child; but this alone is not enough. We must also ensure that all children are physically, emotionally, and socially able to take advantage of the excellence that future schools will offer. This will be possible only if parents, educators, and community and governmental leaders place the well being of children at the top of their list of priorities.

Plans must be developed to mobilize the nation around education. This will require commitment, ingenuity, creativity, money, and hard work, the likes of which have not been seen in recent years. As a parent, you have a key stake in this movement. You will want to continue or even increase your efforts to see that change occurs and that progress is made.

You have been able to apply the ideas presented in this guide to bring about positive change, change you may not have thought possible a short time ago. The chances are that a significant portion of this change has resulted in a much improved education for your child and his or her peers. I hope you will share the ideas and expertise you have gained from *Educational Excellence For Your Child* with others so that, through education, we can become a better society.

Future opportunities for excellence are limited only by your vision of the future and your willingness to continue your efforts. Pat yourself on the back, give yourself an "A+," and move on to new and greater challenges.

Appendix A

THE NATIONAL EDUCATION GOALS

School Readiness: By the year 2000, every child will start school ready to learn.

School Completion: By the year 2000, the high school graduation rate will increase to at least 90 percent.

School Achievement and Citizenship: By the year 2000, American students will leave grades, four, eight, and twelve having demonstrated competency in challenging subject matter including English, mathematics, science, foreign languages, civics and government, economics, arts, history, and geography: and every school in America will ensure that all students learn to use their minds well, so they may be prepared for responsible citizenship, further learning, and productive employment in our Nation's modern economy.

Mathematics and Science: By the year 2000, U.S. students will be first in the world in science and mathematics achievement.

Adult Literacy and Lifelong Learning: By the year 2000, every adult American will be literate and will possess the knowledge and skills necessary to compete in a global economy and exercise the rights and responsibilities of citizenship.

Safe, Disciplined, and Alcohol-and-Drug Free Schools: By the year 2000, every school in the United States will be free of drugs, violence, and the unauthorized presence of firearms and alcohol, and will offer a disciplined environment conducive to learning.

Teacher Education and Professional Development: By the year 2000, the nation's teaching force will have access to programs for the continued improvement of their professional skills and the opportunity to acquire the knowledge and skills needed to instruct and prepare all American students for the next century.

Parental Participation: By the year 2000, every school will promote partnerships that will increase parental involvement and participation in promoting the social, emotional, and academic growth of children.

Joint Statement by the President and Governors of the United States of America, February 26, 1990. Amended by Congress, March 21, 1994.

Appendix B

Blue Ribbon Schools Program

What is the Blue Ribbon Schools Program?
One of the best ways to learn more about some of the excellent things going on in education in America is to visit schools recognized for their outstanding programs and practices. This is exactly what the Blue Ribbon Schools Program team of experts does, and you can do it too.

While there are a number of recognition programs, the Blue Ribbon Schools Program, administered by the U.S. Department of Education, is the best known. Public and private schools may be nominated from all fifty states, the District of Columbia, Puerto Rico, and the U.S. Virgin Islands. Bureau of Indian Affairs and Department of Defense Dependent Schools may also be nominated. As the program has existed for a number of years, there is a good possibility you could visit one or more schools in your area.

How are Blue Ribbon Schools selected?
Schools are chosen annually from those nominated by each state, which administers its own program. The selection process at the national level is performed by a review panel of educators, college and university staff, officials from all levels of government, school board members, parents, the education press, business and professional representatives, and experts from specific areas of interest.

Following a review of all nominations, site visits are made to those schools most likely to receive recognition. Reports of these visits are then considered by the panel before making recommendations to the U.S. Secretary of Education, who in turn announces the schools selected for recognition.

What factors are considered in selecting schools?
The U.S. Department of Education reports the following "Conditions of Effective Schooling" factors are considered by the review panel in selecting schools:
- ✯ student focus and support
- ✯ challenging standards and curriculum
- ✯ teaching and active learning

- ★ learning-centered school contexts
- ★ professional growth and collaboration
- ★ leadership and organizational vitality
- ★ school, family and community partnerships

The review panel also considers these objective "Indicators of Success:"
- ★ student performance on measures of achievement
- ★ daily student and teacher attendance rates
- ★ students' post graduation pursuits
- ★ school, staff, and student awards
- ★ high student retention/graduation rates

How can I find out the names of Blue Ribbon Schools?

Each year, the U. S. Department of Education, Office of Educational Research and Improvement, publishes an inexpensive updated list of Blue Ribbon Schools. From the program's inception in 1982 through 1996, approximately three thousand schools have been recognized, several more than once.

You can purchase a current copy of *Blue Ribbon Schools, Schools Recognized* from the U.S. Superintendent of Documents. This publication includes all schools recognized, except for the most recent year. You can obtain separate lists of the most recent elementary, or secondary school selections by contacting the Blue Ribbon Schools Program directly. These lists have the added feature of including the principal's name, the school address, and the telephone number to call for an appointment. If you are primarily interested in middle or junior high schools, you should ask for both the elementary and secondary school lists, as these schools can apply for recognition at either level. It would also be reasonable to call the Blue Ribbon Schools Program office and request the names of schools in your state or immediate area.

The Blue Ribbon Schools Program has also recognized outstanding practices in geography, history and the arts, and is providing impetus for school reform in a number of other ways. You may wish to inquire about additional information by contacting the Office of Educational Research and Improvement. For information:

> Blue Ribbon Schools Program
> Office of Educational Research and Improvement
> U.S. Department of Education
> 600 Independence Ave.
> Washington, DC 20208-5572

Call the Information Resources Center (800) USA LEARN for current telephone and fax numbers, addresses, and Internet information for U.S. Department of Education offices. To order publications:

> U.S. Government Printing Office
> Superintendent of Documents
> Mail Stop: SSOP, Washington, DC 20402-9328

This information has been abstracted from documents provided by the U. S. Department of Education, Blue Ribbon Schools Program.

Appendix C

Letters and Memorandums

While the telephone is used most often for communications between parents and school personnel and vice versa, there are times when a letter or memorandum (memo) will better serve your purpose. Examples would be when:

- you are presenting a complicated issue
- you wish to present one, or both sides, of an issue without interruption
- you feel it is necessary to refine your words before the other person hears or reads them
- the person has not returned your phone calls
- you wish to document your position, or record an incident
- you wish to keep a copy for your records
- you desire to provide another person with a copy of the information contained in your letter or memo
- you want the recipient to know you have referenced someone else
- you desire to emphasize the importance of your concerns
- you wish to have your letter read in a meeting
- there is sufficient time to use this method

While letters and memos can serve the same purposes, letters are considered more formal. A letter takes more time to prepare, is usually taken more seriously, and if properly prepared, can elicit a response. Memos, especially those dashed off on a prepared form, can be completed in a relatively short time. They are particularly effective if you wish to gain a person's attention, emphasize a single point, or commend someone for a job well done.

Letters and memos can be used for many purposes. Those received most often by schools fall in the following categories:

- inquiry about a procedure, action, or incident
- request for information on one or more matters

Educational Excellence for Your Child

- reaction to report card grades, class assignment, or the like
- request for a service or consideration
- offer of a service or information
- expression of approval or disapproval of something the school has or has not done
- commendation of a staff member or the school in general
- clarification or summary of conclusions following a meeting or investigation

Some people find it helpful to follow a suggested format when writing a school staff member or government official. If you are one of these people, by all means consider the memo and letter outlines and suggested sentences that follow. Each should be customized to fit your particular situation.

Sample memo

Memo forms are available in most stationary stores. They are also included in many word-processing programs. Memos may be either written clearly or typed. This is an example of the way a memo can be used to communicate with the school.

```
                        M E M O


    To: Mr. Jay Brown
    From: Sarah Perrone
    Date:  March 29, 2001
    Copy to: Mrs. Leader, Principal
    Subject: Gymnastics show

       Tony and I would like to thank you and the other physical
    education teachers for all of the work you did in getting the
    children ready for the gym show. It was a great event! Barb and Sal
    enjoyed it a lot, and are looking forward to perfecting their
    unicycle act even further next year.
```

Appendix C—Letters and Memorandums

Sample letter

In this letter Ms. Clark (a) indicates what has occurred, (b) suggests a solution to the problem, (c) states who should take action, (d) encourages a response, and (e) says something good about the school.

---

111 Oak Street
Any Town, State 00000

October 1, 2001

Richard Brown, Principal
Liberty Middle School
222 Education Way
Any Town, State 00000

Dear Mr. Brown:

    It is my understanding that Mr. Woods, John's teacher, talked with you about the removal of his sweatshirt and calculator from locker #452. John is sure several students who previously had lockers in this area know the combination. I believe the head custodian was asked a week ago to change the combination. This has not happened.

    While Mr. Woods was able to get the items back several days later, it is apparent that either the combination must be changed, or a different locker must be assigned. I trust you will be able to correct this situation without delay. If this cannot be done, please call me at 000-0000.

    While this experience has been an unhappy one for John, I feel that overall, our children are off to a good start this year. We appreciate the efforts of you and your staff.

Sincerely,

Mary Clark

Copy to: Willard Woods, Superintendent

Educational Excellence for Your Child

Sample letter

In this letter Ms. Wright (a) provides background, (b) requests information, (c) tells how it will be used, and (d) informs the principal a particular program seems to be working.

1211 River Street, #26
Big City, State 00000

March 13, 2001

June Ramone, Principal
Center Street High School
123 Circle Drive
Big City, State 00000

Dear Mrs. Ramone:

    I have been setting up an Educational Records File for James. While I find I have copies of his standardized test scores for the middle school and his first year at Center Street High, I do not have an adequate description of these tests, or information as to how the results should be interpreted and used. This information will be helpful as he begins to make college plans.

    I would appreciate it if you would send this information to me. As I was a school guidance secretary for five years, I am quite sure I can understand the explanations. If I have any questions, after reviewing the material, I will give you a call. Also, if it is necessary to return any of the booklets or information, I would be glad to do so.

    James has done well at Center Street. Certainly your monthly meetings with his small group have added to his success. I feel he will do even better next year.

Sincerely,

Nancy Wright
Tel. 000-0000

Appendix C—Letters and Memorandums

Sample letter

In this letter, Mr. Parent (a) points out and documents the problem, (b) indicates serious concern, (c) shows he has made an effort to get action, and (d) makes it clear a meeting will be unnecessary if the plan is promptly implemented.

1244 Lake Road
Mount Barren, State 00000

November 1, 2001

Donald Barnes, Superintendent
Mount Barren School District
777 Winding Road
Mount Barren, State 00000

Dear Dr. Barnes:

You will recall we met in August to formalize Kerry's program for the year. I asked you to attend this meeting as there had been some difficulty obtaining services last year. Several others were present, including Kerry's teacher, Richard Howe; School Psychologist, Maria Esteves; and Principal Sarah Richman.

During this meeting, it was agreed that Kerry would receive speech four times a week, remedial reading daily, and thirty minutes a day on the computer, focusing on math. These services were included in his IEP and were to begin in September.

At the conclusion of this meeting I was assured this plan would be implemented. As I told you last Tuesday on the telephone, he has yet to receive speech and remedial reading more than twice a week.

Dr. Wolff and I would like to discuss this matter with you prior to the Special Education Committee's next meeting. If Kerry's program has been fully implemented prior to that time, this will of course, be unnecessary.

I have long been a supporter of the many good things going on in the Mount Barren schools, but could not be more disappointed in the District's failure to deliver these important services. I trust this problem will be resolved promptly.

Sincerely,

Fred Parent
Tel. 000-0000

cc: Richard Howe, Grade 5
    Maria Esteves, School Psychologist
    Sarah Richman, Principal
    Harold Wolff, Special Ed. Committee

Educational Excellence for Your Child

Suggested sentences for letters or memos

If you would like some help in expressing your thoughts, ideas, or concerns, you might consider using one of the following statements to begin your first sentence.

- It has come to my attention that _____.

- I would like you to know how much Josh enjoys the (art, science, math, music, etc.) enrichment program. He has learned new skills and increased his understanding of what has long been one of his favorite activities.

- During a recent meeting (name of person) indicated that (child's name, the school, the curriculum, the school day, other students in the class) _____.

- I would like to take this opportunity to (commend, express my disappointment, point out, make you aware of) _____.

- While reading *Educational Excellence for Your Child*, it soon became apparent the author feels parents should play a significant role in their children's education. This raises the question as to whether Valley Elementary School _____.

- As the leader of a youth group I have often had the opportunity to listen to children talk about their school. I would like you to know _____.

- It is my understanding that the following information _____.

- A recent newspaper article raises the question as to whether the District (has a policy, has failed to recognize, is interested in, has ever considered, realizes the importance of, has received the credit it deserves) _____.

- As a parent of a student who will be attending the middle school next year, I would like to know _____.

- As I have been unable to reach you by telephone, I am writing to remind you _____.

- While developing an "Education Action Plan" with Kelley, it occurred to me that the school could help her meet her long term objective of (becoming a professional dancer, studying computer science, teaching school, etc.) if her schedule included _____.

Resources

To help you become better informed, suggested books, magazines, and other resources have been included in this section. Some items can be obtained from your library/media center or a book store while others are available by computer or mail. You will find a brief summary of the contents of each book and magazine. There are also suggestions for using a personal computer, and the Internet, to locate and obtain resource material. Particular attention has been given to the information available through the Educational Resources Information Center (ERIC). An increasing number of parents are realizing that this comprehensive database is their best source of current information on education and other subjects related to children.

Kay Kimball Gruder has reviewed resources and assisted in the preparation of this section. As a college educator, she helps students acquire the knowledge, skills, attitudes, and practical experiences needed to progress smoothly from high school through college, and on to the world of work. She is familiar with changes that are occurring in schools at all levels, and continues to be an astute observer of parents, children, and teachers, as they participate in the teaching/learning process. She is presently serving on a school council.

Books

The following books have been selected as they can help you achieve your goals of educational excellence and future success for your child. They provide useful information on one or more of the following topics:

- information that will help you better understand your family, child, or school
- steps you can take to improve your preschool or school age child's physical or mental health and abilities, and readiness to learn
- practical things you can do at home or in the community to help your child become better educated
- help you negotiate the maze that often surrounds special education and enrichment programs
- suggestions to improve your child's school

Most of these books have been published in paperback. They should be available from bookstores and libraries.

Adler, Mortimer J., *Reforming Education: The Opening of the American Mind*. New York: Collier Books, 1990.
> One of America's foremost teachers, Adler addresses a variety of controversies about what should be taught in elementary school, high school and college. He also provides insight into how academic material can be presented to ensure optimal learning.

Anderson, Winifred; Stephen Chitwood; and Deidre Hayden, *Negotiating the Special Education Maze: A Guide for Parents and Teachers*. Rockville, Md.: Woodbine House, 1990.
> This book is a comprehensive, step-by-step guide for parents of children with special needs. It helps parents to become effective advocates for their children.

Bennett, Stephen and Ruth Bennett, *365 Outdoor Activities You Can Do with Your Child*. Holbrook, Mass.: Bob Adams, 1993.
> Suggestions for a variety of fun, educational, and inspiring outdoor activities.

Canter, Lee and Lee Hausner, *Homework Without Tears*. New York: HarperPerennial, 1987.
> A parent's guide for motivating children to do homework and to succeed in school.

Cartwright, Madeline and Michael D'Orso, *For the Children: Lessons from a Visionary Principal*. New York: Doubleday, 1993.
> An inspiring account of how a principal, parents, and teachers turned a troubled, inner-city school around.

Collins, Marva and Civia Tamarkin, *Marva Collins' Way: Returning to Excellence in Education*. New York: Putnam, 1990.
> Describes the founding and development of Westside Preparatory School in Chicago. Shares information about the obstacles and successes encountered along the way.

Cookson, Peter W., *School Choice: The Struggle for the Soul of American Education*. New Haven: Yale University Press, 1994.
> Clarifies the many issues surrounding the school choice topic, and examines a variety of school choice plans around the country.

Dodd, Anne Wescott, *A Parent's Guide to Innovative Education*. Chicago: The Noble Press, 1992.
> Explains innovative classroom practices and suggests how parents can work with teachers, schools, and their children to maximize learning.

Dunn, Rita S.; Kenneth Dunn; and Donald Treffinger, *Bringing Out the Giftedness in Your Child: Nurturing Every Child's Unique Strengths, Talents, and Potential*. New York: John Wiley & Sons, 1992.
> Tips on how to identify your child's learning style and optimal learning environment. Identifies how to get the most out of your child's school years.

Ellison, Sheila and Judith Gray, *365 Afterschool Activities: TV-Free Fun for Kids Ages 7-12*. Naperville, Ill.: Sourcebooks, 1995.
> Describes a variety of enjoyable and educational after school activities for elementary and early middle school age children.

Ellison, Sheila and Judith Gray, *365 Days of Creative Play: for Children 2 Years & Up*. Naperville, Ill.: Sourcebooks, 1995.
> Suggests activities using common household items that encourage creativity in children age two and up.

Eyre, Linda and Richard Eyre, *Teaching Your Children Values*. A Fireside Book. New York: Simon & Schuster, 1993.
> Month-by-month program of family and value building activities, exercises, and games for children of all ages.

Faber, Adele and Elaine Mazlish, *How to Talk So Kids Can Learn — at Home and in School*. New York: Rawson Associates, 1995.
> Guides parents and teachers through a technique that will help any parent or teacher talk so children can learn.

Fiske, Edward B., *Smart Schools, Smart Kids: Why Do Some Schools Work?* New York: Simon & Schuster, 1992.
> Profiles schools across the country and describes a variety of successful programs and how they work.

Fuller, Cheri, *Unlocking Your Child's Learning Potential: How to Equip Kids to Succeed in School & Life*. Colorado Springs, Colo.: NavPress, 1994.
> Helps parents understand their child's strengths. Tells how to make the most of them to be successful.

Gardner, Howard, *The Unschooled Mind: How Children Think and How Schools Should Teach*. London: Fontana, 1993, 1991.
> Identifies how our minds and our natural patterns of learning are ill-suited to current educational materials, practices, and institutions which we encounter.

Golant, Susan K. and Mitch Golant, *Kindergarten: It Isn't What It Used to Be: Getting Your Child Ready for the Positive Experience of Education*. Los Angeles: Lowell House, 1990.
> Offers parents insights into preparing a child for kindergarten. Highlights different kindergarten classroom setups.

Harrison, Charles Hampton, *Grade Your Child's School*. Hawthorne, N.J.: Career Press, 1995.
> Information on school programs. Guides one through the process of evaluating schools.

Hirsch, Jr. E. D., *What Your 1st Grader Needs to Know: Fundamentals of a Good First-Grade Education,* vol. 1. New York: Delta Trade Paperback Books, 1993, 1991.
> This is Book 1 in the grade 1-6 Core Knowledge Series. Each book presents the fundamentals of an appropriate education for the grade described.

Lengel, James G. and Diane S. Kendall, *Kids, Computers and Homework: How You and Your Kids Can Make Schoolwork a Learning Adventure*. New York: Random House, 1995.
> A guide to help children get the full benefits of a home computer. Suggestions for equipping a computer and selecting resource materials. Identifies best Internet services for children.

Leonhardt, Mary, *Parents Who Love Reading, Kid's Who Don't: How It Happens and What You Can Do About It.* New York: Crown Trade Paperbacks, 1995.
>   Tells why many children are not avid readers. Describes what parents can do to awaken, or reawaken reading in a child.

Louv, Richard, *101 Things You Can Do for Our Children's Future.* New York: Anchor Books, 1994.
>   Offers practical suggestions and describes techniques that parents can use to improve the environment for children and families.

Martz, Larry, *Making Schools Better: How Parents and Teachers across the Country are Taking Action — and How You Can Too.* New York: Times Books, 1992.
>   Takes a look at what others are doing to improve their schools. Describes what you can do.

McEwan, Elaine K., *The Parent's Guide to Solving School Problems: Kindergarten through Middle School.* Wheaton, Ill.: H. Shaw Publishers, 1992.
>   Provides advice about, and resources for, discovering more about school structure, the learning process, and your child's needs.

Novick, Barbara Z., *Why Is My Child Having Trouble at School? A Parent's Guide to Learning Disabilities.* New York: G. P. Putnam's Sons, 1995.
>   Information on how to recognize problems and effectively deal with them. Tells how to obtain the help your child needs to succeed.

Otterbourg, Susan D., *The Education Today Parent Involvement Handbook.* Boston: Education Today Publishing Group, 1994.
>   Helps parents understand the need for involvement in their children's education. Provides practical suggestions and helpful resources for parents who want to play a greater role.

Perone, Vito, *101 Educational Conversations with Your Kindergartener- First Grader.* New York: Chelsea House, 1993.
>   One of several books in a series, each appropriate for a different grade level. Focuses on conversations that will help you and your child discuss what he or she is doing in school.

Peterson's Summer Opportunities for Kids and Teenagers. Princeton, N.J.: Peterson's Guides, 1996.
>   Identifies hundreds of opportunities in which children can participate. Includes information about summer camps, academic programs, sports clinics, travel adventures, and community service projects throughout the U.S. and around the world.

Rein, RaeLynne P. and Rachel Rein, *How to Develop Your Child's Gifts and Talents during the Elementary Years.* Los Angeles: Lowell House, 1994.
>   A how-to guide to help parents look for and encourage individual strengths and talents that each child has. Includes strategies for stimulating critical and creative thinking abilities.

Seymour, Daniel; Terry Seymour; and 30 Teachers of the Year, *America's Best Classrooms: How Award-Winning Teachers Are Shaping Our Children's Future.* Princeton, N.J.: Peterson's Guides, 1992, 1993.
> Describes how thirty of America's best teachers are making the education system work. You may want to ask about other education, family, test prep, and career books by this education and career publisher.

Silver, Larry B., MD., *The Misunderstood Child: A Guide for Parents of Children with Learning Disabilities.* Blue Ridge Summit, Pa.: TAB Books, 1992.
> Guide for parents who want to understand and help their children. Identifies strategies to implement at home and school.

Smutny, Joan F.; Kathleen Veenker; and Stephen Veenker, *Your Gifted Child: How to Recognize and Develop the Special Talents in Your Child from Birth to Age Seven.* New York: Ballantine Books, 1991.
> Focuses on ways to recognize your child's strengths. Suggests strategies to develop them at home and school.

Tomano, Janice, *Enhance Your Children's Development.* Berne, Ind.: HIS Publishing, 1995.
> Includes information on preparing your child for school and things you can do at home during your child's school years to promote success.

Tovray, Sandy and Maria Wilson-Portuondo, *Helping Your Special Needs Child: A Practical and Reassuring Resource Guide.* Rocklin, Calif.: Prima Publishing, 1995.
> Provides insights, options and answers that will help parents attend to the needs of their children.

Magazines

Despite the apparent concern of many Americans about the quality of elementary and secondary education in the United States, a very limited number of popular magazines devote more than minimal space to this subject. As you might expect, those that do include articles on education tend to be the magazines that focus on parents and children.

The magazines selected for this bibliography can help you improve your family life and raise your children. They usually include one or more articles on education and some feature back-to-school information during late summer. Most focus on a particular age group, often younger children, while others cover all ages. Some magazines may be available at your local library/media center, others can be previewed prior to purchasing at newsstands. Information on the contents of some issues may be found on the Internet.

There are a few general appeal magazines that include articles on children, parenting, families, and education. Examples would be *Better Homes and Gardens, Family Circle,* and *Redbook.* The September issue of *Family Circle* features a back-to-school section. It is, of course, necessary to review individual issues of magazines to determine if they include information you might use.

News magazines like *U.S. News and World Report*, *Time*, and *Newsweek* include articles on children, education, and social change. They are particularly good at presenting issues, interpreting research results, and raising questions that might be of interest to parents seeking excellence.

Another source of current education and parenting information is the Sunday newspaper magazine supplement. *Parade Magazine*, the *New York Times Magazine*, *USA Weekend*, and other national and regional supplements present educational reports and discuss issues of interest to parents. Most local newspapers regularly include school news. They also feature education, or include an education section, prior to the reopening of school in August or September.

Teachers receive professional journals and other publications on teaching, learning, children, and schools. Some of this information could be quite useful in your efforts to achieve educational excellence for your child. Most teachers would be pleased to share their journals with you. If you decide you would like to receive your own copies of a publication on a regular basis, a subscription is probably available without joining the professional association. Also, you could ask if your child's school has a professional library/media center, or has other materials of interest to you. You might be pleased with the resources you will find.

Most parents, or parents-to-be, can benefit from reading at least one of the following magazines on a regular basis. Unfortunately, some are displayed only at larger newsstands. If you don't see the magazine you want, you may need to ask to have it ordered. Fortunately, you can obtain any of the magazines listed by subscription. The telephone number following the mailing address is for subscription information. It is recommended that you call rather than write for current prices, and to hasten the arrival of your first issue.

Black Child
P.O. 12048
Atlanta, GA 30355
(404) 364-9195

> Focuses on the special needs and concerns of parents and others who work with African-American children. Includes current information on nutrition, health and safety, home life, and education. Graphs, charts, and checklists of value to all parents are included.

Child
P.O. Box 3176
Harlan, IA 51593-0367
(800) 777-0222

> Focuses on child development, parenting, health, family life, and living in today's world. Articles range from education to electronic media and clothing to creativity. Provides valuable information and helpful suggestions for parents of preschool through preteen children.

Childsplay
663 Dickinson St.
Suite 10
Springfield, MA 01108-9976
(413) 733-8055

> Regional publication for New England parents wishing to enrich their children's education through discussion, reading, carrying out projects, and attending events. Recommends books and other resources for parents and children. Each bimonthly issue includes calendars of interesting things to see and do in New England. Your region may also have one or more publications that focus on children.

Early Childhood Today
Scholastic, Inc.
P.O. Box 54813
Boulder, CO 80323-4813
(800) 544-2917

> Published by Scholastic, a familiar name to millions of parents, children and teachers; this publication serves as a link between home and school. Information on child development, teaching, learning, health, and useful resources fills each issue. Emphasis is on age six and under.

Family Fun
P.O. Box 10161
Des Moines, IA 50340-0161
(800) 289-4849

> Features practical suggestions on parenting, education, hobbies, games, clothing, collecting, foods, crafts, and travel. Includes reviews of books, videos, and music. Particularly good for parents of elementary and preschool children. September issue features "Back to School" and "Learning Fun."

Green Teacher
P.O. Box 1431
Lewiston, NY 14092
    or
95 Robert Street
Toronto, ON, Canada M5S 2K5
(416) 960-1244

> A magazine on education and the environment. Valuable resource for teachers, parents, and other adults working with children of all ages in North America. Includes ideas for lesson plans. Introduces the reader to dozens of books and other resources available by mail or on the Internet.

Mothering
P.O. Box 1690
Santa Fe, NM 87504-9774
(800) 984-8116

> Stresses the importance of parenting and family life. Provides practical information on mothering, health, and learning. Suggestions for raising children of all ages, with emphasis on early childhood. Includes resource recommendations for parents and children.

Our Children
National PTA Orders
135 S. LaSalle St., Dept. 1927
Chicago, IL 60674-1927
(312) 549-3253

> Includes education news, informative feature stories, and ideas you can use. No advertising. Offers suggestions for parent involvement in education. Describes new resource materials available from PTA and other sources. Summarizes recent PTA activities.

Parenting
Subscription Department
P.O. Box 52424
Boulder, CO 80323-2424
(800) 234-0847

> Includes articles on parenting, learning and education, communicating, health and nutrition and new products. Special reports and information on research developments. For parents of children from birth to ten years, with emphasis under age six.

Parents
P.O. Box 3042
Harlan, IA 51537
(800) 727-3682

> Focuses on parents and children. Features articles on the development and behavior of preschool, school age and adolescent children. Includes information on child care, relationships, parent-child activities, nutrition, clothing, health, and education. Recent research findings of interest to parents are included.

Working Mother
Customer Service Manager
P.O. Box 5239
Harlan, IA 51593-0739
(800) 627-0690

> Focuses on the interests and concerns of working mothers. Presents practical suggestions that mothers can follow to be more effective in balancing work and child rearing. Articles include advice on resources available, and how to make use of them.

Other resources

Many public and private organizations and governmental agencies have information that can help you in working with your child and the school. A phone call to your child's teacher, guidance counselor, or principal; a visit to your library; or an Internet inquiry will give you some insights as to what is available. The following organizations should be kept in mind as you search for information.

- businesses and industries
- colleges and universities
- nonprofit organizations
- foundations

- health organizations
- libraries
- radio and television stations and networks like PBS
- support groups
- professional associations
- PTA
- publishers
- religious organizations
- state education departments
- U.S. Department of Education, Office of Educational Research and Improvement
- U.S. Government Printing Office

Materials available

The following materials are often available to the general public at nominal cost. As when buying any item, it is best to preview the item before purchasing.

annual reports	newsletters
bibliographies	pamphlets
books	periodicals
conference reports	research reports
instructional guides	studies
monographs	tapes and videos

Some organizations publish catalogs listing their resources. Others advertise in newsletters, professional journals, or magazines. Still others depend on the media, word of mouth, home pages or electronic bulletin boards to let parents know they have information on children or education. There are hundreds of thousands of items available.

Computers and the Internet

A computer with access to an information provider and the Internet can link you up with universities, museums, library/media centers, businesses, governments, and individuals around the world. This has become the tool of choice for many who are seeking information. You don't necessarily need to own a personal computer to use these services. Library/media centers, educational institutions, recreation centers, and friends can often provide access to the Internet, and the World Wide Web. There is a good chance that if you make a few inquiries you will not only locate a computer that is "online," but also the help needed to begin searching.

Access to information is what the Internet is all about, and there are definitely growing volumes of information pertaining to education, parenting, and children. In accessing the Internet, one must be a wise consumer, remembering that anyone can display information or sell products and services. The phrase "let the consumer beware" is very important to keep in mind as you access this ever expanding resource. Additionally, you will want to monitor your child's use of the Internet as he or she, without supervision, can quickly access information that is age inappropriate, violent, or sexual in nature. As with other forms of media, parental guidance is often key to the child appropriately using it.

When using the Internet to discover education-related resources, you might want to consider using one or more of the following search terms:

- children
- disabilities
- educational resources
- education (K-12)
- (ERIC) Educational Resources Information Center
- improving education
- kids
- parenting
- PTA (National Parent-Teacher Association)
- schools
- subject areas like math, science, history, and the like
- U.S. Department of Education

The options for search are virtually limitless. Use your imagination, and the chances are you will find what you seek. To help assure that the information you access is "good" information, whenever possible, consult other sources or experts in the field to learn about its validity and integrity. Your child's teacher, principal or guidance counselor might have recommendations about appropriate Internet sites. Reference librarians at schools, colleges or public libraries, state departments of education, U.S. Department of Education, or relevant professional associations might also be able to make recommendations.

Educational Resources Information Center

The Educational Resources Information Center (ERIC) is a comprehensive database of materials pertaining to education and education-related issues. Materials most often include topical brochures of interest to parents and educators, bibliographies, research reports, newsletters, referral services, and a variety of other educational resources. The system is supported by the U.S. Department of Education, Office of Educational Research and Improvement. It is a system that includes multiple clearinghouses, each providing information relevant to specific issues. The following clearinghouses might be of particular interest:

- Assessment and Evaluation
- Disabilities and Gifted Education
- Educational Management
- Elementary and Early Childhood Education
- Information and Technology
- Languages and Linguistics

- Reading, English, and Communication
- Rural Education and Small Schools
- Science, Mathematics, and Environmental Education
- Social Studies/Social Science Education
- Urban Education

Additionally, the ERIC Clearinghouse on Urban Education, and the ERIC Clearinghouse on Elementary and Early Childhood Education, along with a number of other collaborating organizations have developed the National Parent Information Network (NPIN). This network is aimed at providing information to parents and those who work with parents. Information is relevant to parenting, parent-education partnerships, and other areas that could help you do some of the things you wish to accomplish.

Some material within ERIC is provided free of charge, while other information and materials are available at cost. You can access ERIC in a variety of ways, including telephone, the Internet, microfiche and using CD-ROM. You might want to check your local library to find how you can best access this comprehensive resource.

Examples of resources from various sources

The following newsletters and other publications are just a few examples of what you might find after spending a few minutes with an interested friend, your local library/media specialist, PTA president, or on the Internet.

Consortium Connections
The Children, Youth, and Family Consortium
12 McNeal Hall
1985 Buford Avenue
University of Minnesota
St. Paul, MN 55108
(612) 626-1212

> Quarterly newsletter of a consortium developed to bring together University of Minnesota staff and community resources to enhance the ability of individuals and organizations to deal with health, education, and social policy issues. Provides research-based information. Maintains electronic clearinghouse. Check other universities for similar organizations.

Education Today
The Educational Publishing Group, Inc.
Suite 1215
20 Park Plaza
Boston, MA 02116
(617) 542-6500

> Newsletter published eight times a year to help parents support the education of their children. Practical suggestions for local involvement, working with children, and encouraging success. Includes research results, presents issues, and recommends resources for children.

Healthy Kids: Birth-3
Healthy Kids: 3-10
Cahners Publishing
475 Park Ave, S
New York, NY 10016
(212) 689-3600

> Published three times a year. Provides information on keeping your child safe and healthy. Tells how to help your child develop as a positive person. Can often be previewed in physicians' offices.

National Congress of Parents and Teachers (PTA)
National PTA Orders
135 S. LaSalle St., Dept. 1860
Chicago, IL 60674-1860
(312) 549-3253

> Provides current information directly related to teaching, learning, children and schools. Catalog of books, posters, booklets, brochures and videos available. Some publications are offered in Spanish. Maintains "Children First," a World Wide Web interactive on-line forum for all issues affecting children. Headings direct users to topics ranging from "Raising Educated Kids" to "Parent Involvement."

National Parent Information Network (NPIN)
ERIC/EECE
University of Illinois
805 W. Pennsylvania Ave.
Urbana, IL 61801-4897
(800) 583-4135
       or
ERIC/Urban Education
Teachers College, Columbia University
Institute for Urban and Minority Education
Main Hall, Room 303, Box 40
525 W. 120th St.
New York, NY 10027-9998
(800) 601-4868

> Provides information and communications capabilities to parents and those who work with parents. Information available by telephone, mail, or computer via World Wide Web. Maintains "Resources for Parents" and "Parents AskERIC" question-answering service. Newsletter available.

Parent Talk Newsletter
The National Parenting Center
22801 Ventura Blvd. Suite 110
Woodland Hills, CA 91367
(800) 753-6667

> Monthly newsletter featuring columns written by child-rearing panelists. Includes latest information and advice on medical, behavioral and educational topics. Dialog forums for those interested in talking with other parents. Can be accessed via America Online and the Internet.

Parent's Digest
Ladies Home Journal Parent's Digest
100 Park Avenue
New York, NY 10017

> Published annually (fall/winter). Available at newsstands. Features carefully selected articles and information from previously published books and periodicals by today's experts on children and parenting. Offers advice on health, education, and training with focus on elementary age children and younger. Includes reviews of books, other resources, and television, music, and movies.

Pediatrics For Parents, The Newsletter for Caring Parents
Pediatrics for Caring Parents, Inc.
P.O. Box 1069, Bangor, ME 04401
(207) 942-6212

> Monthly newsletter on children's health. Written in language that parents can understand. Provides useful information on diseases; including causes, prevention, and treatment. Includes research findings.

The Single Parent
Parents Without Partners, Inc.
8807 Colesville Rd.
Silver Springs, MD 20910
(301) 588-9354

> Available by mail, six issues a year. Sample issue can be obtained at nominal cost. Distributed to "Parents Without Partners" members. Contains articles on effective programs for single parents; how to raise children alone, legal issues, career development, travel and the like.

Smart Parenting
Meigher Communications
100 Avenue of the Americas
New York, NY 10013
(212) 219-7444

> Newsletter published ten times a year. Reviews thousands of sources and reports information of interest and value to parents of children up to age ten. Practical suggestions on parenting, health and safety, learning, electronics and media, and enrichment activities. Available at some newsstands.

Educational Excellence for Your Child

U.S. Department of Education
Information Resource Center
600 Independence Ave., S.W.
Washington, DC 20202
(800) USA-LEARN

Provides easy access to current information on education. Opportunity to talk with U.S. Department of Education specialists about current programs like Goals 2000, Satellite Town Meeting, Family Involvement Partnership for Learning, or department projects that might be initiated in the future. You can also talk with a publications specialist about ordering publications or videos. When using mail, include name of office on envelope.

Index

- A -
abilities, mental, 44, 45
accomplish goals of this book, xxi, xxiii
action plan. *See* education action plan
activities and interests, 43
activities and resources in the community that increase learning, 193–208
activities in the home that increase learning, 163–192
adult to student ratio, 134
advantages/disadvantages, school survey form, 91
advocate for child, xix
advocate for education, 64
African proverb, village raising child, 112
agenda for school visit, 87
alcohol, 152
appearance of, excellence, 26
appendices, 215–224
asking for information, 30
assessing progress and moving on, 209–214
assigning students, 103
assistance from friends, relatives and professionals, 30
attending, second-level involvement, 127–129
attention span, 59, 60, 69, 153, 154
attitude
    "can do," 154
    of students, 27
attributes
    common attributes of successful schools, 27
    personal, 141
author, about the, 253–254
authority of principals, guidance counselors, teachers, 28

- B -
"back off," knowing when to, 116
backpack, 147
basic school curriculum, 64
Better Business Bureau, 72
bibliography, *see* resources

birth order of children, 31
blue-ribbon schools, 27, 217, 219
board, serving on, 130
book bag, 147
book resources, 225–229
books in home learning center, 158, 159
Boy Scouts, 141
budget process of schools, 131
bulletin board, 124
Bureau of Indian Affairs, 63
bureaucracy, school as, xx, *see also* educational bureaucracy
bus utilization, school day, 69
business
    school/business partnerships, 138
    schools are in business to serve the public, 28

- C -

calendar, 67–69
    See also curriculum, resources and school calendar
    comparing differences in, 76
calling schools, things to do before, 74
"can do" attitude, 154
CD-ROM, 159
challenges
    family, 139, 141
    school, 140, 141
Chamber of Commerce, 71, 72
change
    dealing with, 139–146
    takes time, 116
chaperone, volunteering, 135
checking information, 123
child advocates, xix
children
    See also Know Your Child Worksheet
    See also optimal learning
    average children require extra parent effort, 29
    birth order of, 31
    comprehensive look at, 36, 43
    determining your child's needs, 43–53
    discussing goals with, 99, 100
    education of our nation's children, 25
    exploitation, 142, 143
    functioning ability, 44
    getting to know your child better, 33–41
    involvement in your child's school, 121–132
    key skills, 142, 143
    know who is supervising your, 143
    Know Your Child Worksheet, 36, 47
    most difference are normal, 31
    realizing each child is different, 31
    responsibility for your child's education, 28
    role of school in educating, 64, 65
    schedule of classes, 69

Index

    schools serving, xx, 30
    set high goals, 30
    success indicators, 211, 212
child's interest interview, 33, 35, 36, 40, 41
child's records. *See* records
child's strengths and weaknesses, realism is recognizing, 31
cigarettes, 152
class schedules, 69
class size, 56, 58
classrooms, overcrowded, 59
clerical aide, 135
cocurricular activities, interest in, 126, 132, 143, 144
cocurricular activity advisor, 135
collaboration, 144
committee, serving on, 130
communications, effective, 29
community
    activities and resources that increase learning, 193–208
    educating, 130, 131
    improving education outside of school, 29
    raising a child, 112
    role of, 25
    school programs, before and after, 69, 70
    society and schools, 214
    society's problems, 132
    volunteer, 137
community as school resource, 66, 67
comprehensive list of sources, 71
comprehensive look at your child, 36
comprehensive program, 64
comprehensive school evaluation, 74
computer filing system, 34
computer information services, 159, 160
computers and online services, 65, 125, 130, 160
computers and the Internet,
    resources, 125, 233–234
computers, home pages, 29
computers in education, 58, 62, 65, 66, 155, 159
conducting the child's interest interview, 36
conferences, 113, 114, 129
consumer
    parent, xix, 46, 56, 62
    wise, 46, 56, 62, 122
consumer of education, xix
contacts, sources of information about schools, 71, 72
cost of education, 131
counselor, volunteering as, 135, 136
criticism, 154
curricula, 27
curriculum
    See also resources
    importance of, 64
    resources and school calendar, 63–72

241

- D -

dating the information in filing system, 35
day. *See* school day
definitions
    average student, 61
    children considered average, 29
    curriculum, syllabi, 63
    educational excellence, 26
    several meanings of words, 30
Department of Defense, 63
determinations regarding school visit, 75–78
determining community activities, 193, 194
determining progress, 209
determining your child's needs, 43–53
difference, most are normal, 31
different, realizing each child is, 31
discussing goals with child and others, 99, 100
discussing problems, 112
discussion interview format, 36
distraction, 59
district offices, 71
documents. *See* records
do's and don'ts, school visit, 89
drugs, 152

- E -

educating children, role of school in, 64, 65
education costs, 131
    historical occurrence of, 56
    national goals, 215
    responsibility for your child's education, 28
    U.S. responsibility for, 63
education action plan
    developing, 101–110
    implementing, 111–119
education action plan, 46, 92, 100, 210
education advocate, 64
educational bureaucracy, understanding, 73
educational excellence, 25, 26, 97
    See also excellence
    beginning to obtain, xxi
    introduction to, 25–32
educational expertise, 27
educational records file, 33–35, 37, 75, 101, 113
educators, obligation of to listen to and work with parents, 28
effective ways to use home learning center, 160–162
efforts of parents, average children requirements, 29
efforts of teachers, 27
emotional stability, 154
employers, importance of monitoring, 122
encyclopedias, CD-ROM, 159
enrichment programs, information about, 77
environment
    home learning center, 155, 156
    realizing each child is different, 31

equal access to educational opportunity, 111
equipment, home learning center, 157
evolution of the family, 31
excellence
    See also educational excellence
    appearance of, 26
    future prospects for, 214
    identifying, 26
    in education/life, 97
    journey/destination, 55, 209
    moving toward, achieving, 213, 214
    obtaining need not be difficult, 29
    picture, 26
    some excellence exists in every school, 27
    steps to physical excellence, 150–153
exercise, 150
expectations, school visit, 77
exploitation, 142, 143

- F -

family challenges, 139, 141
feedback, where to get, 210
feeling valued, 147
filing system, 34
first-level involvement, reading/phoning, 123–127
folders, 34, 35, 113, 157
forms. See specific type
formula for school improvement, 212
four 4-H, 138, 141
functioning ability of child, 44
furniture, home learning center, 156
future
    investment in, 157
    prospects for excellence, 214
    volunteer in future school, 137

- G -

getting feedback, where, 210
getting the most out of this book, xxiii
getting to know your child better, 33–41
getting your child's education action plan implemented, 111–119
Girl Scouts, 141
goals
    accomplish goals of this book, xxi, xxiii
    background information on, 97–100
    education action plan and, 102, 103
    look at your child, 43, 45
    national education, 215
    setting high goals, 30
grades included in schools, 56, 57
guidance counselor, 29, 58, 128, 210

- H -

hall plans, school subdivisions, 58
handbooks for parents, 29, 71

handicapping conditions, 35
health, 151
help, offering to, 115
helping others achieve excellence, 213
heredity, realizing each child is different, 31
High Interest Community Activities and Resources List,
    listed alphabetically, 195–208
        auctions
        camping (day or sleep-over)
        clubs/community groups/religious organizations
        concerts and performances
        enrichment programs
        fairs/expositions/field trips
        hobby shows and conventions
        lessons and courses
        library/media centers
        museums/zoos/preserves
        open houses
        physical fitness/athletics/recreation (home and community)
        politics
        safety/survival skills
        shopping
        summer school
        theater
        travel
        tutoring
        volunteering
        work
High Interest Home Activities List,
    mathematics, 167
    reading, 166
    science, 168
    writing, 167
    listed alphabetically, 169–192
        air/space
        animals
        art
        assembling
        astronomy
        automobiles
        baking and cooking
        business
        calendar
        chemistry
        child care
        chores
        collecting
        communications
        computers
        conservation
        constructing
        contests
        coupon clipping
        crafts
        educational games

Index

       educational toys
       electricity and electronics
       entertaining guests
       gardening
       language
       library/media center
       magic
       model building
       music
       photography
       physical fitness/athletics/recreation (home and community)
       puzzles
       radio/television
       recycling
       repairing and maintaining
       scrapbook and family records
       sewing
       shortwave radio
       show and tell
       weather
historical occurrence of education, 56
historical records file. *See* educational records file
holidays, closing schools on, 67
home activities that increase learning, 163–192
home atmosphere, positive, 146
home learning center, 154–162
home library/media center, 159
home pages, computers, 29
home-based volunteers, 137
house plans, school subdivisions, 56, 58
human resources, 66
hygiene, 152

- I -

ideal teaching/learning situation, 59
IEP. *See* individualized education plans
impressions
       of others, 45
       personal, 36
improvement in school, formula for, 212
independent learning, 56, 62
indicators of progress, 211–213
individualized education plans, 61,
individualized instruction, 56, 61
inferiority, feelings of, 28
information
       about community activities, 193
       about schools, sources of, 71, 72
       asking for, 30
       background information on goals, 97–100
       checking, 123
       computer services, 159, 160
       from know your child worksheet, 45
       separated and divorced parents, 125, 126
       world, 65

in-service education, 56
instructor/coach, volunteering, 136
intelligence tests, 44, 45
interest interview, child's, 33, 35, 36
interests and activities, 43
intermediate-term goals, 102, 104
Internet and computers, resources, 125, 233–234
interviews, child's interest interview, 33, 35, 36, 40, 41
introduction to child's interest interview, 35, 36
introduction to educational excellence, 25–32
introduction to parent recommendations summary, 45, 46
inventory form, 35
investment in the future, 157
involvement in your child's school, 121–132

- J -
journey to excellence, 55
judgmental during interview, refrain from, 36

- K -
Kennedy, President John F., 97
know who is supervising your child, 143
know your child worksheet, 36, 43, 45, 47–51
knowing when to "back off," 116
knowing your child better, 33–41
knowledge, value of, 44

- L -
labeling folders, 35
laboratory assistant, 136
language barriers, 44
language skills, 35
large schools, 58
learning
    See also home learning center
    See also optimal learning
    community activities and resources that increase learning, 193–208
    factors affecting, 59
    style, 40, 41, 43, 44, 65
    time in school vs. time learning, 70
legal action, 118
leisure, quality and use, 31, 133, 134
letters, 219–224
library/media aide, 134, 136
library/media centers, 65, 77, 134
    home library/media center, 159
limitation of this book, xx
live to work, 134
long-term goals, 102, 104
look at your child, 43
looking at the organization of schools, 55–62
lost opportunities, 126

- M -

magazine resources, 229–232
making mistakes, 164
making wise choices, 160
materials, home learning center, 158, 159
materials, resources, 233
meeting your child after activities, 144
memorandums, 116, 117, 124, 219–224
mentally ready to learn, 59, 153, 154
mentor, volunteering, 136
metropolitan areas, population, 67
middle child, 31
minimizing serious weaknesses, 31
mistakes, making, 164
modular schedules, 70
monitor, volunteering, 136
monitoring, 118, 119, 122, 123, 209
moral values, 141
moving, changing schools, 56, 64
music, home learning center, 161

- N -

National Congress of Parents and Teachers (PTA), 130
national education goals, 215
nature vs. nurture, realizing each child is different, 31
needs, determining your child's, 43–53
newsletters, value of, 135
newspaper, source of school information, 71
noise, home learning center, 161
notices, 124
nurturing, 31
nutrition, 151

- O -

obligation of educators to listen to and work with parents, 28
oldest child, 31
only child, 31
open house, 128
  See also school visits
opportunities for school volunteers, 67, 133–138
opportunities lost, 126
optimal learning, 68, 147–154
organization of schools, 55–62, 112
orientation program, 29
Our Children, 130
outside of school, improving education, 29
overcrowded classrooms, 59

- P -

papers. *See* records
parent consumer, xix
parent groups, 144–146
parent handbook, 29, 71
parent interest and guidance, 147, 148

parent involvement, xx
parent recommendations summary, 36, 43, 45, 46, 52, 53, 72, 75
parent successes, examples of, 28
Parent-Teacher Organization (PTO), 130
    See also National Congress of Parents and Teachers (PTA)
parental effort, average children requirements, 29
parenting, responsible, 25
parents
    meeting principals, 74
    obligation of educators to listen to and work with, 28
    realism is recognizing child's strengths and weaknesses, 31
    responsibility for your child's education, 28
    schools serving, xx, 30
    separated and divorced, 125, 126
    set high goals, 30
    working, 70
parent/teacher groups, organization, 29, 70, 72, 129, 130
participation, third-level involvement, 129–132
partnerships, school/business, 138
persistence, 154
personal assessment of child, 45
personal feelings dominating the interview, 36
personal hygiene, 152
personal impressions, 36
personal observations, 43
personal traits, 153, 154
personality conflict, 60
persuasion, 115, 116
photocopies, 35, 113
physical characteristics, 45
physical endurance, 69
physical excellence, steps, 150–153
physically ready to learn, 59
picture excellence, 26
plan for action. *See* education action plan
planning ahead, 98
planning your school visit, 75, 76
pleasant demeanor, 154
population, metropolitan areas, 67
portfolios, 35
positive practices list, 147
posture, good, 151
praise, 154
pride, sense of, 30
principals, authority of, 28
principals, leadership and school operation, 73, 74
professional assistance, xx, 30
progress, assessing and moving on, 209–214
protection of records, 35
PTA. *See* National Congress of Parents and Teachers (PTA)
PTO. *See* Parent-Teacher Organization

Index

- Q -
questions
    and answers, school visit appointment, 88
    report card, 127
    school survey form, 75

- R -
ratio of adults to students, 134
reading, first-level involvement, 123–127
real estate agents, source of school information, 71, 72
realism is recognizing child's strengths and weaknesses, 31
reality check; school survey balance sheet, 92
realizing each child is different, 31
realizing school has options, 115
realizing your child's goals, 111
receptionist, 136
recommendation summary. *See* parent recommendations summary
records file. *See* educational records file
records, updating, 35, 45
relaxed interview atmosphere, 36
religion and moral values, 141
remembering, 159
report cards, deciphering, 127
reporting system of schools, 126
resources, 225–238
    See also curriculum, resources and school calendar responsibility
    for education, 63
    for your child's education, 28
    independent learning, 62
    of schools, 131
    principals, 74
rest, adequate, 69, 70
    See also sleep
role of family, 139
role of school in educating children, 25, 64, 65
role of teachers, 62
role you play, 25
roles, realizing each child is different, 31

- S -
safety, 153
schedule of classes, 69
schedules, modular, 70
scheduling school visit, 87
school calendar. *See* curriculum, resources and school calendar
school day, 68, 69
school improvement, formula for, 212
school programs, before and after, 69, 70
school staff, important component, 66
school survey balance sheet, 91, 92, 94–96
school survey form, 62, 64, 66, 70–72, 73–96
school visits, 46, 56, 73–86, 87–96
    open house, 128

249

school volunteers, opportunities for, 67
school year, 67, 68
school/business partnerships, 138
schools
>*See also* computers in education
>*See also* curriculum, resources and school calendar
>becoming involved in, 121–132
>blue-ribbon schools, 27, 217, 219
>budget process, 131
>calling, things to do before visit, 74
>challenges, 140, 141
>excellence exists in every school, 27
>in business to serve the public, 28
>learning about, 56
>modular schedules, 70
>parent handbooks, 29, 71
>reporting system, 126
>role of school in educating children, 25, 64, 65
>serving parents and children, xx, 30
>size, 56–58
>society and, 214
>sources of information about, 71, 72
>successful schools have common attributes, 27
>support staff, 66
>supporting, 131
>time in school vs. time learning, 70
>understanding, 56

schools; looking at organization of, 55–62
scope of the curriculum, 64
scouts, 141
second-level involvement, attending, 127–129
self-contained classroom, 56, 60
self-esteem, increasing, xxiii
self-fulfilling prophecy; think your child is smart, 30
serving parents and children, xx, 30
serving the public, 28
setting high goals, 30
short-term goals, 103, 104
size of class, 56, 58
size of school, 56–58
skills, and mental abilities, 44, 45
skills, 142, 143
sleep, adequate, 69, 151
small schools, 58
smoking, 152
social situations, experienced differently, 31
society and schools, 214
society's problems, 132
sources of information about schools, 71, 72
speaker, volunteering as, 136
special education programs, information about, 77
staff
>important component, 66
>meeting on school visit, 77, 115
>school day, 69

standardized achievement tests, 45, 212
State Education Department, 72
student, average, 61, 62
student population, 57
student to adult ratio, 134
students
    assigning, 103
    attitude of, 27
    identifying excellence, 26
    important component, 66
success
    personal traits, 153, 154
    tests, child, school indicators, 210–213
successful interview, 36
successful, what to do if not, 117, 118
suggestions, school visit, survey, 89, 90
super things to do, 148–140
supervising your child, know who is, 143
supplies, home learning center, 157, 158
support staff, 66
supporting your schools, 131
supportive family setting, 141
syllabi, 63

- T -

take a more comprehensive look at your child, 36, 43
teachable moment, 59, 61, 149
teacher aide, volunteering, 136
teacher observations, 45
teachers
    See also parent/teacher groups
    efforts of, 27
    identifying excellence, 26
    union contracts, 59
teaching
    focus, 61
    team teaching, 56, 60, 61, 70
teaching/learning situation, ideal, 59, 149–150
team teaching, 56, 60, 61, 70
telephone
    first-level involvement, 123–127
    school visit appointment, 89
telephone system operator, volunteering, 136, 137
television, time spent watching, 65
testing skills and mental abilities, 44
tests as indicators of success, 210, 211
textbook publishers, 64
third-level involvement, participating, 129–132
time
    amount requested for school visit, 77, 78
    change takes, 116
    comparing differences in, 76
    time in school vs. time learning, 70
    value of, 69
tobacco, 152

tour of school. *See* school visits
Tourette's Syndrome, 28
tutor, volunteering, 137

- U -

unions, teachers' union contracts, 59
U.S.
    responsibility for education, 63
    school day, 68
    school year, 67
U.S. Department of Education, 25, 27

- V -

value of knowledge, 44
value of time, 69
valued, feeling, 147
values, moral, 141
visits. *See* school visits
volunteers, opportunities for, 67, 133–138
volunteers, third-level involvement, 129–132

- W -

water requirements, 151
weaknesses, minimizing, 31
wise choices, making, 160
wise consumer, 46, 56, 62, 122
words and ways, viii
work habits, 43, 44
work to live, 134
working parents, 70
worksheet, know your child worksheet, 36
World Wide Web, 130, 160
writing goals and strategies, 104–105

- Y -

YMCA, YWCA, 138
year. *See* school year
youngest child, 31

About the Author

Ken Kimball, Jr. credits the positive personal and professional experiences he has had for his desire to help children reach their fullest potential. He realizes these events did not happen by chance, and has written *Educational Excellence For Your Child* to empower a greater number of parents to make a difference in their children's lives.

Ken attended elementary and secondary school in Baldwinsville, New York, where he had a caring family and close friends. He enjoyed learning and quickly found that the entire world could become his classroom. He participated in all levels of scouting, and earned the rank of Eagle. He enjoyed the benefits of working in a number of part-time jobs, and operated successful bicycle repair and photography businesses while still in school.

Ken obtained his B.A. from State University College at Oswego, and his M.S. and Ed.D. from State University of New York, University at Albany. His doctoral thesis, entitled *Leisure and Education for Leisure, A Study of an Emerging Priority*, reflects a continuing interest in the concepts of work and leisure. He taught junior and senior high school for nine years, and served in the U. S. Navy, where he attained the rank of Lieutenant.

Dr. Kimball began his teaching career in North Syracuse, New York. He soon realized the importance of parent input, and in planning his lessons to meet the unique needs and learning styles of his students. Later, while teaching in Stillwater, New York, he made a point of getting to know the parents of all his students, often by visiting them at home. From personal experience, he found the keys to successful parenting were spending time with children, offering support when necessary, encouraging them to act independently when they were ready, being aware of the things affecting their lives, and always trying to set a good example.

Ken served as the principal of Guilderland Junior High School, Guilderland, New York, for five years. During this time, he played a significant role in a study to determine the needs of children age ten to fourteen. At the conclusion of the study, the decision was made to build an innovative three-house middle school named after former Superintendent Alton U. Farnsworth. This school, where Ken served as principal for thirteen years, quickly became recognized for its exemplary programs. During his tenure, Dr. Kimball focused on selecting the best possible staff, encouraging professional growth, stimulating innovation, and creating a positive school climate by involving parents and the community.

Dr. Kimball has served on numerous college and state education department task forces. He taught at the college level in the United States and at Wellington Teachers College in New Zealand. He was a founding member of the New York State Middle School Association and has held offices in many other organizations. He authored a technical handbook for school operations and maintenance personnel and has contributed to other books and publications. For several years, he has written a column for the *Charlotte/AM* bureau of the *Sarasota Herald-Tribune*, a *New York Times* regional newspaper.

Ken and his wife, Betty, reside in Wellfleet, Massachusetts, and in Punta Gorda, Florida, where they enjoy spending time with family members and pursuing a wide range of outdoor activities.